The Theology of St Luke

The Theology of St Luke

by
HANS CONZELMANN

Translated by
GEOFFREY BUSWELL

HARPER & ROW, PUBLISHERS
New York, Evanston, San Francisco, London

Originally published by J. C. B. Mohr (Paul Siebeck)
Tübingen, in 1953 (Second Edition 1957)
under the title DIE MITTE DER ZEIT

Acknowledgement is made to Messrs. Secker and
Warburg for permission to quote, on pages 132 and
162, two passages from M. Burrows' translation of
'The Dead Sea Scrolls'

LIBRARY OF CONGRESS CATALOG CARD NUMBER: 70-172084

Contents

CONTENTS

Introduction

1. This study of St. Luke's theology is, by its approach to the problems, for the most part not dependent on any particular literary theories about St. Luke's Gospel and the Acts of the Apostles, for it is concerned with the whole of Luke's writings as they stand. If these form a self-contained scheme, then for our purpose literary critical analysis is only of secondary importance. Nevertheless, in this secondary sense it is important, and is therefore not to be despised. We must make it plain, however, that our aim is to elucidate Luke's work in its present form, not to enquire into possible sources or into the historical facts which provide the material. A variety of sources does not necessarily imply a similar variety in the thought and composition of the author. How did it come about, that he brought together these particular materials? Was he able to imprint on them his own views? It is here that the analysis of the sources renders the necessary service of helping to distinguish what comes from the source from what belongs to the author.

2. In Germany during recent decades the study of the Synoptics has been dominated by Form Criticism.[1] There are good reasons for this, but even if we take this method not as in the narrow sense aesthetic but in a wider sense as having a sociological trend,[2] it still has its limitations. It does not make literary critical analysis superfluous; on the contrary this is presupposed and must be continued along with Form Criticism.[3]

Form Criticism arose in part from the destruction of the 'framework of the life of Jesus'.[4] This was an event of decisive

[1] The work of literary criticism has continued along with it, but has been greatly overshadowed.

[2] Bultmann, *Synoptische Tradition*, p. 4.

[3] Ibid., p. 3. The appearance of detailed literary analyses is in itself a sign that these problems have not been solved. The English literary critics such as Streeter and Taylor, who at first evidently worked without a knowledge of Form Criticism, developed it further after becoming aware of its existence.

[4] Cf. the work of K. L. Schmidt.

significance. It was only natural that attention should turn almost exclusively to the sections of tradition embedded in this framework. The twofold task presented itself: that of determining the forms and of making a thorough and detailed analysis of the material.[1] However, the study of the framework was at first neglected. It was the question of the historical content of the life of Jesus that was still being investigated, even though there might be scepticism as to the possibility of reaching definite results.[2] Hence interest turned from the framework, now recognized as secondary, to the possibly primary materials, and the attempt was made to discover their original form. It was only later that greater attention was given to the framework itself.[3] This was not an attempt at reconstruction, but a necessary second stage in the study of the history of the tradition. The separation of the framework from the original body of tradition made it possible to see and interpret the framework as an entity in its own right.[4]

3. One of the main insights of Form Criticism was that the Gospels are in their nature and purpose not a historical record or a biography of Jesus; their purpose is the proclamation of saving events, though, it is true, of such as in the author's view have taken place in history. Yet so long as study is directed primarily to the separate parts of the tradition—stories, sayings, and small collections—it can be content with a general statement of the insight that the formation of the synoptic tradition was determined by the kerygma; but if it applies itself more to the form of the single Gospel as such, then it must be more precise. To what

[1] The two tasks cannot of course really be separated. Yet Dibelius is more concerned with the former, Bultmann with the latter.

[2] One must not confuse scepticism as to method with a general scepticism. Cf. Grobel, pp. 105 f. and, for the general background of this scepticism as to method, Bultmann, *Glauben und Verstehen*, p. 101.

[3] Special mention must be made in this connection of the works of E. Lohmeyer, C. H. Dodd and R. H. Lightfoot.

[4] In this respect Lohmeyer's work on 'Galiläa und Jerusalem' represents an important step forward as regards method, although there were of course many earlier attempts. It helped to bring the question of the life of Jesus once again to the fore. Whereas K. L. Schmidt mainly analyses the chronological framework (although with a thorough examination of the geographical aspects), here the main emphasis is on the geographical framework. The examination of the chronological framework is replaced by the attempt to identify the centres to which the local traditions belong. Lohmeyer's work is still of importance, even if the detailed findings cannot be substantiated.

INTRODUCTION

extent does 'belief' influence the development of form? What is the relation of this principle of form to the literary framework of the individual Gospel—not just to the single section of tradition? Do the separate Gospels themselves give any indication of an answer?

In the case of Mark, Dodd answers with a definite affirmative.[1] In the case of Luke there are certain indications. For one thing he preserves in Acts a number of kerygmatic formulae of a particular kind; then in his preface he defines the relation between the object of faith and the Gospel narrative, which is notably different from the definition that is to be assumed in the case of Mark. Whereas in Mark the narrative itself provides a broad unfolding of the kerygma, Luke defines the narrative as the historical foundation, which is added as a secondary factor to the kerygma, a knowledge of which he takes for granted (Luke i, 4). The factual record is therefore not itself the kerygma, but it provides the historical basis for it.[2] This separation of kerygma and narrative makes it possible for each to develop as an entity in its own right. Here is the basis for the consolidation of the form of the Gospel which Luke undertakes, and also for the beginning of the broader development of the formula of belief, such as we see in the Apostles' Creed, the essential affinity of which with Luke's conception is unmistakable.

That the formulations of belief are already determined when the Gospels are composed means that the content of a 'Gospel' is already fixed 'canonically'.[3] Acts i, 1, where the extent of the

---

[1] *The Apostolic Preaching.* Lohmeyer's account is restricted in that he does not make an analysis of the kerygma, but prefers to deal with the Christological titles. But neither a typical formula of belief nor a form of the Gospel can be deduced from these (nor can any particular group of the primitive community be isolated), as from the very beginning the titles overlap. Cf. Bultmann, *N.T.Theol.*, p. 53, and Kümmel, *Th.R.*, 1948, pp. 18 f. It is significant that the development of Christological formulae does not start from a differentiation of titles. The apparent exceptions (Kyrios or Christos Jesus) only serve to confirm this.

[2] Cf. the Apostles' Creed, which presupposes the same circumstances. Cf. also v. Dobschütz, *Apostolicum*, p. 45.

[3] Dodd, *The Apostolic Preaching*, p. 55: 'The kerygma is primary, and it acted as a preservative of the tradition which conveyed the facts.' But of course Dodd applies his thesis systematically only to Mark.

A significant analogy to our approach can be found in the present-day study of the Pentateuch. This has frequently provided a model for the study of the Synoptics as regards approach and method. The phases of the investigation correspond: literary criticism, Form Criticism, study of the composition and of the 'framework'. Reference should be made to the work of Gerhard v. Rad and Martin Noth.

11

first book is laid down as a fundamental division,[1] shows how fully aware of this Luke is. Before anything is composed there is a prevailing picture of the nature and work of Jesus, no doubt an authoritative one, which stamps itself on all the traditional material and even persists where the latter is imperfectly preserved. By defining this prevalent picture we shall, it is true, obtain no material for the picture of the Jesus of history, but we shall for the development of the understanding of Christ in the early Church. The process by which the Gospels were formed proves to be that of the filling out of a given kerygmatic framework with the narrative material about Jesus and the traditional sayings of the Lord. This has been realized for a long time, but it needs to be stated more precisely by bringing out more sharply than before each evangelist's understanding of the kerygma.[2]

The first phase in the collection of the traditional material (up to the composition of Mark's Gospel and the Q sayings) has been clarified by Form Criticism. Now a second phase has to be distinguished, in which the kerygma is not simply transmitted and received, but itself becomes the subject of reflection. This is what happens with Luke. This new stage is seen both in the critical attitude to tradition as well as in the positive formation of a new picture of history out of those already current, like stones used as parts of a new mosaic.

4. In what sense then can Luke be described as a 'historian'? Modern research concerns itself essentially with the reliability of his reporting, but if we are interested in the first place not in what is reported, but in the report as such, the problem takes a different form: what is Luke's conception of the meaning of his account?[3] We must start from a methodical comparison with his sources, in so far as these are directly available or can be reconstructed. What is Luke's attitude to his forerunners and how does he conceive his task in the context of the contemporary Church's understanding of doctrine and history? Our aim is not to investigate the models and sources as such, nor is it to

[1] The connection between 'belief' and the extent of the Gospel is particularly clear in the birth stories. Whether these are present or absent depends on the stage of development of the kerygma.

[2] For Mark, cf. R. H. Lightfoot and W. Marxsen; for Matthew, G. Bornkamm (see Bibliography).

[3] This approach has recently been repeatedly emphasized, in particular by Dibelius. Cf. his *Studies in the Acts of the Apostles*.

INTRODUCTION

reconstruct the historical events. This is of course an indispensable task, but first of all the meaning of the text before us must
be investigated regardless of our idea of the probable course of
historical events, regardless, that is, of the picture which Luke
gives of the latter.

We must of course define Luke's own historical position in
the context of the development of the Church. Only in this way
can we understand how on the one hand he looks back to the
'arché' of the Church as something unique and unrepeatable,
which presupposes a certain distance in time, and how on the
other hand he looks forward to the eschatological events. What
distinguishes him is not that he thinks in the categories of promise and fulfilment, for this he has in common with others, but the
way in which he builds up from these categories a picture of the
course of saving history, and the way in which he employs the
traditional material for this purpose.

Form Criticism has shown to what extent the community projected its own problems and answers back into the reports of the
life of Jesus. It is true that limits were set to this projection both
by belief and by the traditional material itself. But it is not until
Luke that this demarcation, this distinction between then and
now, the period of Jesus and the period of the Church, between
problems of yesterday and those of today, becomes fully conscious. The period of Jesus and the period of the Church are presented as different epochs in the broad course of saving history,
differentiated to some extent by their particular characteristics.
Thus Luke can distinguish between those commands of the Lord
which were meant only for the contemporary situation, such as
the directions concerning equipment given when the apostles are
sent out, which in Luke xxii, 35–7 are explicitly annulled for the
period to follow, and those which are permanent, such as in the
Sermon on the Plain. Therefore he cannot simply project present
questions back into the time of Jesus. His aim is rather to bring
out the peculiar character of each period.

This stage of historical reflection does not represent simply a
result of straightforward 'development'. One could settle even
such difficult problems as the delay of the Parousia, as was done
in 2 Peter, by simply holding on to the old expectation. In Luke
however—and this is the measure of his great achievement—we
find a new departure, a deliberate reflection: he confronts the

13

problem of the interval by interpreting his own period afresh in relation to this fact; in other words, the treatment of his main problem is the result of coming to grips with his own situation. Therefore reflection on the fundamental 'arché' is necessary. The latter, in comparison with Mark's conception in Mark i, 1, is differently defined. The picture of history is thus determined by two factors.

(a) The period of Jesus and the period of the Church are represented as two distinct, but systematically interrelated epochs. Thus the view of Jesus as a historical phenomenon gains positive theological meaning. It is not determined by a Greek conception of history, which aims to instruct as, for example, Thucydides does, by apprehending the typical in the unique events of history (cf. his famous statement of his views, I, 22). It arises rather from the problem of the existence of the Church in a continuing period of time. In order to be able to set out clearly in the person of Jesus a salvation which is timeless, his period must be distinguished from the present period. The Church understands her present existence by recognizing that period as the authentic manifestation of salvation and thereby is enabled to understand not only her present, but also her future existence. And on the other hand, she comes to understand the nature of her Lord by looking back to his historical existence. In other words, Luke is confronted by the situation in which the Church finds herself by the delay of the Parousia and her existence in secular history, and he tries to come to terms with the situation by his account of historical events.[1]

(b) In looking back to the past another distinction emerges even within this present, latest epoch of saving history, a distinction between the present in which the author lives and the 'arché', the foundation period of the apostles and eye-witnesses (cf. the differentiation made in the preface, Luke i, 1–4). Again Luke recognizes the uniqueness of the events of that time, and his picture of the early Church is not meant to harmonize with the present, but stands in contrast. The characteristic summary statements about the life of the early community do not reflect present conditions, neither do they represent an ideal for the

---

[1] P. Vielhauer, *Ev.Theol.*, 1950–1, p. 13: 'How uneschatological Luke's thinking is is proved not only by the contents, but by the very fact of the Acts of the Apostles.'

present. Luke does not wish to reform the present Church by the pattern of the Church of former times. There is no trace of such a desire in his work. Above all the indispensable corollary of such an intention is lacking—a theory of the decline that has taken place in the meantime. A glance at Hermas shows this clearly enough. Luke has no thought of setting out the way in which the Law was adhered to at that time as a model for the present. Rather, this standpoint of attachment to the Law and the Temple cult is part of the unique, unrepeatable situation of the Church at that time; indeed Luke explicitly proposes new relaxations for the future, from the time of the spread of the Gospel to the Gentiles. How, despite this deliberate separation, Luke preserves the positive relationship, the continuity between the Church of yesterday and that of today, is a question which we shall have to consider in detail.

As a result of our considerations so far we can pose certain definite questions. What is the structure of Luke's complete work and the essential meaning of this structure? What is the structure of the Gospel by itself?[1] Is it possible to see in its construction a deliberate agreement with or difference from the available models? Mark occupies the first place of course for the purpose of comparison, but the speeches in Acts are relevant to our question, as Dodd's work shows.[2]

---

[1] We can pass over the question of the structure of Acts itself. It lacks (a) the comparison with the Synoptics, and (b) the influence of a normative kerygma. Instead there is a distinct pattern which has often been pointed out, representing the author's view of Church history. There is one element which mainly interests us: the interpretation of the beginnings from a historical perspective within the framework of the successive periods of redemptive history. E. Haenchen has done the spadework for an understanding of the composition of Acts in his monumental commentary. Cf. also Ph-H. Menoud, *Le plan des Actes des Apôtres* (see Bibliography).

The much discussed question concerning the unity of the whole work can well be linked with the consideration of the two prefaces. It is generally held that the preface to the Gospel points forward to a continuation in a second volume. Cf. Cadbury, *Beginnings*, I, 2, pp. 489 ff., e.g. p. 492: 'It is the real preface to Acts as well as to the Gospel, written by the author when he contemplated not merely one but both volumes.' This thesis concerning the literary unity of the two books has been modified by H. Sal.lin and by Ph-H. Menoud (*Remarques*), but literary observations make it improbable. The Gospel form was already fixed before Luke, and prefaces are found in historical monographs. Other observations also show that Acts was written later than Luke's Gospel.

[2] On the comparison between Luke and Mark, see *ZThK*, 49, 1952, pp. 16 ff. Here the comparison is restricted to the literary differences as between Luke and Mark, but if we include Acts, the problem becomes wider. In Acts Luke comes to terms with his sources in a similar way, but in this case it is naturally difficult to see to what extent he modifies them.

INTRODUCTION

5. C. H. Dodd examines the pattern of the speeches in Acts and compares it with the structure of Mark's Gospel. He concludes that there exists a consistent pattern in the primitive Christian kerygma.[1] If we apply this approach to Luke's Gospel, it becomes evident that Luke takes material from Mark, but certainly not the pattern of the construction. Thus the remarkable fact emerges that there is agreement between the pattern of the speeches in Acts and Mark, but not between the speeches and Luke's outline of the ministry of Jesus.

What is the relation between the two patterns which appear in Luke? What is the relation between tradition and the adaptation of it? Can we see in the outline of the Gospel the real purpose of Luke's work as an author?

6. Corresponding to the two sections of the ministry of Jesus —the ministry on earth and the ministry of the Exalted Lord— there are two carefully described situations in which believers find themselves. When Jesus was alive, was the time of salvation; Satan was far away, it was a time without temptation (cf. Luke iv, 13 with xxii, 3 and xxii, 35). Since the Passion, however, Satan is present again and the disciples of Jesus are again subject to temptation (xxii, 36).[2] In view of this distinction, the continuity between the period of Jesus on the one hand and the period of the Church on the other has to be plainly demonstrated. The plan of the whole historical writing serves this purpose. The story of salvation emerges in three stages:

(i) The period of Israel (Luke xvi, 16).
(ii) The period of Jesus' ministry (not of his 'life'),[3] characterized in passages such as Luke iv, 16 ff., and Acts x, 38.
(iii) The period since the Ascension, on earth the period of the *ecclesia pressa*, during which the virtue of patience is

---

[1] *The Apostolic Preaching*, where he provides comparative tables. Dibelius is also concerned with the scheme underlying the speeches in Acts, e.g. *Formgeschichte*, p. 15; *SBH*, 1949/1, on 'Die Reden der AG'. Grant, *The Earliest Gospel*, pp. 46 ff., discusses Dodd in detail.

[2] *ZThK*, 49, 1952, p. 29, K. G. Kuhn contradicts this interpretation (ibid., p. 221, n. 1). This contradiction is based on a misunderstanding, in so far as I was concerned solely with Luke's interpretation of the sayings about temptation, quite apart from any other possible meaning which the tradition had before Luke. As his note proceeds, Kuhn himself confirms my interpretation of Luke.

[3] Acts i, 1 f., seems to fix the limits of the first book in such a way that the story of the birth and childhood is not included. ἀρχή-ἄρχεσθαι signifies in Luke a quite definite moment of time, namely the 'beginning in Galilee'.

INTRODUCTION

required, and it is possible, by virtue of looking back to the period of Jesus, also to look forward to the Parousia.[1]

The Parousia itself does not represent a stage within the course of saving history, but the end of it. It corresponds to the other extreme, the Creation.[2]

We may say, therefore, that the two books of Luke both belong together and are separate, as a result on the one hand of the continuity of redemptive history and on the other of its divisions.

If in this way the figure of Jesus is fitted into a large framework, and thus interpreted as a historical phenomenon, it is true that at the same time the foundations are laid for greater elaboration in the description of the ministry itself. It is unfolded in Luke in three stages:

(i) The period of the gathering of 'witnesses' in Galilee, opening with the proclamation of Jesus as the Son of God.
(ii) The journey of the Galileans to the Temple, opening with the narrative passage containing the disclosure that Jesus must suffer and the Transfiguration.
(iii) The period of the teaching in the Temple and of the Passion in Jerusalem, opening with the revelation of his royalty at the Entry. This period closes with the dawn of the new epoch of salvation with the Resurrection and Ascension.

We must now substantiate this outline by a detailed examination.

---

[1] It is quite justifiable to speak of 'two advents' in Luke, even though the actual terminology is not found. Cf. Bent Noack, 'Das Gottesreich bei Lukas', *Symb. Bibl. Upps.*, 10, pp. 47 ff.

[2] There is no evidence of any idea of a self-contained world history or cosmic history apart from redemptive history, not even in Acts xvii, where there seems to be a suggestion of a view of world history. But it is given no significance by itself either in the sense of salvation or of disaster, but is entirely determined by the motif of ignorance, which serves as a connecting-link in the missionary approach and which is also applied to Jewish history (Acts iii, 17 and xiii, 27). The application of the idea of creation to the fact that God did not leave Himself without witness is used as a point in the argument, and is not developed for its own sake.

The constitution of the three stages represents the transformation of the original eschatological scheme of the two aeons carried over into history, one of the characteristic motifs in Luke's thought. Just as in the conception of redemptive history the two-fold structure of eschatology is replaced by the threefold structure of historical perspective, so also in the account of the ministry of Jesus. Whereas in Mark the eschatological conception is manifested in the sharp contrast between the two epochs (Galilee and Jerusalem), in Luke there are three successive phases of the ministry.

17

PART ONE

Geographical Elements in the Composition of Luke's Gospel

A. PROLOGUE: JOHN THE BAPTIST

(a) The Place

In the much-discussed passage iii, 1, there is geographical as well as chronological material. We are not so much concerned with determining the separate regions as with the fact that Samaria and Peræa are missing. Klostermann in discussing this passage reminds us that in official language the mention of Samaria would not be necessary. Yet it is questionable whether this can be assumed in the case of Luke. In any case his official terminology is not exact (as the use of ἡγεμών shows). Is there perhaps a connection between the omission of Samaria and other statements? We must bear this in mind as a possibility. The same applies to Peræa. This region is missing not only here, but consistently in the whole book, even where it appears in Luke's sources.

As regards iii, 3–20, the question of the relation between the desert and the Jordan as the scene of John's ministry is clearly answered by Luke in opposition to Mark (and Q?): first he is in the desert, then he appears by the Jordan.[1] The alteration of the locality compared with the source is part of the author's editorial work, whether out of regard for the statement in the prologue or

---

[1] The agreement with i, 80 is a strong argument in support of the view that the prologue formed an original part of the Gospel. Nevertheless we shall not discuss it, as in many respects it requires special treatment, particularly regarding the geographical conception which is assumed.

as a result of reflection on the relation between desert and water. The expression ἦλθεν εἰς πᾶσαν τὴν περίχωρον τοῦ ᾿Ιορδάνου suggests the idea of itinerant preaching, and all the more so, in that it has no support in the parallel passages. It is true that Matthew makes a statement which seems very similar, but it has in fact a characteristic difference: all the region round about Jordan comes to him. Matthew therefore presupposes a fixed locality by the Jordan, as Matt. iii, 6 shows. If the similarity of expression is derived from a source, namely Q, which is quite possible, as the sequel of the story of the Baptist shows, then this variation attains greater significance as being the result of deliberate editing.

On the literary side, it should be noted that Luke omits Mark i, 5, but he presupposes the verse in v. 3 as well as later in v. 21. What is it that Luke objects to? Evidently the statement of where those who come to John have come from. He replaces it by the motif of the 'whole people', which is peculiar to him; even the term 'Judæa' is too narrow for him (or it may be an example of a 'wider' use of the concept, as many think). As will become plain later from the demarcation of the area of Jesus' ministry, the reference to the Baptist's connection with the Jordan serves a special purpose in Luke, viz., the clear demarcation of their two spheres of activity. Later, Luke will omit Mark x, 1. According to Luke, after his Baptism Jesus has no more contact with the Jordan or even with its surroundings. It is true that according to Luke Jesus does in fact come to Jericho, but it is questionable whether Luke knew that this town was in the region of the Jordan. As we shall see later, his acquaintance with Palestine is in many respects imperfect; and from the LXX, of which he made great use, Luke would find nothing to tell him that Jericho was situated in the neighbourhood of the Jordan.[1]

---

[1] From Jos. ii, 7 in the LXX one might infer a fair distance; Jos. ii, 22 f., suggests proximity to the mountain, which is correct, but might give to the person not familiar with the place an inaccurate picture. Cf. also Jos. iv, 19 and v, 10. In the description of Palestine by Strabo and Pliny the Elder the references to this region (the Jordan, the Dead Sea and Jericho) are quite confused. This is partly the result of the compilation of various sources. Cf. also the remarkable description of the country in *Ep.Ar.*, 114 ff., where the Jordan appears as a river forming a boundary. According to Strabo (XVI, 55) it flows between Libanus and Antilibanus into the sea, and the Arabians sail on it. On the Jordan in the Old Testament and in Jewish literature, cf. K. H. Rengstorf, *TW*, VI, pp. 608 ff.

One might even wonder whether he avoids mentioning the Jordan because it is the river associated with John.

The alternative gives rise to a discrepancy in respect of the quotation.[1] Luke is evidently prepared to allow this, in order to implement his idea that the Jordan is the region of the Baptist, the region of the old era, whereas the ministry of Jesus lies elsewhere.[2] In any case 'Judæa', when connected with John, is consistently omitted in contrast with the parallel passages.[3] People do not come to him from Judæa and Jerusalem.

The purpose of this separation from the ministry of Jesus is seen when one compares Luke iii, 21 and iv, 1, 14 with Mark.[4] The distinction of locality corresponds to a fundamental distinction, for John does not proclaim the Kingdom of God, as is made plain in xvi, 16 as a point of principle.

Thus the locality of the Baptist becomes remarkably vague. Luke can associate him neither with Judæa nor with Galilee, for these are both areas of Jesus' activity. Yet on the other hand there has to be some connection, so the Baptist is placed on the border. It is obvious that Luke has no exact knowledge of the area, and this is why he can make such a straightforward symbolical use of localities.

He creates a further discrepancy by introducing a motif of his own: in place of the Pharisees and Sadducees he puts the ὄχλοι.[5]

---

[1] K. L. Schmidt, *Rahmen*, p. 24.

[2] Later we shall see that the lake also has the function of a boundary. Cf. viii, 22 with viii, 40, also viii, 26, 27.

[3] This is in plain contradiction to the prologue, according to which it is the very place to which John belongs. We can only prove that the 'desert' is the desert of Judæa if the prologue is original. Besides, right from his first appearance there is no suggestion that John has been in the desert previously. In any case, the desert in this context is not so much a geographical as a symbolical element, for it signifies the prophet. It is important for us to see that instead of the desert preaching, which has the character of an eschatological sign, the emphasis is on the desert as a place for ascetics.

[4] Luke omits the information as to where Jesus came from. Chapter iv, 1 stresses the final departure from the Jordan and iv, 14 mentions Galilee as the destination. Apart from iv, 1 (and the omission in iii, 21) this is the first mention of Galilee. Therefore John has nothing to do with this region, although Luke knows that John and Jesus are under the same ruler (ix, 8 ff.). Is the disappearance of Peræa from the story of Jesus connected with this demarcation?

[5] A discrepancy, as the speech itself is addressed to Pharisees and similar people. K. L. Schmidt (p. 25) accepts that the Pharisees and Sadducees derive from Q, which is not accepted by most commentators. Our interpretation does not depend on the solution of this question. In connection with the ὄχλος motif as well one

GEOGRAPHICAL ELEMENTS

This might be derived from Mark i, 5, but with variations. Verses 7, 10 and 20 show how consistently this has been done, and in vii, 29 Luke attributes to Jesus the statement that 'all' were baptized.

In other words, all the people are baptized, but their leaders without exception refuse to be baptized.[1] In this way Luke creates a peculiar variant of the idea of the people of God within Israel. We have therefore right at the beginning two distinct groups (in Luke's view, of course, actual historical groups) forming the background to the ministry of Jesus.

The explanatory remark in iii, 15 is to be regarded as an editorial comment by Luke. The verse corresponds both formally and as regards meaning to v. 21.[2]

The reference to the imprisonment in iii, 19 f. divides the section concerning John from the section concerning Jesus in the sense of drawing a distinction between the epochs of salvation, for which xvi, 16 provides the clue. Now the way is open for the story of Jesus. The fact that the activity of the two still overlaps cannot be entirely eliminated, but Luke deprives it of any real significance. According to iii, 21 f. Jesus is baptized as one of the people, like everyone else. Luke excludes any suggestion that John plays an important part in the incident.[3] This is in keeping with his whole conception of the significance of John.[4]

The genealogy has nothing to do with topography, but is important from the point of view of arrangement. As has often been remarked, it is assumed that the name of Jesus is mentioned for the first time, and that there has been no prologue. Yet this fact

might ask whether this is not a creation by Luke. Cf. Schmidt, p. 26. We shall consider the editorial v. 15 later. If Luke found ὄχλοι in his source, he has stylized it and brought out its meaning in connection with the 'true Israel'. Lohmeyer stresses the eschatological meaning of the term 'all' even in Mark (with reference to Mark i, 5). This has to be modified for Luke, as vii, 28 ff. shows. This means that the significance of this event for redemptive history is indicated by the very fact that it is presented as something historical.

[1] iii, 21 and vii, 29.
[2] Schmidt, op. cit., p. 27; Bultmann, pp. 359, 386.
[3] Dibelius makes this point, *Die urchristliche Überlieferung von Johannes dem Täufer*, p. 60. Sahlin's argument (*Studien*, pp. 60 f., n. 2) is untenable.
[4] In contrast to what is generally accepted, we assume that the D variant of v. 22 is secondary.

21

needs the support of other arguments for it to be of decisive significance.[1]

(b) The Significance of John the Baptist according to Luke

In the pre-Lucan tradition John is understood from the standpoint of the dawn of the new eschatological age. He is more than a prophet, he is the forerunner, he is Elijah. Here Mark and Matthew use traditions which Luke himself has preserved for us, so it is all the more striking that Luke's own pronouncements point in another direction. It is true that he does not set out his views coherently, but he indicates it whenever he speaks of John by what he omits and by what he adds.[2]

In the tradition John the Baptist stands on the dividing line between the old and the new epoch. He not only announces the imminent Kingdom of God, but is himself a sign of its arrival. This is what is implied by the interpretation of his figure (not only of his teaching) as that of the forerunner, under the influence of the apocalyptic expectation of Elijah. This is implied by the position which Mark gives him at the opening of the Gospel.[3]

Luke uses the existing material, but transforms it in a characteristic way. Nowhere in his writings is a figure from the past brought into direct connection with the future eschatological events. On the contrary, existing interpretations are rejected. Instead of being directly linked with the eschatological events, the figure is given a definite place in a continuous story of salvation, the end of which is not yet in sight. John no longer marks

[1] Streeter and Taylor make use of this for the support of their Proto-Luke hypothesis, and suggest that the prologue belongs to a second stage of the compilation. The objection to their special theory is that the genealogy is carefully incorporated into a Marcan context (it is not, as the theory would require, that Marcan passages are built around the already existing genealogy).

[2] We are not taking the prologue into consideration here. The view it contains is expressed in i, 17 and i, 76.

[3] In the Acts of the Apostles there is in this connection a specific use of ἀρχή-ἄρχεσθαι which corresponds to Mark i, 1; both in Acts x, 37 and in Acts xiii, 24 the preaching of John is mentioned not for its content, but for its function as an eschatological sign. Cf. H. Conzelmann, 'Was von Anfang war', *Neutestamentliche Studien für R. Bultmann*, 1957, pp. 194 ff. On Mark, cf. W. Marxsen, *Der Evangelist Markus*, 1956, pp. 87 f.

the arrival of the new aeon, but the division between two epochs in the one continuous story, such as is described in Luke xvi, 16. The eschatological events do not break out after John, but a new stage in the process of salvation is reached, John himself still belonging to the earlier of the two epochs which meet at this point. This transformation of the tradition concerning John affects all the different sources, and therefore is to be attributed to Luke himself.

As we have already said, Luke xvi, 16 provides the key to the topography of redemptive history. According to this passage, there is no preparation before Jesus for the proclamation of the Kingdom of God, that is, of the 'Gospel' in Luke's sense.[1] A statement such as Matthew iii, 2 is impossible in Luke. Of course it does not follow that because the preaching of the Kingdom by John is disputed, the preaching of repentance is also disputed. On the contrary, this is his real task. What is more, it is this that persists on into the new epoch. To the traditional verse Luke xvi, 16 there is immediately added the obviously editorial statement of v. 17. Thus even if the original sense of this verse pointed to a break, to the supersession of the old aeon by the new, Luke makes it point at the same time to a continuity: until now there was 'only' the law and the Prophets, but from now on there is 'also' the preaching of the Kingdom. Therefore the preaching of repentance is continued by Jesus. It is John's role to prepare the way for this by preaching and baptism, and his great merit is that he refused to claim for himself the Messianic role. At the same time, however, this makes plain John's limitations: it is only through the proclamation of the Kingdom that John's preaching, and only through the Spirit that John's baptism, are raised to a level appropriate to the new epoch.[2]

---

[1] One cannot appeal against this view to the word εὐαγγελίζεσθαι in Luke iii, 18. In this context it means simply 'to preach'. See Bultmann, *N.T.Theol.*, p. 86 (for the contrary view, cf. Klostermann, ad loc.). In Luke John is thought of as quite unconnected with the message of the Kingdom. The *praeparatio* is not conceived by Luke in eschatological categories, as in the other Synoptics, but is seen in the simple fact of the preaching of repentance, which is valued therefore not because it is a sign, but because of its content.

[2] The emphasis on the priestly descent is not found anywhere outside the prologue. Here it is a question of a very slight special tradition, and scarcely that. The manner in which it is present is more significant than the fact that it is present. The motif is taken from a source, but is not made full use of even in the prologue itself. It is a remnant, not a developed theological motif.

GEOGRAPHICAL ELEMENTS

Apart from the prologue Luke recognizes no typological correspondence between John the Baptist and Jesus. One might even wonder whether he did not deliberately exclude any indications of it.[1] The fact is that two epochs meet at this point, and although they have a connection, they have to be all the more clearly distinguished because even in the new epoch it is a question of a continuation of the one redemptive history. Yet John has to be described in the categories of the old epoch, as a 'precursor', as Elijah, or as a sign of the 'arrival'.[2] If his baptism is described as a baptism of repentance, the accent does not lie so much on the fact of its being an advance over earlier times, as on how it falls short compared with Christian baptism with the Spirit. To what extent this distinction concerns the author is shown by the continued reference to the problem in Acts (i, 5; xi, 16; xviii, 24–xix, 7). We have already mentioned the motif which is of importance for the composition of redemptive history, viz., that all the people submit to John's baptism.[3]

Thus John has a clearly defined function in the centre of the story of salvation. As it is his ministry rather than his person that serves as a preparation for Jesus, he is subordinate to the work of Jesus in the same way as is the whole epoch of the Law.

Luke recognizes neither earthly precursors of the Parousia nor those appearing from heaven. In iii, 16 he even omits ὀπίσω μου. John is great, but not in the Kingdom of God. In addition to this fact, we must also consider Luke's view of Moses and Elijah. Again it plainly contradicts the prologue, where in i, 17 John is linked with Elijah. Luke's own view stands out here particularly clearly. Luke can find apologetic on behalf of the Baptist in his sources. Yet in respect of these two figures he is quite independent, but consistent, as a result of his eschatology.

---

[1] Why does he omit the account of John's death? Perhaps in order to avoid a possible typological parallel. Why does he emphasize so strongly in another passage that John is dead and cannot return?

[2] In Luke's view there is only one prelude to the Parousia: the Resurrection of Jesus. And even this is separated from the Parousia by a long interval.

[3] Luke finds in this the explanation as to why Jesus himself does not baptize. John has performed it extensively—and a new stage of baptism presupposes the sending of the Spirit. Is the omission of the confession of sin (in contrast to Mark i, 5) linked with the fact that baptism is connected with the earlier period?

The apologetic note is strengthened; cf. the addition in
iii, 15, and the contrast brought out in passages such as Acts i, 5,
xi, 16 and xiii, 23 ff. Luke's sources use the precursor-motif in
their apologetic: John is not the Messiah but 'only' the pre-
parer of the way. He may be Elijah. Luke's argument, however,
is the reverse of this: John is not the precursor, for there is no
such thing, but he is the last of the prophets (cf. the omission
from Mark i, 7 already mentioned). Luke ix, 8 informs us that
John is dead and appears no more. Nothing definite is said about
Elijah: but this applies only in the actual historical situation, that
is to say, in the case of Herod. He does not wish to commit himself to do anything about John. We have to distinguish between
what Luke makes Herod say and what he himself thinks. The
argument concerning John presupposes the general doctrine that
before the Parousia there is no resurrection apart from that of
Jesus, no return to earth of figures from the past. As far as
Elijah and Moses are concerned, Luke answers the undecided
question in the story of the Transfiguration, ix, 28–36. With
their appearances here the role of both of them is completed.
Luke emphasizes, by way of correcting his source, that this is in
fact their role: they come as heavenly messengers to Jesus, but
only to him, not publicly. According to Luke they do not even
speak in the hearing of the three disciples. Therefore it is foolish
to look for precursors; the Kingdom does not come μετὰ
παρατηρήσεως, it comes suddenly. In Luke's view evidently this
element of surprise is a refutation of the apocalyptic idea of the
precursor. Luke xvii, 30 ff. is relevant to this. Any suggestion of
a false interpretation has to be removed. As a consequence therefore Mark ix, 9–12 is omitted. The Elijah-motif is excluded also
from the account of Jesus' death, hence the absence of Mark
xv, 35.

The tension between tradition and the adaptation of it can be
seen in Luke vii, 18–35. Verses 28–30 presumably contain the
author's interpretation, although perhaps influenced by the
source. In the tradition John was more than a prophet; now he
becomes the greatest prophet. This agrees with xvi, 16. He is
included within the saving events, for it is God's will that
men should be baptized, but not that one should think of
John in an eschatological sense. The people fulfil God's will,
whilst the leaders keep themselves apart; in this way John

gives support to the claim made by Christians that they are Israel.[1]

Already before Luke one of the main themes of the tradition concerning John is that he marks a division in the story of salvation, so now Luke proceeds to build up his scheme of successive epochs (xvi, 16). Acts x, 37 and xiii, 25 show how he does it.[2] Because of the emphasis on the separation of the epochs, the fact that the ministry of John and that of Jesus overlap to a certain extent in time is lost sight of. This is shown by the statement in Luke iii, 19 f., which contains nothing new and yet provides the key to Luke's composition. It is true that it is not in the 'right' place from the historical or the literary point of view. Yet this position is not the result of following a source, so we must conclude that it has been fixed by the author.[3] These verses form the dividing line between the section about John and that about Jesus, and their purpose apparently is, in view of the temporal overlap, to make clear the fundamental separation.

The exit of John has no particular significance, and we learn of his death incidentally in ix, 9. His fate is that of the prophets,[4] and is not an eschatological event.

The account of John's preaching completes the picture. By the insertion of this special section we are given the pattern of his preaching:[5]

(1) The threat of judgement, which provides the motive for
(2) The challenge to repent and be converted (which to Luke's mind are separate conceptions).
(3) Exhortation.

In Matthew John's teaching has a definitely Christological

[1] In anticipation we may say that as a result of this the leaders are thought of as a merely secular factor, along with all those who support them. Luke xx, 1–8 is closely related to vii, 18 ff.

[2] The formulae of course have at first a different bearing from the fuller historical account. Their purpose is only to bring out the antithesis, not to go into the details of the relationship.

[3] K. L. Schmidt. We can go even further than Schmidt does. In his view, Luke is not interested in the figure of John the Baptist as such. This means rejecting the idea that the 'figure' has any importance as a sign. It is going too far to say that this account is self-evident, for the 'self-evident' interpretation of John is the eschatological one. It is a matter of considerable significance when Luke recasts his material to give it a historical perspective.

[4] Luke xi, 47; Acts vii, 52.

[5] This of course corresponds to a common primitive Christian pattern.

bearing. In Luke it is directed to conversion, baptism and exhortation. The Christological reference, on the other hand, is made relatively independent by the insertion of v. 15, and thus acquires a more polemical and apologetic flavour.

To sum up, we may say that Luke employs geographical factors for the purpose of setting out his fundamental conception, and that he modifies his sources to a considerable extent. This modification takes the form of a conscious editorial process of omissions, additions, and alterations in the wording of the sources. It is plain that his purpose is to keep separate the respective localities of John and of Jesus. As far as the outline of Jesus' life is concerned, it is the beginning of his own ministry that marks the 'arché' not, as in Mark, the appearance of John. It is not until now that the region of Galilee is mentioned, Luke having omitted it from Mark i, 9.

B. THE COURSE OF JESUS' MINISTRY

(a) GALILEE

1. The Temptation (Luke iv, 1–13)

The course of Jesus' movements, the departure from the area of John the Baptist—the desert—Jerusalem, no doubt has its basis in the source, but it is obvious that it has been modified. The much-discussed change of position of the second and third temptations gives rise to the idea that Jesus' travels begin in Jerusalem.[1]

The Temptation is the first event in the life of Jesus since the descent of the Spirit, and the desert forms an episode between the Jordan and Galilee, symbolizing the separation. It is pointless to attempt to locate it.

Whereas Mark i, 13 and Matt. iv, 11 suggest that for the time being the Temptations come to an end in the desert, Luke

---

[1] Klostermann interprets ὑπέστρεψεν as referring to the 'return' to Galilee. Schmidt, however, interprets it as 'he withdrew'. Klostermann overlooks the fact that v. 14 makes no mention of a 'return'. One cannot harmonize this with Mark, for why has Luke, in contrast to Mark i, 9, omitted 'Galilee'? This omission shows that his alterations are intentional.

omits this suggestion and goes straight on to Galilee. The Temptation is finished decisively (πάντα), and the devil departs. A question of principle is involved here, for it means that where Jesus is from now on, there Satan is no more—ἄχρι καιροῦ.

It is significant that according to Luke Jesus is not 'led by' the Spirit, but himself acts 'in the Spirit'.[1] This is in keeping with the view contained in the words ὧν ἤρξατο ὁ Ἰησοῦς ποιεῖν τε καὶ διδάσκειν (Acts i, 1) and which is suggested by the conclusion of the Temptation story in v. 13, where its place within the pattern of redemptive history is made plain: a period free from Satan is now beginning, an epoch of a special kind in the centre of the whole course of redemptive history. What is now beginning therefore is not the last times, but the interval between the period of the Law, or of Israel, and the period of the Spirit, or of the Church.[2]

The expression συντελέσας πάντα πειρασμόν can scarcely be overemphasized. It really means that henceforth there will be no temptations in the life of Jesus. Thus his life as a whole is not regarded as a temptation either. It is not until the moment indicated by ἄχρι καιροῦ that temptation recurs. Luke xxii, 3 and the prompt reappearance of the πειρασμός motif in the farewell speeches in Luke show how important it is to emphasize this.

This particular interpretation of the life of Jesus is without doubt Luke's own interpretation. The expression ἄχρι καιροῦ is Luke's, and its meaning can be deduced from Acts xiii, 11 (cf. Klostermann, ad loc.). As further evidence of Luke's editorial work there is the fact that he builds up this pattern, by means of which he links the story of the Temptation with that of the Passion, from material from different sources, sometimes from Q material, sometimes from Marcan material.[3]

---

[1] ἤγετο ἐν τῷ πνεύματι appears to be a correction of the source, signifying that Jesus is not subject to the Spirit.

[2] This new epoch opens with the announcement of 'the Kingdom of God'. One should not read into Luke's phrase the idea of 'proximity'. This period is described in Luke iv, 18 ff. as the fulfilment of Scripture. (See below.) The period of Jesus the time of which is sharply defined (cf. iv, 13 and xxii, 3), is meant to be a clear manifestation of salvation.

[3] This is a further argument against the Proto-Luke theory. Hirsch, II, p. 251 uses the occurrence of διάβολος in the one case and σατανᾶς in the other, as the basis for literary analysis. His reference to Q is of course correct, and the expression σατανᾶς in xxii, 3 may also come from a source. In this case we see all the more clearly how Luke builds up his unified structure from a variety of elements.

28

GEOGRAPHICAL ELEMENTS

In Luke iv, 5 it is noticeable that, in contrast with Matthew, the mountain is not mentioned, although the theme is suggested in the expression ἀναγαγών. Is this connected with the fact that in Luke 'the mountain' is more stylized than in the other evangelists and has a fixed meaning? It is the place of prayer, the scene of secret revelations, of communication with the unseen world. No temptation can take place on it nor any public preaching.

2. The Summary in Luke iv, 14 f.

The way in which the transition from vv. 9 ff. to v. 14 implies the remoteness of Galilee does not create a favourable impression of the accuracy of Luke's identification of the separate regions such as is generally assumed.[1]

In each case the Spirit serves to motivate the change of place, and K. L. Schmidt rightly sees in this a motif peculiar to Luke, by means of which the evangelist gives the change of place significance for redemptive history.[2]

The real problem of our investigation emerges with the first mention of Galilee. We shall see from it the great extent to which geography is involved in the composition of the Gospel.

It has long been established that Mark i, 14 is based on a scheme of redemptive history.[3] The aims of both Matthew and Luke is to make a smoother transition from Mark i, 13 to i, 14,[4] but they do it independently of one another.[5] It is worth noting

[1] Cf. Klostermann on Luke i, 5.

[2] K. L. Schmidt, p. 37. We need only add to his reference to the Acts of the Apostles, where the same motif is found repeatedly, that one modification arises from the special nature of Luke's Christology: in Acts the Spirit 'commands', because it is men that are involved, but the Son of God receives no 'commands' from Him.

[3] Ibid., p. 34.   [4] Ibid., pp. 34 f.

[5] Streeter, p. 206, stresses the remarkable agreement concerning the strange form of the name Nazara in Matt. iv, 13 and Luke iv, 16. This is of course important from the point of view of a possible connection between Matthew and Luke in their editing of the context, perhaps on the basis of a common Q tradition (alongside the Marcan source). It is of interest to Streeter to establish a Q source, in order to prove in accordance with his theory a Proto-Lucan S/Q compilation. Yet apart from the form of the name we have mentioned, there is no similarity between Matthew and Luke. Streeter himself makes particular reference to the later process of assimilation of textual forms, particularly in the case of place-names. We must therefore be wary of drawing conclusions from literary similarities.

Even if Luke found it in his source that Jesus went to Nazareth right at the

that we have here a passage where the editorial work of Luke can be proved independently of any theory concerning sources.

This passage is often quoted to illustrate the carelessness with which the editorial work is generally done in the Synoptics: Jesus comes to Galilee, his fame spreads, he is active; now he is appearing for the first time (the fact that the appearance in Nazareth is depicted in Luke as the first appearance holds good), but this gives rise to the difficulty that in iv, 23 Luke inadvertently presupposes an earlier ministry in Capernaum. Is not this interpretation the result of introducing an attitude to history which does not do justice to the text?

K. L. Schmidt rightly points out (pp. 37 f.) that at first it is not easy to appreciate the order of the events in vv. 14 f.: 'More than the summary reports of Mark and Matthew, Luke's verses have the character of a heading for what is to follow.' The attempt to demonstrate that there is an uncertainty in the order of events is the result of importing the meaning of Mark's version into Luke's verses. The latter look forward and provide a survey of the whole of the first period of the ministry of Jesus ($\kappa\alpha\theta$' $\ddot{o}\lambda\eta\varsigma$, $\dot{\epsilon}\nu$ $\tau\alpha\hat{\imath}\varsigma$ $\sigma\upsilon\nu\alpha\gamma\omega\gamma\alpha\hat{\imath}\varsigma$ $\alpha\dot{\upsilon}\tau\hat{\omega}\nu$, $\delta\sigma\xi\alpha\zeta\acute{o}\mu\epsilon\nu\sigma\varsigma$ $\dot{\upsilon}\pi\grave{o}$ $\pi\acute{\alpha}\nu\tau\omega\nu$).

There is more here than a mere reference to the next story, for the whole first stage of the ministry is envisaged. Later Luke marks the end of this stage and the beginning of the next, that of the 'journey', just as distinctly. The expression $\delta\sigma\xi\alpha\zeta\acute{o}\mu\epsilon\nu\sigma\varsigma$ contains more than just a factual statement of his success, for the success leads his followers into misunderstanding. This misunderstanding of the disciples will accompany him as he proceeds. 'Galilee' has, beyond its geographical meaning, a symbolical meaning which brings out its true significance as expounded by Lohmeyer, pp. 41 ff. But of course we must also consider the positive function of this locality—see below.

Thus Luke replaces Mark's account of the content of Jesus' preaching by the summary description of a definite period. This is significant for his far-reaching new conception of the 'life of Jesus', or rather, for the transformation of the existing accounts

beginning of his public ministry, then it is all the more interesting to see what he makes of this simple item—nothing less than a main pillar of his whole structure (see below). On the important function of the place in Matthew, although of an entirely different sort, cf. Lohmeyer, *Galiläa*, pp. 36 f., and Klostermann on Matt. iv, 13.

into such a 'life of Jesus'. Of course Mark's synopsis at this point could not satisfy him even in its essentials. (Klostermann, ad loc.) For Luke, 'the gospel of God' is no longer that of the nearness of the Kingdom.[1] Why does Luke emphasize ἐδίδασκεν ἐν ταῖς συναγωγαῖς αὐτῶν so much in his summary? We are reminded of the standard point of contact in the Acts of the Apostles, according to which Paul first of all regularly goes into the synagogue. This connecting link derives from the relation of the Church to Israel within redemptive history. This is another pre-Lucan motif, which is stereotyped by Luke.

The area covered by Jesus' ministry embraces the whole περίχωρος; what is the significance of this?[2]

In Luke's view we have to distinguish the region in which Jesus himself is active (which is more sharply defined in Luke than in the other evangelists) from the region into which his fame spreads. In other words, one must distinguish the region into which he goes from that out of which people come to him. According to Luke he never goes beyond the region of Galilee and Judæa. He enters neither Samaria (this will be discussed later) nor Phoenicia, nor Decapolis nor any other part of Peræa.[3] The sole exception, the journey to the region of Gadara, is indicated as such. On the other hand, the people come to him from regions which he never visits. On the whole the summary accounts of his first public appearances have a unity of style which suggests a very definite geographical conception.

3. The Beginnings (Luke iv, 16–30)

In the series of supposed discrepancies in chapter 4, the reversing of the order of Capernaum and Nazareth holds an important position. We have to leave aside the question as to what the historical facts were if we are to understand Luke's account. We are concerned with its inner consistency and meaning.

[1] On the essential meaning, cf. Schlatter, pp. 46 f. What he thinks should be ascribed to the special source could be Luke's own contribution.

[2] Schlatter, p. 47: 'ὅλη ἡ περίχωρος indicates that the περίχωρος has fixed boundaries'. The normal usage suggests rather the opposite. Cf. Bauer on this subject. Josephus is of no assistance here.

[3] Lohmeyer notes the restriction of the area of Jesus' travels, but when he writes: '. . . but instead a new region opens up: Samaria' (op. cit., p. 42), he shows a misunderstanding of the nature of the itinerary. The extension is brought about by the inclusion not of Samaria, but of Judæa (and only of Judæa).

31

GEOGRAPHICAL ELEMENTS

The section iv, 15–v, 11 forms the point of intersection of some of the essential lines of Luke's account, and we must attempt to interpret exactly the geographical references. The structure is as follows:

(1) Preaching and rejection—at home.
(2) Miracles and popular acclaim—in other parts.
(3) Miracles and call—of strangers.

The literary critical question primarily concerns the problem, whether the passages iv, 16–30 and v, 1–11 are derived from a special source or whether they represent a free adaptation by Luke of Mark's version. If the latter could be proved, we should possess not only a striking illustration of his own theological outlook, but also of the degree to which he has modified his sources. But we are in a vicious circle, for the requisite proof presupposes a knowledge of these very factors, i.e. of Luke's own views and of the degree to which he has adapted the sources.[1] The question is whether, quite apart from these problems, we can recognize the essential meaning of the present plan, which can in any case certainly be ascribed to Luke.

The investigation into the historical course of events is faced in this section with a practically insoluble problem: even if Luke has replaced Mark's account by a variant from another tradition, the fact remains that he was familiar with it. Why does he not adhere to Mark's course of events? When Streeter suggests that he is following the order in the other source, the question remains as to why he did so. Which view of the course of events do we see here? In this instance an incident is definitely moved to a position which expresses some essential meaning (within the present context of the Gospel, that is, not an earlier 'Proto-Lucan' context).[2] If we explain the present order as deriving from 'Proto-Luke', assuming in other words that the account of the appearance in Nazareth was already an initiation story, how is the occurrence of the place-name 'Capernaum' to be accounted

[1] Streeter, Schlatter and Hirsch ascribe the passages to their sources of course. They are in fact quite different from the usual rendering of Mark's reports.

[2] The explanation, that Luke only adopts the sections in Mark for which he has no variants in the Proto-Lucan section does not solve the problem of what function the story has in the present context. We shall see that the passage has a function in that very arrangement of Jesus' life in which the Marcan elements are already present.

for? On the basis of this theory it can only be referred to future events, which in fact turns out to be correct. But then the theory no longer applies in another respect, for these future events belong in fact to the Marcan material, and thus presuppose its presence. Therefore at any rate Luke has Mark before him when he introduces this account here. But what is the significance of this choice of position?

The position is all the more surprising, as the incident is not a typical one. Its significance lies indeed in its very uniqueness. It may provide a symbolical presentation of the relationship of Jesus or of the Church to Israel, but this is not its sole significance. It has been observed more than once, that two levels of meaning are present. What, according to the author, is the primary meaning?

Luke makes no separation between chronological and soteriological significance. On the contrary, to him the historical sequence as such is of fundamental importance. Yet he is not a modern, 'secular' historian, he is a man of faith. In other words, when he has discovered the redemptive significance of an event, he can go on to deduce from it the 'correct' chronology, which means, among other things, that he can begin to modify Mark. In contrast to Mark, we find in Luke not 'historical plausibility' for its own sake, but the basic pattern of a complete Christological conception, which is consistently set out in the chronological sequence of events in the life of Jesus. (For a different view, cf. K. L. Schmidt, p. 47.) The correctness of the chronology cannot be demonstrated 'historically'. In Luke's understanding the proof of its correctness is to be found in the fate of Jesus.

The locating of the story in Nazareth is part of its original content.[1] The elimination of the place-name contradicts the findings of both literary and Form Criticism. By omitting the reference to place one can do away with the alleged inconsistency in v. 23 and bring out clearly the 'typical' meaning of the passage.[2] But for one thing, Luke himself identifies this account with the Nazareth story of Mark, as he has a gap where the Marcan passage occurs.[3] For another thing, this view overlooks

[1] For the contrary view, cf. K. L. Schmidt, p. 41. Klostermann, e.g., states the position correctly.
[2] K. L. Schmidt, p. 40.   [3] Klostermann, ad loc.

GEOGRAPHICAL ELEMENTS

the fact that for Luke the meaning of the story lies precisely in
its historical uniqueness. There is no unrestrained symbolism in
Luke; only what is in his opinion a historical event can possess
genuine typological meaning. To reduce events to 'meaning' is
a modern procedure.

In its present form the story has two main points,[1] one, which
expresses the typical meaning and proclaims salvation to the
Gentiles,[2] and the other, which is bound up with the locality of
Nazareth. Jesus does not now turn to the Gentiles, but he goes
to Capernaum, to strangers; that is, however, not to a foreign
people but to those who are not his immediate compatriots or
relatives. Here, over and above the historical report, Luke's idea
of election is set out, which is also found in the passages
viii, 19–21 and xi, 27 f. Verse 23, which is usually rejected as
belonging to an earlier stage,[3] is vital for this second point;
but it is by means of this second point that the section is built
into the whole Lucan arrangement, which is therefore a reflection of Luke's own purpose. If the verse is derived from a source,
Luke in any case makes an independent use of it.

The general opinion, that the verse represents a reminiscence
of previous events, rests on an inadmissible interpretation of
history. It is a view which is not suggested by the text, is
scarcely conceivable from the point of view of literary criticism
and is disproved by Luke's structure. The future tense ἐρεῖτε
points to a future rather than a present utterance by those who
are being addressed.[4] We cannot assume that Luke has been

[1] Bultmann, p. 31, n. 2.

[2] Schmidt, who stresses this in particular, does not mention the fact that Jesus
does not go to the Gentiles. The move in this direction has its definite place in
Luke's whole work—after the outpouring of the Spirit. What this story says concerning salvation for the Gentiles is said in anticipation of the mission of the Church,
and does not refer to the historical ministry of Jesus in his lifetime; Luke makes it
particularly clear that there is no extension of the ministry to Gentile territory.

[3] According to Klostermann, ad loc., Luke was not able to remove the traces.
This suggests a remarkable procedure: he completely alters Mark's outline, but
to make it plain to the attentive reader, he deliberately inserts the additional
reference to Capernaum, which is not found in Mark!

[4] Klostermann's objections to the reference to future deeds and a future utterance are not plausible. There is no question of a future return to Nazareth. There
is no 'split' in Luke's narrative between present and future events. It is a question
of a clearly executed arrangement of the passage as an introductory sermon, in
which only future deeds can be mentioned. To what extent Luke uses Marcan
material for this is relatively unimportant for our purpose. Cf. R. H. Lightfoot,
History and Interpretation, p. 201.

careless here, as he would not find the decisive word Capernaum in Mark, which is the only place where previous events in Capernaum are described. The passage can only be explained as a conscious piece of composition. So far no particular deeds have been recorded in Luke, but they follow immediately upon this story and are deliberately set over against it—in Capernaum.[1] It is decisive for our interpretation that we observe this fact about Luke's composition: that the saying is in fact fulfilled in the course of the account. They come to Jesus later and wish to see him again in Nazareth (viii, 19–21). The speakers are his own relatives. In this passage the introduction of Mark's meaning for the purpose of harmonizing has a disastrous effect. Contrary to his custom Luke has removed the passage from its Marcan context, and has also omitted the motivation provided by Mark iii, 21. This omission is generally taken to have a softening effect, which may be true. Other passages, however, which show a polemical tendency towards the relatives, suggest otherwise. In any case, the whole point of Mark's account, namely that they come to divert Jesus from his ministry, disappears with this omission. Luke's context shows clearly that whosoever hath, to him shall be given; and whosoever hath not, from him shall be taken away even that which he thinketh he hath. The arrival of the relatives serves to illustrate this saying. There is no mention of their wishing to take him back into private life, but they wish to 'see' him. Exactly the same wish is expressed by Herod not long afterwards (ix, 9). Chapter xxiii, v. 8 provides the explanation, which is that they want to see miracles performed. They want to take him to Nazareth in order that he may work miracles in what they consider the proper place. The meaning of the passages iv, 16 ff., and viii, 19 ff., is brought out by their position within the general construction. In the one case the Marcan text is simply taken over, in the other Luke is at least acquainted with it.[2]

---

[1] We have already mentioned the difficulties the Proto-Luke theory finds itself in here. One difficulty is that it has to explain 'Capernaum' as an addition by Luke.

[2] We must consider briefly the literary problem. Dibelius (*Formgeschichte*, pp. 106 f.) traces Luke's version directly from Mark. We can add in support of this that the additions reveal typically Lucan motifs and in fact give the impression of being a mere series of them. Thus we have a number of particularly important sayings, but the compactness of the narrative is lost. The motifs not found in Mark are:

(*a*) The scheme of promise and fulfilment (Scriptural proof).

GEOGRAPHICAL ELEMENTS

The theme of promise and fulfilment is set out by means of two Scriptural quotations. The first one, vv. 18 f. expressly speaks of fulfilment in 'the present'. Schlatter (p. 221) describes its contents as follows: 'What Jesus said to the people of Nazareth was the Gospel without any concealment. He brings to them the time of salvation.' One is reminded of 2 Cor. vi, 2: ἰδοὺ νῦν καιρὸς εὐπρόσδεκτος, but when according to Luke Jesus says: σήμερον πεπλήρωται ἡ γραφὴ αὕτη, then we see the difference. Paul identifies his own time as the eschatological one, but Luke sees salvation already as a thing of the past. The time of salvation has come about in history, as a period of time which, although it determines the present, is now over and finished. The analogous passage, xxii, 35 f., which distinguishes between the period of Jesus and the present in order to bring out their individual character, shows that Luke has no doubt about this. The meaning of this, however, is simply that the End did not come with Jesus. The truth is that in the life of Jesus in the

(b) The demarcation of the period of Jesus as part of redemptive history (from Luke's standpoint the 'today' of v. 21 is already a date in history).

(c) The rejection in Jesus' home town is taken over, but the combination with the motif of the relatives (in conjunction with viii, 19 ff.) is new.

(d) Luke's view of the relation between teaching and miracle is introduced, and also the idea of election in the specific form which we shall consider later.

(e) The Capernaum motif, which is linked with the choice of the 'witnesses' of the ministry which follows.

(f) The universalist tendency (although any suggestion that Jesus goes beyond Jewish territory is consistently avoided).

However, if Luke did not start from Mark's version, but from a variant of it, this affects the literary aspect to some extent but not the actual meaning of the passage. If this is so, then Luke must have found certain of the motifs we have mentioned already present, preferred this particular variant of Mark's narrative for this reason and emphasized the motifs still more. In support of a non-Marcan source one can adduce the Aramaic colouring (Violet, ZNW, 1938). It is impossible to look into the historical reliability of the two versions.

Hirsch (II, pp. 38 ff., cf. pp. 409 f.) reconstructs it as a 'pointedly anti-Jewish story'; but in the same volume he points out that henceforth Jesus will go neither to the Samaritans nor to the Gentiles.

There is one further observation concerning method on the question of the historical reliability of this account. The fallacy that one can draw conclusions concerning the historicity of events from the accuracy with which customs and conditions are described, seems ineradicable (Violet, op. cit.). According to this method, the next step is to draw from such accuracy of description the conclusion that the work of revision was done by someone familiar with the conditions. But the earliest narratives of the Synoptic tradition have no interest at all in giving a detailed description of the milieu. Besides, over against the much extolled accuracy we must set Wellhausen's reservations concerning the narrative.

36

centre of the story of salvation a picture is given of the future time of salvation—a picture that is now the ground of our hope: his life is an event which procures for us forgiveness and the Spirit, and thereby entrance into a future salvation. Yet this in no way alters the fact that the period of Jesus, like the present, is not yet the End. The Good News is not that God's Kingdom has come near, but that the life of Jesus provides the foundation for the hope of the future Kingdom. Thus the nearness of the Kingdom has become a secondary factor.

In a significant way miracle is set above preaching. This is expressed in the sequence Nazareth—Capernaum—call. It is instructive to compare the plan of Matthew and Luke, particularly at the start of their accounts. In Matthew's order teaching comes first. It is only after the Sermon on the Mount that miracles are reported. Luke also starts with a sermon, but it contains not teaching, but a reference to the function of miracle. The result is rejection. Then the actual event of choosing disciples is immediately linked with miracles, and the first call is preceded by one.[1]

With reference to the universalism of this passage, we may note that Lohmeyer strongly rejects the idea that there is a universalist trend in Luke's account of Jesus' ministry.[2] In fact Luke deliberately removes the time of the mission to the Gentiles from the period of Jesus, and uses for this purpose the method of delimiting the locality. It is only through the Spirit that the mission becomes possible, but the essential presupposition, namely the idea of election, does play a part in the Gospel and in fact one of peculiar complexity. It is seen in the fact that Jesus has around him not his relatives, but those who have been freely called. One belongs to Jesus only by call and discipleship. If the preaching of John the Baptist destroyed the possibility of a call based on descent from Abraham, now the ministry of Jesus carries this a stage further: one can be a 'relative' of Jesus *sola gratia*. The special features of Luke are the explicit emphasis to the point of polemic and the particular relation of word and deed in the call of the disciples. These two elements are also found in Luke's conception of the witness. As the witnesses have

---

[1] Cf. Luke's preference for the order ποιεῖν-διδάσκειν, ἔργον-λόγος with Matt. iv, 23 and ix, 35.

[2] Lohmeyer, op. cit., pp. 44 f.

to be present 'from the beginning' (Acts i, 21 f.), it is most important that the first deeds of Jesus and the calls should be connected. It now becomes clear what it is that the people of Nazareth, including the relatives, have missed—the beginning. Even if they come to him later, they cannot rectify this omission. They cannot now be 'witnesses'. It must be borne in mind that originally the idea of the witness did not have this exclusive connotation, but was used for the witness of the Resurrection, as can be seen even from certain Lucan passages. There was of course nothing to prevent the Risen One from appearing to his relatives as well. The restriction of the idea to those who were eye-witnesses of his whole ministry is unmistakably polemical and is an indication of disputes in the primitive community, in the course of which declarations such as Acts xiii, 31 were made (N.B., in a speech by Paul).

It is therefore unnecessary to suggest that the meaning of the antithesis between Nazareth and Capernaum is to be found in the symbolism of the turning to the Gentiles. It is true that this has something to do with it, but the primary meaning is that provided by the immediate context: Jesus now turns to the task of gathering the disciples, the group which will later be simply designated 'the Galileans', or as those who 'came up' with him from Galilee. Here we link up again with the geographical thread. Now the meaning of the first phase of Jesus' ministry becomes clear: it is during this time that the later 'witnesses' are assembled. It is no accident that they are designated 'Galileans'. This serves in particular to denote their later position in Jerusalem.[1]

4. The Beginnings: Capernaum (Luke iv, 31–44)

We will note in the first place certain geographical details. It is of course geographically correct to say that Jesus comes 'down' to Capernaum, but this does not necessarily imply an accurate geographical knowledge on Luke's part. κατά might

---

[1] In Jerusalem they remain the Galileans. Lohmeyer's view needs correcting at this point. The term 'Galileans' in the Lucan traditions at least does not refer to a community in Galilee, but to the primitive community in Jerusalem. The heart of the Galilean idea is that the Galileans know that they have been led to Jerusalem by Jesus and that now they are to stay there. Luke makes no mention of Galileans in Galilee.

well be deduced from the incorrect idea that Nazareth stands on a hill. A fuller elucidation of the geographical reference (πόλιν τῆς Γαλιλαίας) is not of itself of significance (cf. the statements concerning Bethsaida and Nain); but the question arises whether the phrase might not have a special point in view of the contrast drawn between the two towns, no doubt in line with Luke's ideas concerning the Galileans. Most remarkable of all, however, is the fact that we are not told anywhere in Luke that Capernaum is situated by the lake. Yet the fact that it is situated here is part and parcel of many of the traditions. Simon the fisherman has his home here (iv, 38). It cannot be an accidental omission, as it occurs all the way through. Manuscript D is aware of the omission and supplements from Matthew. A glance at v, 27 shows how consistent is Luke's practice. He leaves out Mark's phrase πάλιν παρὰ τὴν θάλασσαν and thus transplants the call of Levi into the country. In Luke the lake is only a boundary and is treated as such (viii, 22, 26, 37, 40), although this gives rise to difficulties, as certain local settings cannot be separated from the lake, that of v, 1–11 in particular.

If one were not familiar with Mark, one would have the impression that Capernaum was in the middle of Galilee. Is that Luke's idea, thinking that Jesus would not choose as his centre a place at the edge of this region?

Verse 37 harks back of course to v. 14, and provides the first confirmation of that statement.

Verse 38 has to be altered as a result of the omission of Mark i, 16–20, as v. 31 has already been altered compared with Mark i, 21, where the plural is replaced by the singular. The controversial question as to whether Luke presumes that Simon was previously acquainted with Jesus is to be answered in the negative.[1] One might wonder in fact whether it is not Luke's intention to use this statement to explain their acquaintance. It is true that in v, 1–11 he does not refer back to it and that he makes no mention later of any connection between Simon and Capernaum. In the light of v, 1 ff., it becomes doubtful whether one can use iv, 38 f. as evidence for locating the town by the

[1] It is pointless of course to ask how Jesus comes to be in this particular house. This statement is in fact made in very general terms. What is significant for Luke's conception is the postponement of the call, even though the logical sequence suffers.

lake. Verse 43 brings out the significance of a declaration by Mark: "δεῖ"! ὅτι ἐπὶ τοῦτο ἀπεστάλην. The phrase εὐαγγελίζεσθαι τὴν βασιλείαν τοῦ θεοῦ is the typically Lucan, non-eschatological form of the proclamation of the Kingdom, a substitute for the original form ἤγγικεν.[1]

καὶ ταῖς ἑτέραις πόλεσιν signifies the fixed area in which he is to appear, as is shown by the definite article. It indicates a boundary beyond which he does not go.

The region is positively stated in v. 44, which is exceptionally important for our investigation: is Jesus' ministry set in Galilee or in Judæa? And what areas are meant by the two terms? As far as textual criticism is concerned, one has here, as often, the impression that the decision is for the most part only the outcome of a conception which is already present.[2] In this passage the external evidence is in fact of little help in arriving at a decision.[3] It is a debatable point which reading represents a modification. So we have to fall back upon arguments as to the basic meaning. 'Galilee' fits in with the plan of Mark and Matthew, but not with Luke's (even if we ignore this particular passage for reasons of method).[4] This can be seen from the two

---

[1] See below on x, 9. For examples of typical terminology, cf. ix, 2, 11, 60; xvi, 16; xviii, 29; xxi, 31.

[2] Klostermann speaks of 'intentional extension of the activity of Jesus to the whole of Jewish territory' and refers to Luke i, 5 and to the evidence contained in Luke of the usage of 'Judæa'. K. L. Schmidt sees that the external evidence cannot be decisive, and turning to the 'higher textual criticism', states that Judæa is 'simply excluded' by the context. If this is so, then it applies to the whole of Jewish territory. Zahn and Wellhausen prefer Judæa as the more difficult reading. Hirsh (II, p. 10) considers 'Judæa' to be a wrong correction, which takes vv. 43 f. incorrectly as a 'complete programme of Jesus' public ministry'. Schlatter, p. 51: 'Referring to the new source Luke had no thought of restricting Jesus' ministry to Galilee.' Lohmeyer also (p. 42) reads 'Judæa'. It is pointless to quote more opinions. We shall attempt to formulate a new argument.

[3] It must be admitted that Codex D with its tendency to make corrections makes us suspicious rather than favourably inclined towards it. It is the geographical references in particular that make us suspect its special readings.

[4] Grant, p. 136: 'The real center of Jesus' ministry in Luke is "Judæa", that is, the Jewish populated part of Palestine . . .', a definition of Judæa which is questionable. One problem is the relation of the term 'Judæa' to the important motif of the 'beginning in Galilee' and the 'anabasis' of the Galileans. In the passages which mention it, it is difficult to separate the source from the editorial adaptation of it. In any case the source definitely mentioned only Galilee. Luke modifies this by making Jesus preach in Judæa as well at an early stage. But what then becomes of the 'journey' to Jerusalem? This question becomes more acute if we read 'Judæa' here. On this matter, see below.

passages vii, 17 and xxiii, 5 which prove that in this section the original reading is Judæa. For Luke, in contrast to Mark, Jesus' ministry covers the whole of Jewish territory, and is all the more rigidly restricted to this. Yet Galilee and Judæa are throughout clearly distinguished as regions (contrary to Klostermann's comment on Luke i, 5).

This seems to be contradicted by the report of the journey, in so far as it appears to assume that Jesus crossed from Galilee to Judæa, and that he spent some time in Samaria. We shall consider these questions later.[1]

'Galilee' has no fundamental significance for Luke as a region (cf. by contrast Matt. iv, 14 ff.), but only on account of the 'Galileans'. It is Judæa that has a significance of its own as a locality, especially Jerusalem as the place of the Temple.[2] The manuscripts do not appreciate this distinction, but make corrections from the parallel passages (especially D; cf. its variants for iv, 31; v, 14, 27.

5. The Call by the Lake (Luke v, 1–11)[3]

As regards the sequence, it is not demanded by the text that Jesus must already have known the disciples. Such an interpretation is the result of pragmatic reflection. The draught of fishes seems rather to be an initiatory miracle.

The style of the call is very different from Mark. It follows upon a miracle, whilst Mark bases it on the ἐξουσία expressed in the call itself. Whereas in Mark the idea of the creative word

[1] We will refer here in passing to an idea which we shall have to examine in greater detail later (cf. comments on Luke xvii, 11), viz., that in interpreting Luke's geographical references we cannot just take for granted our knowledge of the map. In all probability Luke had no exact idea of the country. On the one hand Galilee and Judæa are clearly distinguished, and on the other hand he implies they are close to one another. Does he imagine the two regions to be adjacent, so that to his mind Samaria does not lie between them but alongside them? If this is so, the idea contained in iv, 44 no longer presents any difficulty in connection with the report of the journey.

[2] Lohmeyer, op. cit., especially pp. 41 ff.

[3] The literary problem is solved in this section in the same way as in iv, 16–30. Bultmann rightly points out (p. 232) that there has been considerable modification by the author. It is obvious that vv. 1–3 are modelled on Mark i, 16–20 and iv, 1 f. We need not concern ourselves with the question concerning the history of the tradition, as to whether or not the origin of this passage was an Easter story. In any case it did not come down to Luke as such.

appears, in Luke the mighty deed and the word of the Kingdom are two separate factors. In Mark the call comes at the beginning, as part of the eschatological preliminaries, but in Luke it has to be preceded by a miraculous demonstration.

In v, 1 we meet for the first time the term used by Luke for the 'lake of Galilee', i.e. λίμνη.[1] We have already mentioned that Luke makes little use of the setting of the shore.[2] Whereas in Mark the lake is the centre for Jesus' teaching,[3] in Luke he appears publicly on the shore only on this one occasion, and here it is in connection with the scene of manifestation; even then it is separated by v. 4 from the scene where he is teaching. In what follows there is no further mention of the people.[4] Whether it was Luke himself who turned the call into a miracle of manifestation, or whether it had already taken place, it is a development that is in keeping with the trend of his thought.[5] Throughout Luke the lake is more a 'theological' than a geographical factor. It is the place of manifestations which demonstrate the power of Jesus.[6] Never again is he seen in public by the lake.[7] It has mysterious features. It is like a 'dead sea',[8] therefore it cannot be a place where Jesus stays for any length of time. Once again we see how a special geographical detail is connected with Luke's interpretation of Jesus.

Omitting the report concerning Capernaum, the story of the call should be read together with the Nazareth story, of which it forms the positive completion. The critical attitude in his home town serves as a foil to the presentation of what is the only genuine relationship to Jesus: that which is the result of a call.

---

[1] θάλασσα no doubt seems inappropriate to one who sees Palestine from the perspective of the Mediterranean.

[2] Bultmann, p. 381.

[3] Lohmeyer, *Markus*, p. 83. Mark ii, 13; iii, 7; iv, 1 f.

[4] The history of the tradition of the passage, e.g., that v. 5 presupposes a morning scene, does not prove anything for our purpose.

[5] It is difficult to say why he created this particular setting.

[6] The manifestations on the mountain, though they also are in secret, are quite different. They do not demonstrate Jesus' power, but show him in communication with the unseen world. On this subject, cf. *ZThK*, 1952, pp. 16 ff.

[7] And never again do we find another boat on the lake accompanying Jesus. Cf. viii, 22 with Mark iv, 36.

[8] This does not mean, of course, that Luke locates the scene by the 'Dead Sea', nor does it mean that he completely symbolizes it, as Bertram suggests ('Le chemin sur les eaux considéré comme motif de salut dans la piété chrétienne primitive', *Revue d'histoire et de phil rel.*, 1927, pp. 516 ff.).

When we compare the two scenes, we can detect again a polemical note reflecting the rivalry of two groups, one evidently gathered round Peter (and the sons of Zebedee) and another round the relatives of the Lord.

In conclusion we must consider two other suggested explanations. Klostermann suggests that Luke has forgotten to mention a return to Capernaum following upon iv, 44. He overlooks the fact that according to Luke Capernaum is not situated by the lake, and so the call cannot be located there.

K. L. Schmidt (pp. 46 ff.) traces in the early chapters the following scheme: Nazareth—Capernaum—Galilee, and suggests that because of this Luke could not mention the lake before this point. This is only begging the question. The point is, why does Luke follow this scheme which he himself has created? Nazareth and Capernaum do not stand together as equals, and Capernaum and Galilee cannot be separated, but are bound together, as was made clear in iv, 31. And further, Jesus' ministry is not confined to Galilee, neither according to Mark, where he goes as far as Phoenicia and Decapolis, nor according to Luke, where Judæa is included.

6. Luke v, 12–26

The editorial verse 12 refers back to iv, 43 f. Codex D takes Jesus back to Capernaum again in v. 14 and thus assimilates the setting of the story of the paralytic to the parallel passages. But this contradicts Luke's account, which does not think of Capernaum as a fixed abode; in fact Luke is now reporting the preaching tour in Judæa. He is quite consistent, and omits the place-name from Mark ii, 1.[1] Instead, the area covered by the ministry is once more described: Galilee—Judæa—Jerusalem.[2] No doubt stylistic factors play some part in the formulation of this pattern. The account corresponds in essentials to the statement in iv, 43 f.[3]

[1] Wellhausen's explanation, that Luke is indifferent as regards the itinerary fails to take into account how consistent Luke's omissions are.

[2] D leaves out Jerusalem, presumably because it is thought of as being included in the term 'Judæa'.

[3] Galilee—Judæa—Jerusalem is a fixed pattern in Luke, with modifications of course, e.g. vi, 19; Acts i, 18; x, 39. In any case it presupposes a definite geographical conception, without which this combination would not be possible, and also a particular conception of the relationship of Jerusalem to Judæa.

GEOGRAPHICAL ELEMENTS

7. The Call of Levi (Luke v, 27–36)

As we have already mentioned, Luke removes the scene from
the shore. Evidently no normal human activity takes place by
the lake, therefore there are no tax-gatherers there. The people
are omitted from the scene.[1]

8. The Itinerary in Luke vi, 1–vii, 50.

The references to time in vi, 1 and vi, 6 serve simply to mark
the progress of the tour. The first references to place are in
vi, 12 (the mountain) and vi, 17 (the plain). It is useless to discuss the exact position of the level place in relation to the
mountain.[2] The similarity with ix, 37 makes any suggestion
only tentative.

Even in Mark 'the mountain' is a place of revelation.[3] Its
symbolical significance is increased still more by Luke. Thus
there is no question of locating 'the' mountain. It is a mythical
place, to which 'the people' cannot come. This links it with the
lake. The people remain behind when Jesus ascends the mountain alone or with his disciples (cf. ix, 37 with the parallel
passages).[4] It has become the type of the place of prayer and
heavenly proclamation and therefore plays a special part in the
story of the Passion, such as Luke did not find in his sources.[5]
Consequently the plain also attains a special character as the
place of meeting with the people.

If the mountain motif has a model in Mark, the motif of the
lake is Luke's own creation, and is apparently intended as a
counterpart. In both cases Jesus is alone with his closest associ-
ates. In both settings manifestations take place, although of a
different kind. The mountain reaches up to Heaven, the lake

[1] D 'corrects' this.

[2] Schmidt (p. 112) and Hirsch (II, p. 45), suggest a hillside. In considering this,
one must at least give the aorist its full weight. The separation from the people is
stressed clearly enough in v. 12.

[3] Lohmeyer on Mark iii, 13.

[4] Lohmeyer, loc. cit., discusses the typological connection with the events on
Sinai. On the history of the tradition of the mountain motif as such, cf. Riesenfeld,
especially pp. 217 ff., 243 and 293. On the parallelism of mountain and lake, cf. the
parallel between the two scenes describing a call. Does the conception of the desert
in Q correspond to the mountain and lake symbolism in Luke?

[5] Luke vi, 12; ix, 28 ff.; the Mount of Olives.

GEOGRAPHICAL ELEMENTS

down to the abyss (viii, 26 ff., especially 31 ff.). The significance
of the mountain is more fully brought out by means of this
contrast. The divine messengers descend upon it, and Jesus
ascends it for the purpose of secret disclosure to his disciples.[1]

The lake motif is indirectly involved again when Luke replaces the shore in Mark iii, 7 by the plain. And also why does
he reverse the order of the scenes vi, 12 ff., and vi, 17 ff.? Surely
for literary reasons, in order to prepare the setting for the
Sermon.[2]

In Luke's description of the circle of influence (not merely
where Jesus himself has appeared) 'Galilee' is omitted in contrast with Mark. The list seems to belong to a picture of the
spread of Christian communities at a later time. If this is so, we
may suppose that the silence concerning Galilee is connected
with its absence in Acts.[3] Idumæa also seems to lie beyond
Luke's horizon. Finally, Peræa is missing throughout Luke. On
the other hand, the παράλιος does appear in the Acts of the
Apostles as a region where there are Christian communities, so
it is surprising that nothing is related of a mission of the primitive community in that area. These communities seem to be
traced back to the ministry of Jesus himself. The consistency
with which Luke refuses to allow Jesus to enter this region in
person is therefore all the more striking. Again the country
seems to be seen from the perspective of one living abroad.

The real relation of Luke's version to the Marcan source is
well described by Lohmeyer (*Galiläa*, p. 42): 'The description
in Mark iii, 7–9 is stripped of its secret eschatological meaning;
what are for Mark the most important regional names, Galilee
and Peræa, are missing. . . .'

In the present sequence the pattern is as follows: secret manifestation—public revelation. It is composed of material from
Mark and Q. There are two aspects to a manifestation, for it has

[1] The term τὸ ὄρος is found in Mark iii, 13 and vi, 46. Cf. Lohmeyer on Mark
iii, 13. There is at least a suggestion of the Sinai typology. There is possibly a
connection also with the hill on which the Temple stands. ἀναβαίνειν is a technical term. Cf. Bauer, ad loc., and Schneider in *TW*, I, pp. 516 ff.

[2] Does seeing a miraculous demonstration also play a part? Cf. the course of
events from v. 17 to v. 20. By the transposition the scene in vv. 17–19 becomes at
the same time a programme for the ministry of the apostles.

[3] Lohmeyer, *Galiläa*, pp. 51 f. On the other hand, however, the description of
Samaria in Acts as a missionary region shows that in Luke's opinion this is a region
that is not covered by the ministry of Jesus. On this point Lohmeyer is inconsistent.

both a secret meaning and a public meaning. This corresponds to Luke's twofold idea of the Church, with its secret celebration and its public preaching, and to the twofold aspect of the Kyrios, as Lord of the Church and Lord of the world.

The statements in vii, 1 and vii, 11 do not add anything new. In Luke vii, 17 Judæa appears again. It is pointless to attempt an exact definition of the περίχωρος of Nain. Again the area indicated is not that where Jesus has appeared in person, but that of his φήμη, and naturally this cannot be a strictly defined 'region'. Luke probably imagines that Nain is situated in Judæa.[1]

9. Luke viii, 1–ix, 9.

viii, 1–3

Klostermann considers the break at viii, 1 'more strongly marked than at ix, 51 where the turning towards Jerusalem begins'. If this can be established as correct, it has far-reaching consequences for the understanding of the whole composition of the Gospel. In fact it can be shown that Jesus has been engaged in incessant travels before ix, 51, and that this fact is specially noted by the author. In addition there is less evidence of a real change of place after ix, 51 than before.

Nevertheless, this explanation by Klostermann (among others) overlooks a factor which is of central importance in Luke's account. The 'tour' in the first part of the Gospel is different in kind from the 'journey' in the second part. The 'tour' is really just a matter of a change of place, but the

[1] The place-name 'Nain' is probably part of the tradition. Cf. K. L. Schmidt p. 115. The arguments against this are not plausible.

Schlatter raises the question of the περίχωρος. The question is important for him, for he ascribes the term to the 'new narrator' who is familiar with the geography. The word 'περίχωρος', however, is not found in the vocabulary of the special material; it is derived from Mark (Mark i, 28, cf. Luke iv, 37) and taken over by Luke and used more extensively than in the source (Luke iv, 14 and viii, 37). The only passage where it appears in the context of the special material is vii, 17, which is a typical editorial comment by Luke. It is impossible to gain an exact idea of the position of Nain, especially as the comment does not refer to where the event takes place, but to its effect. As regards the technique of composition, we note that after a Marcan section there follows a Q section, beginning at vi, 20. The special material is clearly inserted as a supplement. The placing of the story of the raising from the dead is motivated by vii, 22. The Proto-Luke theory is again in difficulties here.

'journey' primarily serves another purpose, that of representing a stage of Christological development. However strange it
may sound at first, change of place does not play a vital part in
it. We shall go into this more fully later. For the time being we
need only note that viii, 1 should not be regarded as the beginning of Jesus' travels. He has been a traveller for some time.
The appearance of the Galilean women assigns the passage to
the first epoch of Jesus' ministry. The mention of them of
course points forward to the Passion, but that is not all, for they
also have a function as 'witnesses from Galilee' similar to that
of the disciples, as we see from the part they play later. As Acts
i, 22 shows, we cannot restrict the circle of witnesses to the
'apostles' in the sense of Luke vi, 13. In view of this the women
have to be present in the first period. The Mission of the Twelve
in ix, 1 ff. points in the same direction. This incident belongs to
the first part, as the Mission of the Seventy to the second. The
expression ἐν τῷ καθεξῆς, to which Klostermann refers, does
not necessarily mark a new phase in the ministry, but may simply
be a connecting·link, as vii, 11 shows (Bultmann, p. 386).

The motif of the Galilean women is of course connected with
Mark xv, 40. The fact that the names vary no doubt indicates a
subsidiary tradition, but not necessarily a new 'source' in the
specific sense. Why does Luke mention the women as early as
this, and why just at this point, where he is again going over to
Marcan material? Why does he move Mark's report concerning
Jesus' relatives from its place and introduce it elsewhere?

The position it occupies in the general arrangement gives this
small section a particular significance. Here we can see both the
positive concept of the Galileans and the polemical concept of
the relatives, emerging as a motif not only from the source, but
also as part of Luke's own adaptation. Women have their share
in the 'anabasis' of Jesus, and later they witness the Crucifixion
and the Resurrection. Therefore they must be mentioned in
Galilee in the circle of those around Jesus, which is what is done
here.[1] Just as Luke with his narrow interpretation of the concept of witness and apostle (the strict definition of Luke vi, 13 is
in fact adhered to in the Acts of the Apostles) forestalls the

[1] Features from the primitive community have naturally been projected back.
Just as the male followers are turned into apostles, so the female followers are
turned into deaconesses (v. 3).

claims of Jesus' brethren, so it is possible that by his emphasis on the women he forestalls those of Mary. The Galilean women and Mary seem to stand in a similar relation to one another as the Twelve and the Lord's brethren.[1]

The section viii, 4–18 is again removed from the lake. As we have already noted in connection with v, 1–11, Luke may have used Mark iv, 1 for the composition of the scene there; therefore he does not repeat the setting here.

viii, 19–21

We have already pointed out that this section has been moved from its Marcan context. But why is it introduced just here? It is because it follows upon the mention of the Galilean women and upon viii, 9 f., where what it means to be a disciple is described for the first time, and where Jesus speaks of the privilege of the disciples in regard to the μυστήρια (N.B., plural) of the King-dom of God. Above all, the scene serves as an illustration of v. 18. The very position of the scene indicates that the relatives are excluded from playing any essential part in the life of Jesus and therefore also in the Church. This is made even more emphatic by the manifestation to the disciples which follows. Here events take place of which the relatives have no know-ledge, but of which they would need to know if they were to be able to act as witnesses.

The term 'mother and brethren' is derived from Mark; it is more easily understood, when it is not preceded by a birth story.

The relatives do not really wish to turn Jesus aside from his activities, they want to 'see' him and bring him to Nazareth. To 'see' means that they want to see miracles, as becomes plain from the Herod episode, which follows shortly afterwards. However, as Luke repeatedly makes clear, miracles cannot be

[1] From the literary angle we may note that at Mark iii, 20 Luke abandons Mark's plan. Apart from the purely literary aspect, there are two basic reasons for the alteration, the one already mentioned, viz., that Luke has his own opinion of the relatives (see comment on viii, 19 ff.), and also the fact that Luke has his own view of Jerusalem. In this connection there is a considerable degree of editorial adaptation by Luke.

The omission of Mark iii, 20 shows that for Luke Jerusalem is not just the place of the hostile power, although it certainly is that, but also the future goal of Jesus, and not only for himself but also for the Church.

had on demand; they can be had only as a free gift. This corresponds to the way in which one becomes a 'relative'—by a free choice.[1]

10. The Lake (Luke viii, 22–39)

This material is derived from Mark, and Luke does not need to make much alteration. In view of the fact that the lake has already disappeared from the centre of the sphere of activity, the setting therefore has a different character than in Mark; it becomes a setting on the border, on the edge of solitude. Luke does not even relate that the people are sent away—it apparently goes without saying by the lake. The accompanying vessels are simply omitted. The lake is the given setting for the manifestation of power. The mysterious features are heightened, and Holtzmann and Loisy (ad loc.) are probably right in their view that the storm descends like a demon into its element.[2] The disciples however are obviously spared, in comparison with Mark, for v. 25 presupposes that they still have faith.

The theme is continued in vv. 28 ff., where there follows the manifestation of power over the forces 'on the other side', 'over against Galilee'. Only on this one occasion does Jesus go beyond Jewish territory and the lake. The remark ἥτις ἐστὶν ἀντιπέρα τῆς Γαλιλαίας indicates that this is an exception; here we have Luke's counterpart to the part played by Peræa and Decapolis in Mark.[3] This precise reference indicates that what follows is in some way exceptional. If, in spite of this, Luke did not omit the incident, then this—one is tempted to say— 'katabasis' into 'strange parts' must have a special meaning. What is its meaning? Among other things it no doubt serves as an example of a demonstration of power outside Jewish

---

[1] Klostermann thinks the relatives are spared in Luke. The context and the statements suggest otherwise. Besides, in contrast to Mark vi, 3, they are reduced to a 'group'. It would be easier to find evidence of special consideration in the Nazareth story. This question, however, is connected with the literary question concerning the source.

[2] On the 'katabasis', cf. ix, 54; Acts xi, 5; xiv, 11, and the technical sense of ἀναβαίνειν.

[3] The question of the place-name, which belongs to textual criticism, is not important for our purpose. The important thing is the part played by the 'other side'.

territory, which was of fundamental importance for the Gentile mission.[1]

The character of the lake is, compared with Mark, made more distinct by the allusion in v. 31. Evidently the devils are sent to where they do not wish to go, into the 'abyss'. Is the 'lake' their proper abode, from which they emerge?

ἀπεπνίγη refers to the herd, not to the devils, for the latter are not yet destroyed, but driven away, sent out of the world back to the place to which they belong. Of the other geographical references in the passage, we note that in v. 37 περίχωρος occurs again, and that in v. 39 Decapolis is missing. The latter is omitted in Luke as consistently as everything else that lies beyond the lake and the Jordan.[2]

In the section viii, 40–56 only v. 40 requires comment. Here the fact that the people were waiting is noted.

For the rest, the word 'Galilee' disappears from viii, 26 to xvii, 11. Instead, the theme of the journey starts in chapter ix. The fact that even during the 'journey' Galilee is thought of partly at least as the scene, will be considered later.

11. The Mission of the Disciples (Luke ix, 1–6)

This Mission is different in its nature and its purpose from the second Mission (cf. x, 1). It does not come under the 'journey'. Is it intentional, that the Twelve are not sent out in pairs? Are they an exception to the general early Christian rule?

The instructions given in vv. 3–5 serve according to Luke to describe the period of Jesus as a time during which his followers are fully protected, and it is in fact interpreted in this sense in xxii, 35 f.

Between the Mission and the Return of the disciples nothing essential can be reported about Jesus, because there would otherwise be a gap in the testimony of the witnesses. The further question arises as to whether the Mission of the Seventy during the journey means that the Twelve stay with Jesus during this

---

[1] The motif of rejection, which appears in iv, 16 ff. and ix, 51 ff. as well, is also typical. In any case, Jesus does not come here again. Can we trace in the background disputes in the Church about the country east of the Jordan?

[2] When Hirsch (I, p. 40) suggests that ὅλην τὴν πόλιν is a faulty transcription of Δεκάπολιν, he overlooks the fact that Decapolis is not found anywhere in Luke.

GEOGRAPHICAL ELEMENTS

time, because they have to 'come up with him' (Acts xiii, 31; cf. Luke x, 1—ἑτέρους).

12. The Herod Episode (Luke ix, 7–9)

This passage points forward to the Passion story (xxii, 6–16), but the immediate reference is to xiii, 31–3. However obscure the meaning may be there, it is obviously the intention to make it clear that there is an interval in between the present and the Passion, as part of the whole pattern of events.

We have already met the expression ἐζήτει ἰδεῖν, which also points forward to the Passion (cf. xxiii, 8). The figure of Herod is treated psychologically. He is not in eschatological anguish, but is troubled by the people's opinions. He has no pangs of conscience on account of John. His rational way of arguing is very different from the role he plays in Mark, which is determined by the saving events.

Any thought of precursors and of the return of figures from the past is excluded.[1]

The reason why Herod wishes to 'see' Jesus is a pragmatic one: Luke needs this motif in view of the part which Herod plays later in the departure of Jesus from Galilee and in the Passion. Thus he appears in a significant scene in each of the three sections.[2]

13. The Feeding of the Five Thousand[3]

The curious statement in v. 10 b, that Jesus withdraws to a city, has often been noted,[4] as well as the fact that there is no mention of a voyage. Again there is no connection with the lake. Instead, in contrast to Mark, Bethsaida is introduced; again,

[1] We cannot object that these are Herod's words and are meant to be taken as characterizing only Herod. They are certainly meant to do this, but Luke takes the saying as generally valid. We find mention of resurrected prophets in Mark ix, 13 and Matt. xi, 14. Luke consistently omits them.

[2] It is impossible of course to say how far the picture of Herod is historically accurate.

[3] The question of traces of Q tradition in the story can be mentioned here in passing, but we need not go into it.

[4] D at least improves this into a village, evidently following v. 12, according to which there is no 'city' in the vicinity. The original text of Codex Sinaiticus goes further: τόπον ἔρημον.

51

one cannot prove from the map that this town lies by the lake and the text gives no indication of it. It is in this connection that we must consider the hypothesis first ingeniously propounded by Streeter, that this local setting is to be explained by reference to the familiar great Marcan omission which follows. We shall shortly discuss this latter question separately, but here we will anticipate the discussion in so far as it touches on this section. When Streeter and others assume a defective text of Mark to be the source (pp. 176 ff.) and make this the explanation of the differences between Mark and Luke, they overlook the fact that certain elements in this different setting in Luke are not isolated, but typical: e.g. the part played by the lake, which makes it impossible to place by the shore a scene where the people are present, the consistent omission of Decapolis, and the restriction of Jesus' activities to the region on this side of the lake.[1]

14. The Great Omission

It is a well-known fact that the section Mark vi, 45–viii, 27 is not included by Luke. As the explanation of this 'omission' is vital for the problem we are concerned with, we will consider it now. The suggested explanations of the omission can be divided into two main groups, which cut across all schools of literary criticism:

(*a*) That Luke is not acquainted with the Marcan passage. Again, two explanations are put forward: firstly, that he is working with a shorter *Urmarkus* (e.g. Bussmann), and secondly, that he is working with a defective text with a purely accidental gap (Streeter and Hirsch).

(*b*) That it is an intentional omission (Taylor—who differs from Streeter on this point—and Schlatter).

We will now consider in greater detail the explanations suggested by Streeter on the one hand and on the other by Taylor.

Streeter[2] first reduces the omission to Mark vi, 53–viii, 21, for in vi, 45 the disciples are sent to Bethsaida, in vi, 51 Jesus joins them after walking on the water, and in viii, 22 they

---

[1] Taylor as well as Lohmeyer stresses this (*Behind the Third Gospel*, p. 91). Cf. Grant, pp. 125–47.

[2] pp. 176 ff.

arrive in Bethsaida. These are facts which Luke takes for
granted.[1] Streeter rejects the idea that the omission is intentional. He holds that there is no real foundation for it, and that
such an omission would be out of keeping with the way in which
Luke normally uses his sources, for he usually omits passages
from Mark only when he already has a variant in the Proto-
Luke material to put in their place.

Streeter also rejects the *Urmarkus* theory, and suggests that
this passage was missing in the version of Mark which Luke
possessed. The style of this section is Marcan, and Matthew is
familiar with it.[2]

Streeter's own explanation is that the copy of Mark which
Luke used was defective; in his view the lost ending of Mark
makes this quite plausible.[3]

Streeter emphasizes the importance of arguing not from
general principles, but from observation. Let us consider his
proposals.

The following points have to be explained:

(i) The locating of the Feeding of the Five Thousand at Bethsaida.
(ii) The omission of Caesarea Philippi.
(iii) The fact that Jesus prays alone in ix, 18. What is the
correct reading in this verse? According to Streeter,
συνήντησαν; but if this is correct, how does Luke arrive at
it?

These points are all explained, if Luke's source extends as far

[1] Otherwise the mention of Bethsaida and the setting of Luke ix, 18 becomes
unintelligible. What has to be explained is why Luke includes the place-name, but
not the lake. Is this the result, as Streeter suggests, of the sheer accident that there
was simply no mention of the lake in Luke's copy? To say this one would need to
be able to determine very precisely the extent to which the text was defective. This
is exactly what Streeter attempts, but there is a danger of confusion between what
can be assumed and what still remains to be proved.

[2] On this point Hirsch appeals to his theory that Matthew used a quite different
version of Mark from Luke.

Bussmann rejects the idea of an accident (*Syn. Studien*, I, pp. 50 ff.). He also
believes that we cannot attribute to Luke an intentional omission for fear of
creating doublets, as Luke has more doublets than any of the other evangelists.
Bussmann's demonstration of the doublets in Luke is impressive, but he cannot
point to any narrative doublets. The twofold reports, e.g. two instances of raising
from the dead, are not really 'doublets'.

[3] His arguments are inconclusive. Literary criticism can still fall back upon the
Urmarkus.

as αὐτὸς μόνος in Mark vi, 47, and starts again at καὶ ἐν τῇ ὁδῷ ἐπηρώτα in Mark viii, 27. From these fragments Luke builds up a reasonable sequence of events.

(i) He concludes from the incomplete text that Bethsaida is nearby 'so that the disciples would be able to land and come back to meet our Lord by road, after he had dismissed the multitude'.[1] It is quite natural that he should put the place-name right at the beginning of the story of the Feeding.

(ii) It also helps to explain without difficulty the absence of Caesarea Philippi. To explain it as the result of an indifference to geography is unsatisfactory, for there is no other evidence for such an assumption than that provided by this passage.

(iii) If Luke is using a defective text, then in stating that Jesus is alone he is not setting himself in deliberate opposition to Mark. This is important for determining his relationship to Mark.

We cannot but agree with Streeter in his caution concerning hypotheses based on Luke's alleged pragmatic considerations. But against his suggested solution there is the fact that the picture of the locality which emerges is in remarkable agreement with other data.[2] In this connection Taylor's arguments attain greater significance,[3] namely, that Mark vi, 45-52 is a doublet of another story, and that Luke thinks of Gennesaret not as a region, but as a lake. On vii, 31 he remarks that according to Luke Jesus cannot minister in Phoenicia and Decapolis, and that the idea of a journey outside Jewish territory is unthinkable. According to Taylor it is not so much the content as the framework of these passages that causes the omission. Chapter viii, vv. 1 ff. and viii, 22 ff. are also doublets. 'It may be significant

[1] p. 176.

[2] It cannot be argued that this is the result of the omission, and that it is because of the omission that Luke possessed too few facts about a ministry of Jesus in places beyond the region. He had sufficient facts about the ministry by the lake, and about Decapolis, etc., but he suppressed them. Against Streeter, who has to associate the Feeding closely with Peter's confession, there is also the fact that Luke usually locates a manifestation to the disciples and a manifestation to the people in different places, as they are different in kind. In other words, manifestations in Luke have a twofold aspect, a secret one and a public one. Cf. v, 1 ff.; Draught of Fishes— healing; vi, 12 ff.: mountain-plain; viii, 22 ff. and viii, 40: Mission—Feeding of the Five Thousand; the Transfiguration and ix, 37. Streeter does not explain the omission of Mark vi, 31, which nevertheless is closely connected with the question of the locality. There is a typically Lucan motif here.

[3] *Behind the Third Gospel*, esp. p. 91.

54

that the only indications in Mark which point to any place or district outside Galilee are in Luke omitted'; Caesarea Philippi is lacking, also the location of the Mount of Transfiguration, and there is nothing corresponding to Mark ix, 30. 'The consequence is that in Luke Section C[1] is a Galilean Section throughout.' 'It appears, then, that the omission of Mark vi, 45–viii, 26 and the treatment which St. Luke has accorded to Mark viii, 27–ix, 40 in Section C, stand upon the same plane in respect of the movements of Jesus.'[2]

Taylor's reference to the framework and the agreement with the other parts of the Gospel is worthy of consideration.[3] We can go even further, and add that the close connection between the Feeding, the Confession and the Transfiguration is vital for Luke. In his geographical scheme there is no place for such a journey as Mark describes in the first stage of Jesus' ministry, nor in the next stage either. Of course Luke knows that Phoenicia is a region containing Christian communities, as is shown by the Acts of the Apostles (and is implied in Luke vi, 17), but according to him Jesus himself does not enter the region.

Does Luke realize that by making Bethsaida the scene of a manifestation he is laying the foundation for the lamentation over this town in x, 13? Does he know that Bethsaida was outside Herod's jurisdiction? We should not speak at this point of Jesus' withdrawing from Herod, for such a withdrawal is explicitly indicated at another point; but there might be at least a suggestion of a withdrawal in view of Herod's desire to see a miracle.

15. Peter's Confession and the Prediction of the Passion (Luke ix, 18–27)

If Luke is familiar with the section omitted from Mark, he must have intentionally replaced Caesarea Philippi by Bethsaida; our view of this, however, depends on the view we take concerning the omission. We will consider first what can be established

---

[1] Taylor's term for this section in Luke, arising from his Proto-Luke hypothesis.
[2] All the quotations, op. cit., p. 91.
[3] Taylor's own arguments really show how questionable the Proto-Luke theory is. In Block C the Marcan material is presupposed for the insertion of the other passages. If this is connected with the omission, then it means that Luke used Mark from the beginning.

quite apart from this latter problem. It is clear that the Feeding, the Confession, the Prediction of the Passion and the Transfiguration form a complete cycle, to which Luke assigns a prominent function in his whole structure. The geographical approximation of these incidents, whatever the cause of it may be, produces a series of Christological statements which Luke harmonizes one with the other by altering his sources and introducing variations of Marcan motifs. For example, he turns Mark's Messianic secret into a misunderstanding of the Passion.

Mark viii, 32 is missing. As a result, the difference stands out all the more clearly; on the one hand, Jesus speaks only to the disciples, on the other hand to all (Luke ix, 23—cf. the Marcan form). In Luke's context the people are the same as those at the Feeding. Therefore the sayings in vv. 23 ff. stand in strong contrast to the 'glory' that was seen in the miracle, and in this way the correct understanding of miracle is made plain. In Mark the distinction between disciples and people seems to depend on the theory of the secret, which does not exist in this form for Luke. This is how Mark is modified: in certain instances Luke sets out the same facts as Mark, but the difference is in the manner, depending on the audience. (Cf. the heightening of the contrast in v. 18.) In ix, 21 Luke bases the command of secrecy on the inevitability of the Passion, whereas in Mark the secret is a matter of fundamental principle. It is the same form of the motif of silence as appears in ix, 31 and later in the deliberate discontinuance of miracles in the Jerusalem period. Peter's protest is omitted, and in place of it is another motif, that of the secret of the Passion. The disciples do not protest about the way which lies ahead of Jesus, for they have no understanding of it (ix, 45 and xviii, 34). This idea has been imported into the text by Luke. From the psychological point of view it is scarcely conceivable that they should not understand these clear utterances.[1]

The abbreviation of Mark ix, 1 is connected with Luke's conception of the Kingdom, for instead of the event of the arrival of the Kingdom Luke stresses the state of affairs that it represents. Luke knows that nobody of Jesus' generation has experienced the Parousia, but it is granted to them to see the Kingdom. This conception of the Kingdom is in accordance with

---

[1] The emphasis on the failure to understand is unmistakable. It is true that Luke has the support of Mark ix, 32, but he both underlines it and repeats it.

that expressed in xvii, 21 and xxii, 15 ff. (cf. also xxii, 69 with Mark xiv, 62).

16. The Transfiguration (Luke ix, 28-36)

We come now to the classical mountain-scene in the Gospel.[1] Once again, Jesus is separated from the people (vv. 28, 37).[2] As regards the position of the particular mountain we learn no more than in other cases. It is pointless to attempt to identify it geographically, for Luke gives no indication and is not interested in this aspect.[3] What matters for him is that the mountain is a place of manifestation. He has obviously realized the difficulties of the Marcan form, but he has not achieved a satisfactory sequence himself.[4] However, he makes the story serve his particular point of view.

The purpose behind the heavenly manifestation is the announcement of the Passion, and by this means the proof is given that the Passion is something decreed by God. This is of particular importance for the Lucan type of the kerygma.[5] It is true that we are immediately confronted by the difficulty, that on the one hand the Passion is here disclosed to Jesus as something new, but on the other hand he has already spoken of it himself. The problem cannot be solved by literary analysis, as the difficulty is obviously created by Luke himself. It arises from the fact that on the one hand he adheres to Mark's order, and on the other connects the scene with the Passion. If we take the context seriously—which is necessary in Luke—then the story

[1] We can pass over the question of the source and the problem of the history of the tradition (e.g. whether it was originally an Easter story—cf. Bultmann, p. 278). Riesenfeld's investigation of the 'myth pattern' is not relevant for our purpose, for our concern is with Luke's work as editor.

[2] In this passage the expression τὸ ὄρος has been interpolated by Luke, in place of ὄρος ὑψηλόν. P. Schubert (*Neutest. Studien für R. Bultmann*, 1954, pp. 181 f.) correctly points out that compared with Mark, Luke has modified the relation between the Confession and the Transfiguration by inserting in v. 28 the words: μετὰ τοὺς λόγους τούτους.

[3] The eight days cannot be used for locating the incident. In any case they do not indicate the distance to the mountain.

[4] On this point, cf. the commentaries.

[5] Consider the meaning of the Passion in the formulae of belief in the Acts of the Apostles, and the attempt to prove its 'necessity', also the role of the word δεῖ in Luke in this connection. See Luke xxiv, and, for the analysis of this chapter, cf. P. Schubert (see Bibliography).

provides the heavenly confirmation of Jesus' prediction of the Passion.

It is related to the story of the Baptism. The one introduces the period of Jesus' Messianic awareness, the other the new period of Jesus' awareness of the Passion. The Transfiguration represents in Luke a new demonstration from heaven, which supersedes the earlier one. Luke's main aim is to bring out its special meaning, and he does so by connecting it with the Passion-phase in the development of Jesus' life. At the same time he differs from his source, for according to Mark it is the intercourse with the heavenly beings itself that testifies to who Jesus is. What is of importance is not the content of the conversation, but simply the fact of it. It is this to which the disciples react. Luke, however, is interested to know what the heavenly figures say, and he finds his answer in the context. The connection with the story of the Passion greatly influences the account. The prayer on the mountain, for example, points forward to the last of such prayers by Jesus on the Mount of Olives (xxii, 39—N.B., not Gethsemane), as it also points back to the Baptism (iii, 21).

The Passion is spoken of only to Jesus himself. Therefore there is no question of demonstrating its necessity to the disciples, but of ratifying it to Jesus himself to prepare him for his path of suffering. This also corresponds to the composition of the story of the Baptism, which in Luke, more so than in Mark, is centred on Jesus himself rather than on the spectators and John.

Other motifs, which suggest a connection with the story of the Passion, are the sleeping of the disciples, the fact that the incident takes place at night,[1] the heavenly apparition and the psychological explanation of the sleeping, an explanation appropriate to the situation here, but different on the Mount of Olives.

The whole scene has a double meaning and a corresponding twofold structure:

(i) The heavenly announcement to Jesus concerning the Passion.

(ii) An announcement to the disciples concerning the nature of Jesus.

---

[1] Cf. Klostermann on vv. 28 f.

GEOGRAPHICAL ELEMENTS

As regards the past it is a corroboration of Peter's confession, and as regards the future it is a means of strengthening them for the road that lies ahead. In contrast to the story of the Baptism, the voice speaks in the third person, which is quite in keeping with the context. The command to the disciples to hear him has, in this context, the special meaning that they are to hear his prediction of the Passion. The subsequent misunderstanding of the disciples stands out all the more by contrast.

The conversation during the descent is omitted, and together with it the idea of Elijah as the forerunner is suppressed. Luke's conception of the eschatological drama has no room for this idea.[1]

The whole episode therefore has a typological meaning which points forward to the events in Jerusalem. We find all together the suffering, the sleeping of the disciples, and the fact that on 'awaking' they see his glory. The Mount of Transfiguration foreshadows the Mount of Olives, in both its aspects, for it is the place of prayer and arrest as well as the scene of the Ascension.[2]

17. Luke ix, 37–50

There is a similar pattern in vi, 12, 17. The people again seem to be waiting on the typical 'plain'. The correct reading and translation of v. 37 are important for the understanding of the episode of the Transfiguration.[3] In connection with v. 43, it

[1] Grant, p. 101, commenting on Mark ix, 13: 'Luke significantly omits the section, while the Fourth Gospel flatly denies the identification of John with Elijah, i, 21.' So also does Luke.

[2] The sleep motif creates a difficulty, for it is not introduced until v. 32. which means that it is an editorial addition. Yet the disciples have evidently seen the two figures (v. 33), although they have not heard what they said. It is interesting to see how Mark ix, 6 is altered in v. 33. What appears in Mark as a dilemma resulting from fear is represented in Luke as the typical lack of understanding such as we find in ix, 45 and xviii, 34.

G. H. Boobyer, *St. Mark and the Transfiguration Story*, 1942, sees in the story (in all three Synoptics) a reference to the Parousia. J. G. Davies, 'The Prefigurement of the Ascension in the Third Gospel', *JThS*, N.S., 6, 1955, pp. 229 ff., connects it with the Ascension. The latter suggestion is more in keeping with Luke's intention, but Luke is not thinking just of the one event of the Ascension, but of the whole series of events, the Passion, the Resurrection, the Ascension, and the subsequent 'glory' of the Lord.

[3] Klostermann, ad loc. Did D imagine that the event took place by day or by night? Klostermann's preference for D is open to question. On the night motif, cf. the prayer by night in vi, 12. It is a typical setting for prayer.

59

should be noted that Mark ix, 28 is missing.[1] Mark's statement διὰ τῆς Γαλιλαίας and the motif of the secret journey through this region, are absent. Luke goes so far as to replace the note of secrecy by emphasis on the public nature of the journey. The scene is still set at the place of healing (ix, 37 ff.). Thus the close connection with the Transfiguration is preserved, which is now enclosed, more distinctly than in Mark, by two predictions of the Passion.[2]

The omission of the reference already mentioned appears again to have a specific geographical cause. Other passages, notably xvii, 11, suggest that Luke thinks of Galilee and Judæa as a continuous whole. Might it not be that the reference in Mark ix, 30 is not included in his version, because in his opinion one does not go from the Mount to Jerusalem via Galilee and Samaria, but past Samaria to Galilee and Judæa?

Mark ix, 32 is underlined by Luke and linked with the whole plan of the saving events of Jesus' life by bringing out the underlying principle.

Just as Luke cannot include Galilee in v. 43, so neither can he include Capernaum in v. 46. Evidently Jesus is now on the edge of the Galilean region, but Capernaum is thought of as being in the middle of the region.

(b) THE JOURNEY (LUKE ix, 51–xix, 27)[3]

1. General Survey

Two of the essential questions that we must consider are controversial: in the first place, there is the question of defining where the section begins and ends, and then there is the question as to whether it is possible to speak of a report of the 'journey' at all.[4]

[1] Wellhausen, ad loc., points out that in Luke Jesus never withdraws into a house with the disciples.

[2] On the omission of Mark ix, 30, cf. Taylor, *Behind the Third Gospel*, p. 91. Why is there nothing in Luke corresponding to Mark ix, 31b? Is it a subsequent addition introducing the customary phrase? Or is it Luke's aim to work up to the climax of the third prediction?

[3] Among recent analyses we may mention those by F. Blinzler, C. F. Evans, L. Girard and J. Schneider (see Bibliography).

[4] On the basis of their theory Streeter and Taylor examine the sources and the principle of composition. For them the section up to xviii, 14 is the outstanding

GEOGRAPHICAL ELEMENTS

Let us consider the opinions of certain critics. Wellhausen remarks that the public and the opponents are the same as previously in Galilee.[1] According to Schlatter, 'It would be foolish to call this section of the Gospel a "journey report".'[2] K. L. Schmidt writes:[3] 'In view of the meagreness of the material, it was not possible for Luke to compose a proper report of the journey. One cannot avoid being struck by the fact that although Jesus is travelling to Jerusalem all the time, he never really makes any progress.' In Bultmann's view,[4] the Samaritan journey is a fiction created by Luke, but, he continues (p. 388), he was 'not able to maintain the fiction of the Samaritan journey'. Underlying these views is the fact that the insertion of the material into a plan of a journey for which it was not originally intended creates a certain lack of harmony. In only one passage is the journey context inherent in the material, in ix, 51–6, where the arrival in a Samaritan village is an essential part of the story. Only two other reports contain a place-name as part of the original material, xviii, 35–43 and xix, 1–10.[5] Finally, there is one further passage (xiii, 31–3) which requires a local setting, that of Galilee. By its very nature it could be used to provide the motivation for the start of a journey, but in its present position it comes in the middle.[6]

example of a 'non-Marcan' composition. It is on the basis of the sources that Streeter propounds his view that we have here the 'Central Section' of the Gospel (p. 203), but on the question as to whether it is the report of a journey, he goes on: 'But the geographical notices are of the vaguest.' (Ibid.) Here we see once again how the Proto-Luke hypothesis creates its own difficulties, for it is in the present plan that the section is 'central'. According to the theory, what precedes it must have already been present at least in Luke's plan. Therefore the central section is a literary insertion, which explains its prominent position in the present construction. The Marcan elements form part of the basis.

[1] Introduction, p. 53.

[2] p. 331. It has to be admitted that there is some obscurity, as Schlatter bases his argument on the sources, not on the present text. 'Neither Q nor L (Luke) pictures Jesus as "a traveller", but rather as a wanderer who, since Galilee has rejected him [sic], has neither homeland nor habitation.' This view flatly contradicts the text.

[3] *Rahmen*, p. 269. Similarly Streeter, p. 215.   [4] *Synoptische Tradition*, p. 24.

[5] The geographical reference for the one story is found in Mark. For the other story, cf. K. L. Schmidt, pp. 264 f.

[6] Schlatter's reference to the source only obscures the problem. The fact that even after the departure in ix, 51 ff., Jesus is still in Galilee is overlooked. Besides, from the point of view of method, the present text and the reconstructed sources should be kept separate. If, e.g., the source suggests a short period for the journey (p. 270), this proves nothing as regards Luke's conception. The account of the

GEOGRAPHICAL ELEMENTS

We have to start from the fact that Luke develops the idea of a journey, for which there is little support in the material available to him.[1] This most characteristic journey motif is a piece of deliberate editorial work.[2] For the critics interested in the historical aspect this proves the 'secondary' character of the journey. This conclusion is no doubt valid, but from our point of view this very fact gives the motif outstanding importance, for here we are in touch with something specifically Lucan. The discrepancy between form and content does not lead us to 'reject' the journey, but helps us to discover what is Luke's Christology.

It is not possible to reconstruct the length of this period from the sources.[3] The present text suggests a considerable period of time, equal in importance to the preceding one.[4]

journey offers perhaps the most instructive example as to how form-critical analysis should be carried out. It is characteristic of all the views we have quoted that they start from the historical question: Did such a journey take place? Has Luke succeeded in making it plausible? It is in this way that Bultmann arrives at his opinion. There is value in this approach, but by itself it is inadequate. What we are concerned with is Luke's picture of Jesus. The question therefore is: What is Luke's purpose in constructing the scheme of the journey? His intention is all the plainer because of the fact that the scheme does not harmonize with the material. This means, then, that Luke is determined to carry it out at any cost. Why is this? Contrary to Schlatter's opinion, he does picture Jesus as a 'traveller', from ix. 51 onwards. This agrees neither with the fact that it is at this point that the real change of place ceases, nor with the fact that Jesus was already travelling. The position therefore is that there is a 'scheme', which we are investigating. It was not Luke who created the journey motif, for he found it in Mark (more likely than in the special material), but he was the first to develop it into a scheme. The discrepancy between the material and the scheme is the clearest indication by which we can recognize Luke's own composition and see what is his special interest.

[1] Bultmann assumes a connection with Mark (p. 361), and refers to Mark ix, 30, x, 17, and x, 32, 46. We can see how meagre the material is by the fact that only the two Jericho stories—one of which comes from Mark—indicate a real change of scene. In the special material there is scarcely any support for the motif. Even Schlatter admits (p. 390): 'The topographical framework, which enclosed the separate reports, cannot be reproduced.' K. L. Schmidt writes (p. 270): 'But it is the peculiarity of this tradition, that it provides individual pericopae without reference either to place or time.'

[2] Bultmann, pp. 361, 388; Schmidt, pp. 246–71.

[3] Schlatter's argument (p. 270) that the time of the journey is short as the period of suffering has now begun is unacceptable. It is not the period of suffering that has begun, but the period in which Jesus is aware that he must suffer. Besides, Luke breaks up Mark's scheme of the week in Jerusalem (Bultmann, p. 386) and replaces it by a longer period of activity in the city.

[4] The chronological references are few: x, 1, 21, 25, and xiii, 1, 31. It is as impossible here as in the first section to calculate the length of a period on the

62

GEOGRAPHICAL ELEMENTS

These considerations suggest that we should regard the author of the present Gospel as the creator of the scheme of the journey, and the arguments to the contrary only serve to strengthen this view.[1] The literary analysis points to the same conclusion, for the scheme covers all the layers of material employed.[2] We must now substantiate our view by reference to the text, but first we must discuss the second of the questions that have been raised: How should we define the limits of the journey report?

Where does it start? Klostermann suggests viii, 1, but this does not take into account the systematic character of the journey references, which do not begin until ix, 51. From the linguistic point of view also, it is only at ix, 51 that there is a main division.[3] Furthermore, if we begin this section at ix, 51 we can see how the section ix, 18–50 leads up to it, and how this latter passage shows the journey to be a progress towards the Passion. It is this that distinguishes the journey from the earlier travels.

As regards the end of the report,[4] K. L. Schmidt, with reference to 'Luke's geographical plan', marks the division at xix, 27.[5] Schmidt's argument is worthy of consideration, because he does not argue from observations concerning the sources, but from the present structure. The extent of the typical 'journey references'[6] supports his marking of the division. In any case

basis of these few observations. What it is important to see is that the journey is described as a comprehensive ministry and that in many passages Luke draws an analogy between this period and the previous period of Jesus' travels, as, for example, in the parallel Missions.

If the journey is conceived to be of brief duration, then the enigmatic verses xiii, 31–3 lose their last trace of intelligibility. Cf. Schlatter's view (p. 332) that according to xiii, 8 f. Jesus could not of his own free will shorten the period of time.

[1] Schlatter considers the geographical references to be the more or less accidental outcome of the combination of sources (pp. 219 f.). He suggests that this is also the cause of their lack of clarity, that the sources considered separately are exact, and that Luke wished to be the same. This explanation does not do justice to the systematic nature of the geographical references in the course of the journey, which stand out so clearly as a distinct group.

[2] One of the weightiest arguments against the Proto-Luke theory.

[3] This is the view of most commentators; cf. Schmidt, pp. 246 f. '. . . considering ix, 51–xix, 27 as a continuous section. Only by so doing can we do justice to Luke's geographical plan' (p. 247).

[4] Klostermann on Luke ix, 51 ff.   [5] Cf. n. 3.

[6] Luke is no more aware of the fact that Jericho is closely linked in local traditions with Jerusalem than of the fact that his route for the journey partly assumes a journey through Peræa. He particularly omits Mark's Peræa. Jesus' route cannot be reconstructed on the map and in any case Luke did not possess one.

we cannot place the division at xix, 11, for ἐγγύς means precisely that they are not yet at their destination. This statement does not serve to mark the end of the journey, but to represent the Lucan 'misunderstanding'.

Both the sections concerned open with a divine revelation, and, as we have seen, the two reports are assimilated to one another. Both are connected with the self-awareness of Jesus, with his Messianic awareness and the awareness of his suffering. In both periods his ministry begins with a rejection and, as a result, a change of scene (from Nazareth and from Samaria). On two occasions disciples are sent out, the same traditional material being employed. In both instances, there is a scene involving Herod, which serves indirectly to characterize Jesus, and in both instances there is a discussion about Jesus' close relatives. It is against the background of these parallels that we have to see the differences which Luke brings out. In neither case does Jesus make a secret of his self-awareness, but the sayings about the Passion give rise to the disciples' misunderstanding. This is another example of a motif that has been imposed upon the material, for in Jesus' sayings there is nothing that lends itself to misunderstanding.

In Mark the disclosure is meant to prepare the disciples. This is the reason for the repetition. On the first occasion Peter protests, and on the second they still do not understand (Mark ix, 32), therefore a third announcement follows. On this occasion too a scene of misunderstanding is added, but there is no question of a principle of the inevitability of misunderstanding; they are not yet on Jewish soil, where the final disclosure is given, at the Last Supper. Luke presents a different picture. In the first period there is no secret, for misunderstanding cannot arise until it becomes clear what kind of Messiah Jesus is to be—a suffering Messiah. This remains hidden from the disciples, until the Resurrection. In Mark the important thing is that he is the Messiah, in Luke what kind of Messiah he is.[1]

[1] The dispute concerning precedence after the second announcement and the incident concerning the sons of Zebedee after the third announcement serve in Mark as indications that despite Peter's Confession the secret has not really been discovered. Thus Luke's account is already foreshadowed in Mark, but Luke shifts the emphasis to the special theme of the Passion. The omission of the incident concerning James and John is connected with this. It is placed later, at the Last Supper, but then all the Twelve are involved.

GEOGRAPHICAL ELEMENTS

The theme of misunderstanding has a specifically Christological bearing, not a psychological one. The 'journey' begins after the fact of suffering has been disclosed, but not yet understood. Now the destination is fixed as the place of suffering required doctrinally. This requirement is expressed in xiii, 31 ff., a passage which interprets the journey as a circumstance necessary from the Christological point of view. In other words, Jesus' awareness that he must suffer is expressed in terms of the journey. To begin with he does not travel in a different area from before, but he travels in a different manner, for he now has before him the goal which, it is clear from xiii, 33, will not be attained immediately. The essential principle on which the account in this section is based, as well as the three-fold arrangement of the whole Gospel, is contained in this saying. It also suggests that the three sections are meant to be roughly equivalent in time.

2. Detailed Exegesis.

ix, 51–6: The rejection by the Samaritan villagers.

It is on the basis of this section that the journey is usually located in Samaria. In this case the 'other village' in v. 56 must be Samaritan. 'It is a misunderstanding of the meaning of the narrative to think that v. 56 refers to a non-Samaritan village, e.g. to a Galilean village situated on the border with Samaria.' (Schmidt, p. 267.) Schmidt can quote in support v. 52, according to which Jesus has preparations made for a stay in Samaria, the implication being that Jesus does not break with these people. It is plain that he is not rejected by the Samaritans everywhere. Against Schmidt's views it may be argued that Luke opens his first main section with a rejection in Nazareth, and that Jesus never enters this town again. It is not stated that Jesus 'does not break' with these people, and it is not implied in the rejection of the disciples; it is in fact a purely subjective interpretation. No analogies to such supposed behaviour on the part of Jesus are quoted, but there are analogies for the final

Miraculous proof has significance of course only in relation to Messiahship as such; it cannot prove the necessity of suffering. Proof is provided by the Resurrection and by Scripture, but only subsequently, after Easter.

withdrawal of Jesus where he is rejected, as in Nazareth and Gadara. It is not really a question of the people, but of the description of Jesus' ministry from an objective, Christological point of view. From now on Jesus avoids these places, thus providing an illustration of the rule which he immediately proceeds to give to his disciples (x, 10).

This locating of the journey in Samaria, which is almost universally accepted (with significant exceptions), is based not on the text, but on the map. Passages such as xvii, 11, however, make us wonder whether Luke might not have had an inaccurate picture of the country.

The section ix, 51–6 is a traditional passage, but in v. 51 we see the characteristic terminology of Luke's journey references.[1] This introduction, formulated in a typically Lucan way, sets the tone for what follows, and provides the opening for an entirely new section of the ministry. Verse 53, following upon v. 51, is for the purpose of emphasis. Schmidt rightly stresses the liturgical, cultic quality of the style.[2]

ix, 57

καὶ πορευομένων αὐτῶν is out of harmony with the material of this section, and a comparison with Matthew shows it to be an editorial contribution.[3]

---

[1] The question therefore arises, whether it was not Luke who first inserted the passage into this context. Cf. Bultmann, p. 388. His argument on p. 24, that it cannot be an old tradition, as the journey is something constructed by Luke, is not plausible. If we grant the latter, how can it prove anything concerning the antiquity of the tradition? It is precisely at this point that the Samaritan setting is original and pre-Lucan, and this is why Luke could make use of it in this passage. One cannot of course speak of a Samaritan 'local tradition', for the whole trend is anti-Samaritan. The style suggests a secondary insertion into this context (ἐγένετο + καί + finite verb—cf. Schmidt, p. 259).

Schlatter points out the 'Palestinian' character of the wording (p. 273), but he has to concede that the expression συμπληροῦσθαι τὰς ἡμέρας is Lucan. The second half of the verse is obviously Semitic. Did Luke perhaps find the passage already in existence as part of an account of a journey to Jerusalem, which meant that he was able to make use of it without difficulty? We cannot decide definitely whether v. 53 was inserted by him as an interpretation. The Semitic turn of phrase suggests the contrary. On the other hand this can be shown to derive from the LXX, which certainly exerted a strong influence on Luke's style.

[2] p. 260. For his view of the pericope, see p. 209. Cf. J. Starcky (see Bibliography).

[3] Schmidt, p. 260.

GEOGRAPHICAL ELEMENTS

x, 1

Even if the Mission of the Seventy is not, as Wellhausen thinks, an invention by Luke, it is true that the idea that it should in a special sense be a preparation for the journey to Jerusalem does derive from him. Further, x, 1 introduces into the scheme material which in itself does not belong there, but which presupposes a fixed centre of operations, as is shown by x, 17. The difficulty arising from the compilation of the different sources can be seen in the editorial word ἑτέρους.[1]

x, 38

Here is a further reference to the journey, without there being any reason for it in the material. Cf. the typical phrase εἰς κώμην τινά. Any identification with the Johannine setting in Bethany should be avoided, for it would be an attempt to reconstruct the historical facts. Luke is not familiar with the exact place.

In what follows references to the journey are missing, until they reappear in chapter xiii, again without any apparent cause. xiii, 22 gives an indication of how Luke thinks of the journey, not as a brief operation, but as a long period of activity directed to a definite goal.[2] The form of v. 22 is typically Lucan. A comparison with Matthew shows that Q material has been introduced into the scheme.

The journey motif and the description of Jesus' ministry are not only not integrated with one another, they are positively incompatible, yet this very combination is a basic characteristic of Luke's account. Jesus does not make directly for Jerusalem. The journey is simply one of the forms that Jesus' ministry takes. It is not the outcome of the fact that Galilee has rejected him, but of the fact that it is God's will that he should suffer.

---

[1] Does this mean that the Twelve stay with Jesus during this time, as sharers in the 'anabasis' as his closest companions? This is probably so.

We cannot say that the journey does not begin until after the return of the Seventy, thus obviating the difficulty. In Luke's conception, ix, 51 marks the beginning of the journey, and he further underlines it by the addition of ἑτέρους, which is a reference to the earlier messengers from the period of Jesus' travels.

[2] Streeter, p. 215: 'a slow progress towards Jerusalem'.

xiii, 31–3

The tradition presupposes a stay by Jesus in Galilee, and Luke is aware of it. He is familiar with the connection between Herod and Galilee (xxiii, 6). The question arises, whether this passage originally explained the reason for a journey to Jerusalem. If this is so, then the position Luke gives it is all the more strange.

It is certainly not a journey report. However, it not only expresses the necessity of the journey from the doctrinal point of view, but also the necessity of a fairly long duration. The purpose of the journey is not merely to bring about the inevitable change of place, in order to reach the place of suffering; it is also in itself something of divine appointment, which may not be brought to an end too soon, because it has a function of its own. Here again Luke has the support of existing tradition, but he develops it by producing from the available materials a new plan of the life of Jesus in three stages.

xiv, 25

The appearance of the people shows that the emphasis is still meant to be on the ministry, but as part of the journey.

xvii, 11

This is the most remarkable of these references, particularly on account of the order of the place-names. The commentaries usually start from the actual geographical situation, but can we take it for granted that Luke had such knowledge? Whether we translate 'through the midst of' or 'between', it is strange that Samaria is placed first.

Hirsch attempts to explain it by suggesting (II, p. 227): '. . . only a native of Judæa or Jerusalem could use such an expression . . .'. This means attributing the statement to a source, against which we must set the fact that it agrees with the other journey references. Here again this particular reference is not rooted in the tradition, but is an editorial insertion. The expression πορεύεσθαι is specifically Lucan. The other Gospels prefer ἀναβαίνειν. In order to make his thesis plausible, it would be necessary for Hirsch to prove that there is a journey context throughout the special material. It is also not a man from Jerusalem who would express himself in this way, but a man who is not familiar with the country. What is more, the style shows that the statement derives from Luke himself. He has set it out in a very simple way, by combining two facts:

(a) Jesus is on the journey from Galilee to Judæa.
(b) He meets a group of nine Jews and one Samaritan, and is thus on the border between Galilee and Samaria.

Most explanations take account of this, but the further question must be considered, whether Luke really has a quite definite but incorrect conception.[1] The expression indicates that Luke imagines that Judæa and Galilee are immediately adjacent, and that Samaria lies alongside them, apparently bordering on both the regions. This idea is not inconceivable for a man who knows that the inhabitants of Galilee and Judæa are Jewish and that the Samaritans are distinct from them. The main evidence in support of our interpretation is Acts ix, 31, where we find the same sequence of regions, in the reverse order. This hypothesis becomes all the more probable by virtue of the fact that Pliny has exactly the same idea of the country. (Pliny, *Nat. Hist.*, V, 68 ff.) First he describes the coast, in which he includes (V, 69) the country from Askalon and Asdod to Samaria, whilst in V, 68 Samaria lies inland. Then he continues (V, 70): 'Supra Idumäam et Samariam Judäa longe lateque funditur, pars eius Syriae iuncta Galiläa vocatur, Arabiae vero et Aegypto proxima Peraea. . . .' Cf. also Strabo, XVI, 760: Τοιοῦτοι γὰρ οἱ τὴν Γαλιλαίαν ἔχοντες καὶ τον Ἱερεικοῦντα καὶ τὴν Φιλαδελφίαν καὶ Σαμάρειαν ἣν Ἡρῴδης Σεβαντὴν ἐπωνόμκαεν. From these geographical details we can explain the course of the journey without difficulty: Galilee—along the border of Samaria—Jericho—Jerusalem; and also a number of otherwise strange statements. In Luke Jesus can alternate without difficulty between Galilee and Judæa, without any thought of journeys to Jerusalem in the Johannine manner. This explains iv, 44, and also the fact that there is no transition marked

[1] Hirsch begs the question. He assumes, what has to be proved, that the author has an exact understanding of this statement, and on this basis he then seeks to explain the expression. But this assumption becomes improbable if the passage is part of Luke's editorial contribution.

between the stay in Galilee, xiii, 31 ff., and the arrival outside Jerusalem. It is popularly assumed—although it cannot be proved—that 'Judæa' is used in a narrower and in a broader sense, but this assumption becomes unnecessary if the two regions are thought of as adjoining. According to Luke's idea, they are a unity from the geographical, national and religious point of view, and politically they are divided into the Roman province and Herod's domain. Luke makes use of this political distinction in the Passion story.

The whole country seems to be viewed from abroad. Luke is familiar with the coastal region of Phoenicia, and in Acts with the connection of Judæa with the coast. He appears to think of Galilee as inland, but adjoining Judæa, and of Samaria as being to the north of Judæa; this is suggested by the account of the mission in Samaria in Acts viii and by the statement in Acts xv, 3.

The question arises, whether the phrase 'Judæa and Jerusalem' might not perhaps be explained as the outcome of a particular conception held by Luke. In the story of the Passion the Sanhedrin could be taken for the city council of a free city. Does Luke think of Jerusalem as a free 'polis' in the Roman constitutional sense, so that it stands as a separate entity over against Judæa, the procuratorial region? The fact that the 'enemies' Pilate and Herod meet here is in keeping with this idea, and. of course, an official stay by the procurator in such a 'polis' is quite feasible. It is possible that this insight will help us to understand the strange proceedings between the governor and the city in Luke's account of the Passion. The following picture emerges:

(a) the Jews as a religious unit centred on the Temple;
(b) politically, they are divided into a procuratorial region, a dependent state and a 'polis'.[1]

The course of Jesus' trial, in which all the courts have their part—Pilate, Herod, and the city council of Jerusalem—corresponds to these divisions.

To this picture of the scene of Jesus' life must be added the 'typical' localities, mountain, lake, plain, desert, the Jordan, each specially employed in a way peculiar to Luke. In a word,

[1] This in fact is not what Jerusalem was. Cf. Schürer, II, pp. 79 f., p. 208.

the process by which the scene becomes stylized into the 'Holy Land' has begun.

If Galilee is directly adjacent to Judæa, then it is no longer necessary to make Jesus go through Samaria or Peræa. We need no longer try to explain the strange route through Samaria via Jericho. Luke can reproduce statements from his sources without sensing any difficulty. It also becomes clear how he can employ summaries such as xxiii, 5, which embrace a ministry in Galilee and Judæa. The course of the journey seems to be the following: Jesus comes from the 'mountain' to the border of Samaria, he is rejected, returns to Galilee, where he continues his ministry, now in the context of the journey; then he goes to Judæa, which is also an old sphere of activity; when the time comes he enters the Temple, and later the city. He does not touch the Jordan, and Peræa is avoided, as a comparison with Mark shows. Mark x, 1 is omitted, although Luke is acquainted with the verse and presupposes it in ix, 51.

That Jesus passes through Samaria can be deduced from only one passage, ix, 51–6. And as here it is a question of rejection, even this argument falls to the ground. All the other observations support the idea of a direct transition from Galilee to Judæa.

There is, it is true, another argument in support of a stay in Samaria, from the angle of the history of tradition, namely that stories concerning Samaritans are only to be found in the central part of the Gospel.[1] How much weight does this carry?

Samaritans appear in two passages, x, 29–37 and xvii, 11–19. Neither passage, however, represents a local Samaritan tradition. Their meaning has much in common with that of the parable of the Pharisee and the Publican, which is a local Jerusalem tradition. In both passages the viewpoint is definitely the Jewish one, for the Samaritan is at first assumed to be inferior, in accordance with the general opinion; but then on occasion this Jewish viewpoint is abandoned. But there is no evidence for the contention that they are local Samaritan traditions. The fact that Samaritans are the subject is no proof. The important thing

[1] Hirsch in particular employs this argument; cf. II, pp. 117 ff. and 347 ff. He deduces from it that the journey is set in Samaria, and that the author has a Samaritan point of view. This is the result of disregarding form analysis. The latter shows that they are Jerusalem traditions. See above.

is how they are depicted. The centre of the tradition is in both cases Jerusalem. This is shown by the scene of the parable and the part played by the Temple in the story.[1] It is from the standpoint of Jerusalem that the Samaritans are judged. In other words, these passages prove the opposite of what Hirsch, for example, suggests.

It is important from our point of view that Luke adapts local Jerusalem traditions. In these the Samaritans seem to serve the purpose of justifying the mission which is being undertaken in Samaria by certain circles in the early Church. This is in complete accordance with the report in Acts. Whatever may be one's view of the historical reliability of this report, the account remains consistent throughout both books.[2]

The statement in xix, 11 is important on account of the view of eschatology it contains. This will be discussed later, but the verse must be mentioned here because of its significance for the Proto-Luke hypothesis. It stands between a section of special material and of Q material, and serves to link the two, but it clearly presupposes Mark xi, 1.[3] Again we see how Luke's editorial work affects all the material from the sources.

To sum up, we may say that the extent of the journey report is not determined by the source material employed, but by the work of arrangement carried out by the author. It is he who stamps

[1] On Luke xvii, 11 ff., cf. Schmidt, pp. 262 f. The same applies to the other passage.
[2] There would be a further argument if the Galileans in xiii, 1 had originally been Samaritans. This report also points to Jerusalem as the place of its transmission (cf. the Temple and the Tower of Siloam). But how exactly do Galileans come to be in Jerusalem traditions? It is in the very Jerusalem material of which Luke made use (especially in Acts) that the Galileans play a prominent part, one even of doctrinal significance.
The story of Mary and Martha is not to be reckoned among the Jerusalem traditions.
[3] According to the Proto-Luke theory, the Bartimaeus story must have been placed before the Zacchaeus story later as an interpolation from Mark. Then after the Parable of the Pounds Mark is taken up again. In reality the Zacchaeus story is clearly linked to the Bartimaeus story by v. 1, in other words Mark is taken for granted. Otherwise Luke would have been more likely to make the Bartimaeus story follow after the Zacchaeus story. The Parable of the Pounds has also been interpolated later, for Luke does not make it follow on the Jericho stories, but on the reference to Jerusalem. In other words, the manner of compilation again points to the priority of Mark.
Luke xix, 11 shows how Luke binds all his sources into the unity of a 'journey report'. This view is confirmed by xix, 28, where Mark is taken over, obviously by the same person to whom the earlier journey references are to be ascribed.

GEOGRAPHICAL ELEMENTS

the 'journey' on the existing material, for his editorial work affects each group of sources, Q, Mark and the special material. The more meagre the material, the more distinct does the author's intention become. It is true that he does receive from his sources, particularly from Mark, suggestions for the drawing up of a journey, but in the elaboration and use of the motif for the arrangement of Jesus' life he is quite independent. The journey is therefore a construction, the essential meaning of which has yet to be brought out. It will not do to dismiss it by pointing out the geographical discrepancies. According to the editorial journey references, ix, 51–xix, 27 should be fixed as the extent of the section covering the journey.

(c) JERUSALEM

1. The Problem

The description of Jesus' itinerant preaching served to present an account of the assembling of witnesses, and it presupposed Jesus' Messianic awareness. The account of the journey that followed described a journey undertaken in the full awareness of the Passion, thus showing itself to be a symbolical entity, meant to set out a certain conception of Christology. Is topography used also in the story of the Passion as a means of setting out certain Christological facts?[1]

[1] The literary critical problem cannot be fully considered here. Of course the findings of source and form analysis must be borne in mind throughout. It is a moot point whether the source Q contained a section on the Passion; it is an assumption that has recently found fresh support—cf. the confident view of Schelkle, p. 285. It is more generally assumed that Luke had an additional source at his disposal for the Passion. As examples of analysis leading to opposite views, we might quote on the one side Finegan, who sees the whole of Luke's account of the Passion as a literary revision of Mark by Luke. Unfortunately he does not go into the question of the provision of a framework or of any uniformity of theological conception. On the other side there is Taylor, who traces back large sections not to Mark, but to a variant of Mark. P. Winter (*The Treatment*—see Bibliography) expounds a modified form of the Proto-Luke hypothesis in respect of Luke xxi–xxiv. In his analysis he agrees to a large extent with Taylor, but in contrast to the latter he declares that the authors of Proto-Luke and of Luke cannot be identical.

As regards method Taylor simply begs the question. Arguing for the superiority of the Lucan version (*Behind the Third Gospel*, p. 47), he writes '. . . it must be allowed that the story as such reconstructed [by which he means the reconstruction of the "Proto-Luke" version after the exclusion of obviously Marcan material] has much probability.' This simply pragmatic approach merely proves that Luke is concerned with improving Mark's account, that compared with the latter, in other words, his account is secondary.

73

GEOGRAPHICAL ELEMENTS

2. The Geographical Transition (Luke xix, 28–39)

The geographical references in chapter xix are either completely editorial or have undergone editorial revision (vv. 11, 28, 37 and 41). In v. 11 there was mention for the first time not merely of Jerusalem as the goal, but also of the fact that they are now near to it. Here there emerges the motif which occupies a prominent place in Luke's thought, for it is in relation to 'Jerusalem' that Luke develops his eschatology.[1] Taken together with ix, 45 and xviii, 34 the verse represents a further step in the account of the 'misunderstanding'. Once again we see that this is not a merely psychological matter, but something that concerns redemptive history, for the disciples interpret the approach to the city as the approach to the Parousia instead of to the Passion. They have a wrong conception of both Christology and eschatology. It is not yet—not for a long time—the 'kairos' of the Parousia. Above all, Jerusalem has nothing to do with the Parousia, though it has with the Resurrection.[2]

A literary analysis shows that the motif is introduced here by Luke himself. It is a question of statements which serve to link the special material and Q. As a result of this particular statement the parable that follows is given a new meaning, for its main point is now that of the delay of the Parousia. The statement also has a bearing on the special eschatological discourse in chapter xxi, and on the political note in Luke's account of the Passion. It is made clear in advance that the Entry into Jerusalem is a non-eschatological, non-political event, and Jesus is here rejecting any other view of it. He does not intend to set up 'the Kingdom' in Jerusalem. The alternative remains to be considered.

The reference to 'Bethphage and Bethany' simply comes from Mark, but in what follows there appears a complete and independent topography. What is its origin?[3]

---

[1] In answer to Lohmeyer, this means that the significance of 'Jerusalem' is not to be understood from the angle of Christology, but from that of eschatology; it is not a question of merely deducing this connection as a hypothesis, for it is given by Luke himself.

[2] This might sound surprising, but it is in accord with Luke's adaptation of Mark xiii and the story of the Passion.

[3] Bethany disappears from now on (see below). Verse 37 presupposes no special knowledge of the place. Schmidt's view that the geographical reference is a later interpolation (p. 297) applies also to Mark, if we are to take the longer text here.

74

GEOGRAPHICAL ELEMENTS

3. The Mount of Olives and the Temple

Whereas Matthew sets out the Entry as a type of the Parousia (xxiii, 39), Luke's main purpose is to stress the distinction between them, as we can see from xix, 11, and later from the discourse on the Parousia. He does not connect the Entry with the city at all—according to Luke Jesus never enters it before the Last Supper,[1] but he connects it exclusively with the Temple. The Entry is not an eschatological event, but the inauguration of the period of the Passion which is now dawning (we are obliged to speak of such a period). Matthew emphasizes the typological meaning of the event and its significance for the spectators, and the public demonstration of the Messianic claim. In Luke it is quite different: Jesus goes to the Temple. This has direct significance only for himself, in so far as he has arrived at his destination, and takes possession of it.

It is true that there is some typology in the story, but, characteristically, it does not relate to eschatology, but to Church history, for it is here that the foundation of the Church's claim to be the true Israel is laid. This is important, too, for the political apologetic, which from now on comes to occupy an important position. As a result of this, the part played by the public is restricted in v. 37: only the disciples rejoice, while the people watch.[2] Luke's purpose in altering the acclamation in v. 38 seems to be to avoid any contradiction between his emphatically non-political Christology and the fact of the Entry.[3] The Davidic Lordship is omitted. This seems to be connected with xix, 11, and throws light on that passage.[4]

---

[1] Taylor (*Behind the Third Gospel*, p. 142) thinks that if Mark were the basis of this story it would be hard to understand why Luke omits the climax, the Entry into the city, and he also thinks that the other source, which existed before Mark and has only been completed from Mark, did not describe Jesus' Entry, 'but rather the exultation of the disciples as the city came in view'. Taylor fails to see that the entry into the city is intentionally avoided, and that this very feature is characteristic of Luke's conception. This is a clear example of how literary critical conclusions are drawn from a preconceived interpretation. The objection might be made that in order to enter the Temple one would first have to enter the city, but Luke hardly had an accurate idea of the position of the city and of the Temple. The story in Acts iii, 1 ff., for example, proves this.

[2] This is contrary to Schmidt's view (p. 279). He corrects himself on p. 278, but then goes on: 'The difference is not very great.' On the contrary, it is the difference which is significant. Luke interprets Mark differently from Matthew.

[3] Cf. on the other hand the D text, which here again proves to be secondary.

[4] It is a feature of Luke's account that the typological meaning of significant

75

The account of the Entry into the city and the Temple, which in Mark is one complete account (Mark xi, 11), is divided in Luke by the insertion of xix, 39–44 into the scene of acclamation at the Mount of Olives—the symbolical 'mountain'—where Luke brings out the separation resulting from the coming of Jesus, and the Entry itself, the sole purpose of which is that Jesus may take possession of the Temple (v. 45). This form of the story cannot be explained from the use of different sources, but is the result of consistent editorial adaptation by the author. There is no need to assume that there are any sources other than Mark. How deliberately Luke has introduced this particular interpretation is proved by the fact that it not only underlies all that follows, but also that it is plainly expressed in the editorial statement of xxi, 37 f. Here we have another example of a scheme imposed by Luke.[1]

By the omission of the episode of the Fig Tree it is possible for the Cleansing of the Temple to be presented as one complete event.[2] Behind this omission there is also the idea that Jesus performs no miracles in Jerusalem,[3] the reason being that nothing should stand in the way of the Passion.

passages is brought out at a later point without any express reference to the earlier passage. The allusions are meant to speak for themselves. They are particularly numerous in the story of the Passion. xxii, 3 takes up iv, 13, and xxiii, 2 is an echo of xx, 25. The acclamation fulfils the saying in xiii, 35. We are immediately faced with the problem of the prologue. Between it and the Passion there are many connections: ii, 7–xxii, 11; ii, 14–xix, 38; ii, 38–xxiii, 51. If the prologue is an original component, then we have before us in the Cleansing of the Temple the fulfilment of ii, 14, but in this case the alteration of the Davidic concept, which cannot really be separated from the scene xx, 41 ff. is hard to explain. Merely on the basis of a comparison of form, ii, 14 gives the impression of being an amplification of xix, 37 rather than vice versa. But this is not enough to prove whether Luke modelled the acclamation on the words in the prologue, or whether they are a later formation based on the Lucan form in the Entry. The question immediately arises of course as to how far the Entry is intentionally described as the fulfilment of the stories of the Presentation in the Temple and of the Boy Jesus in the Temple.

[1] This manifestation also is followed by a rejection. In this way the beginning of the third section is made to correspond with that of the first and second, but we must beware of trying to force the parallels into too rigid a pattern.

[2] It is pointless to argue about what is primary and what is secondary as between Mark and Luke. This is one objection in particular that must be raised against Streeter and Taylor. It is obvious that Luke had Mark in front of him. The consistency of his account is not the result of better information concerning the event, but is the result of the author's having a definite theological conception.

[3] What he actually does is fully reported in xxi, 37. In Mark also there are no miracles performed in public, but the reason for it is different. For Mark, miracles are simply out of the question in Jerusalem, as this city is a place of evil (Loh-

GEOGRAPHICAL ELEMENTS

The positive meaning of the Cleansing of the Temple appears in v. 47. According to Luke, Jesus teaches 'daily' in the Temple and goes each night to the Mount of Olives.[1] There is neither the place nor the time for an anointing in Bethany.

By breaking up the daily routine that is found in Mark, Luke creates the impression of a fairly long period of activity, of a third epoch of Jesus' ministry, equal in importance to the two earlier ones[2], and which again is clearly marked by its special character, e.g. by the absence of miracles and on the positive side by a special kind of teaching. Everything leads up to the ministry in this important place, which gives to the teaching a special quality.[3] That this special arrangement is something brought about by Luke is proved by the fact that it can be seen not only in additions, which one could always attribute to an extra source, but also in omissions, as e.g. in that of Mark xiii, 1.[4] Mark's criticism of the cult from the eschatological standpoint is greatly modified.[5] In Luke it is not a question of the eschatological end of the Temple, but of its cleansing; in other words, Jesus prepares it as somewhere he can stay, and from now on he occupies it as a place belonging to him. The Cleansing is no longer an eschatological sign, but a means of

meyer, pp. 33 f.). Luke's reason, on the other hand, is a psychological one, arising from his conception of miracles, according to which a miracle of itself has convincing power. Thus we find appearing all the more prominently in Luke legendary features, the purpose of which is to demonstrate that the Passion is in accordance with God's will. The principle on which Luke's account is based can be seen in ix, 21 f., where the command of secrecy rests on the necessity of the Passion. In Luke's account of the Passion we can see this principle applied.

[1] Cf. xxii, 39 as well as xxi, 37 f. It is not an adequate explanation to say (Bultmann, p. 389) that xxi, 37 f. is a compilation by Luke on the basis of Mark xiv, 26.

[2] Cf. xx, 1, another editorial contribution. What according to Mark takes place on the third entry into the city (Mark xi, 11, 15) happens according to Luke on any day in a fairly long period of time.

[3] On the literary aspect, Luke xix, 47 is formed from Mark xiv, 49. By the duplication the verse now has the effect of being a preparation for xxii, 53. Mark xi, 19 does not appear until Luke xxi, 37. In other words, Luke builds a new structure with materials from Mark. It is pointless to enquire into sources for the details in these editorial compilations, and it is even more so to attempt to enquire into the historical reliability of Luke's form of report. Luke has composed in his own way, on the basis not of additional information, but of theological reflection.

[4] This is important for deciding to what degree Luke has modified his sources, and this cannot be decided merely from the extent of the alterations but from the nature of them.

[5] On this whole topic, cf. Lohmeyer, *Evangelium und Kultus*, Göttingen, 1942.

taking possession, and therefore of itself it has no significance.[1]
Luke xx, 2, in contrast to Mark xi, 28, is now strictly relevant
again.[2]

It is in the Temple that the final manifestation of who Jesus
is is now given in view of his imminent Passion. In this way the
pattern of promise and fulfilment emerges and the Passion is
interpreted in advance. With the Church in mind, the claim of
the Jews is refuted. Their appeal to the Temple and to tradition
is unfounded. As since the rejection and death of Jesus they
occupy the Temple unlawfully, it is quite just that it should be
taken from them by destruction, as chapter xxi makes plain.
This destruction is the clear refutation of Judaism, and is not an
eschatological event. In the hands of the Jews the Temple is
merely a profane building. The saying about the Temple in
Mark xiv, 57 f. is omitted.[3]

4. The Opponents of Jesus

The disappearance of the Pharisees from the Passion is
noticeable. They play the part of opponents as late as xix, 39 ff.,
and their hostility is along the lines of the picture given of the
Pharisees in the special material.[4] Whereas Matthew transfers
the dispute to Jerusalem, in Luke there is only the small
amount of Marcan material by way of polemic, and this is no
longer directed at the Pharisees, but at the scribes. This alteration can be seen in Luke xx, 20 (contrast Mark xii, 13), as a
result of which the resemblance to the Sadducees is lost.[5] For
the most part the opponents in Luke are those portrayed in
xxii, 2—the chief priests and the scribes.

[1] Along with the absence of the incident of the Fig Tree the reference to the
Cleansing as a 'sign' is also missing. The present continuous course of events
provides a context for the Cleansing, but gives it no meaning of its own.

[2] 'Again', as the passage evidently referred originally to the Cleansing of the
Temple. As a result of the interpolation of the incident of the Fig Tree it is irrelevant in Mark. Luke restores the old context. We cannot of course say whether this
is historically correct, as it rests on secondary theological considerations.

[3] It probably has a symbolical meaning even in Mark; cf. xv, 29, and Lohmeyer,
Markus, ad loc. In Luke the saying occurs in the story of Stephen, again as a false
witness.

[4] On this point, cf. in particular Schlatter, e.g. pp. 303 ff., 333 ff., and 346 ff.

[5] This is in accordance with the description of the Pharisees and the Sadducees
in Acts.

GEOGRAPHICAL ELEMENTS

5. The Temple Discourse

The theme is limited to two subjects, the Law and the Last Things, in particular the connection of the latter with Jerusalem. These two factors, the Eschaton and Jerusalem, should be kept apart. The setting of Mark xiii, 1 is altered. According to Luke, Jesus speaks only in the Temple, and for this reason Mark xiii, 3 is also omitted. The Mount of Olives is not the place of teaching, but of prayer by night. In clear contrast to Mark, the eschatological symbolism of the setting ($\kappa\alpha\tau\acute{\epsilon}\nu\alpha\nu\tau\iota$ $\tau o\hat{v}$ $\iota\acute{\epsilon}\rho o\hat{v}$) is abandoned. Mark and Matthew present Jesus' teaching as a secret revelation, and therefore they remove it from the Temple, and the fact that it is set at a distance has a symbolical significance. According to Luke, Jesus addresses the speakers of xxi, 5 publicly in the Temple.

6. The Summary Statement in Luke xxi, 37 f.

Cf. p. 76, n. 3 and p. 77, nn. 1 and 3.

7. The Events up to the Last Supper

As in the statement just mentioned, the wording of xxii, 1 indicates a fairly long period of time in Jerusalem. But here a special note is struck. Mark states expressly that Jesus should not be killed 'at the feast', but as according to Luke he has already been there some time, it is obvious that he is to die 'at the feast'. We almost have the impression of a ritual act, an impression which is also given later by the Barabbas episode. Reference should also be made to xxii, 53.

We have already remarked that the omission of the Anointing is connected with the typical setting that we find in Luke. Has Luke any other reasons for this omission? Perhaps it is unacceptable to him because of its eschatological reference. He is prepared to accept it, as in his variant in vii, 36 ff., only as a demonstration of love and as a sign of repentance. It is not a human being that strengthens Jesus for the hour of death, but an angel. The body is evidently not to be anointed until after death (xxiii, 55 f.), and only by his own followers; but then the anointing is no longer necessary, for he is alive.

79

GEOGRAPHICAL ELEMENTS

Chapter xxii, v. 3 completes the circle of redemptive history, for Satan is now present again. Now the period of salvation, as it was described in iv, 18–21, is over, and the Passion, which is described by Luke, and also by John, as a work of Satan, is beginning.[1] This motif seems to take the place in Luke of the Marcan aspect of the Passion as it is seen in the Anointing.

We cannot now go into the chronology of v. 7. In v. 10 there is the first mention of the entry into the city, and immediately it takes place. For now the time of the Passion has begun, and already the Supper looks back to the period of salvation (xxii, 35–8). The angle from which the Supper is seen is that it is a strengthening for the πειρασμοί that are now beginning again even in Jesus' lifetime, now that Satan is once more present.[2] We need not go into the complicated problem of the sayings at the Last Supper, apart from considering the meaning of καθώς in v. 29. Does it suggest the idea that for the disciples the Supper takes the place of what Jesus himself has to suffer? In other words, that there are two ways into the Kingdom of God, through martyrdom and through the sacrament, and that the latter in a special sense represents an appropriation of the Passion?

8. The Sayings at the Last Supper.[3]

These are not directly connected with the setting, but with the particular ideas which help to determine its pattern, and which in turn are expressed by it. Here the πειρασμός theme predominates (cf. xxii, 28, 40). We must beware, however, of deducing from v. 28 a picture of Jesus' whole life as a temptation, for this would be false. It is now that the πειρασμοί hold sway.[4] Previously they were far away. It is this fact that

[1] On this subject, cf. Noack, *Satanas und Soteria*.

[2] xxii, 18 is peculiar. The time is not defined. An interval is assumed, in which Jesus does not drink, evidently the present period of history (the period of the Church) until the Parousia. Is there no feast in Heaven whilst the Church on earth is suffering?

[3] For a detailed analysis, cf. H. Schürmann, *Der Paschamahlbericht* (Luke xxii, 15–18), 1953; ibid., *Der Einsetzungsbericht* (Luke xxii, 19–20), 1955; ibid., *Jesu Abschiedsrede* (Luke xxii, 21–38), 1957.

[4] In order to avoid misunderstanding, we repeat that in the following exposition we are concerned solely with the meaning that these sayings have for Luke (on the objection raised by K. G. Kuhn, cf. p. 16, n.2). To what extent the whole ministry of Jesus was thought of as a 'temptation' before, at the time of, and after Luke, is a question we can leave open at this point.

underlies v. 35, in agreement with the thought of the rest of the Gospel. The framework which extends from iv, 13 to xxii, 3 depicts the ministry of Jesus in this way. Verse 36 emphasizes strongly that an epoch is 'now' dawning. The time when the disciples were protected is over, and the conflict is now starting, when they will need wallet and purse,' when ·they will suffer want and have to face conflict. Since the beginning of the Passion—and only since then—to be a Christian means to be engaged in conflict, and the apostles are they who stand fast now. This is the meaning of the Perfect in v. 28. In keeping with this is the fact that, according to Luke, they do not flee. There is therefore all the more reason for mentioning temptation by Satan (vv. 31 ff.).[1] The scene on the Mount of Olives is constructed with this in mind.

It is not an adequate explanation of the absence of the place-name 'Gethsemane' in xxii, 40, to attribute it to an 'invincible aversion to Semitic place-names'.[2] The phrase κατὰ τὸ ἔθος brings out the contrast with Mark. Verse 39 now serves to explain how the traitor knows the place. The episode now takes place at the familiar place of prayer, which makes the intrusion seem all the worse. The familiar motifs recur. The disciples must pray for themselves, for prayer is the weapon against temptation. Mark's trio is omitted. The disciples sleep out of sorrow, which is an echo of the sleeping at the Transfiguration. Here again the heavenly apparition is granted only to Jesus himself. In comparison with Mark's account the disciples are spared, for they do not need to be 'awakened' three times, but are only once admonished, that this is not the occasion for sleeping. The following passage is therefore omitted, for the apostles' spirit is not weak.

On the themes of temptation and of the sword, we may note that in Mark temptation is something eschatological, connected with the 'hour', whereas in Luke it is connected with martyrdom, but not with any particular time. The context suggests a symbolical interpretation of the sword, in connection with the Christian's daily battle against temptation, particularly in times of persecution—in other words, in connection with the battle

[1] Cf. the treatment of the incident of the Temptation. Does 'Satan' come from a special tradition? The saying casts little light on this matter.

[2] Thus Wellhausen, ad loc.

against Satan, who has 'asked to have' the disciples, and whom they have to withstand.[1] There are no previous references in the Gospel to the conflicts, sacrifice, and victory of the disciples. A comparison of Jesus' words of farewell in xxii, 35–38 with the two Mission charges (ix, 1 ff. and x, 1 ff.) confirms this fact.

There is no doubt that the critics are right when they regard these speeches as influenced in their form by the circumstances of the community. Yet Luke does not see in them a picture of his own time, but of the time of Jesus, a definite period in the past—in other words, of an ideal past. In the passage under discussion this is very marked.[2]

Whereas in Mark and Matthew the equipping of the apostles symbolizes the eschatological readiness for the End, as a sign to men, in Luke it is interpreted as a sign of security. It serves to present the period of Jesus as an ideal period, as a contrast to the present with its tribulations. The preparation which took place then is set over against that which is now required. Here, at the Last Supper, when the time of security is past, Jesus discloses the redemptive significance of the directions which were then given. The situation of v. 36 (ἀλλὰ νῦν) persists right until the time of the author.[3]

The scene is based on the Lucan misunderstanding, which emerges in connection with the sword, in the form of the question: a fighting or a suffering Messiah? Thus the disciples' reply concerning the two swords becomes a sign of the misunderstanding which leads to armed resistance when Jesus is arrested, whilst their real task now is to suffer. This misunderstanding is in keeping with that resulting from the predictions of the

---

[1] A similar image is found in ix, 23 in the application of the Cross to the 'daily cross'. Any search for historical reminiscences in the mention of the swords is doomed from the start. In Luke's view the sword, which they are to procure, can have no political significance. Taylor, *Jesus and His Sacrifice*, p. 192: '. . . Jesus is speaking metaphorically. He is thinking of the position in which the disciples will find themselves after His death.' P. 193: 'That Jesus should have been misunderstood by the Twelve is part of the dramatic irony of a tense situation. The cry: "Lord, behold, here are two swords", reveals the fact that they have merely caught the surface meaning of His words.'

[2] Bultmann comments (pp. 155 f.) that even Mark feels that the instructions are no longer appropriate and tries to make a compromise. As a matter of principle Luke connects them with a past which is radically different.

[3] Is there an allusion here to the fact that the Twelve were sent out singly?

Passion and with xix, 11. What the disciples have to face is not battle and victory, but temptation.[1]

Verse 28 does not mean 'You are the heroes who have persevered', for nothing has yet happened, but 'You have come with me to Jerusalem and now have had to face temptation with me' (and still do—N.B., Perfect). And in fact they are the ones who still continue. A typical eschatological prospect emerges from this temptation.

Verse 29 expresses the analogy the Father—Jesus: Jesus—the disciples. Verse 37 provides the interpretation, and points to the misunderstanding that follows (by reference to Isaiah liii, i.e. to the one who does not fight).

9. The Arrest

In contrast to Mark, the scene appears to be given the stylized setting of the Mount of Olives, and depicts the situation of the martyr facing the decision as to whether he should accept martyrdom. In xxii, 52 Luke deduces from the presence of the servants that of the masters. A new factor emerges: the στρατηγοί.[2] On account of the changed setting, Mark xiv, 43 is altered. Here the kiss is explicitly the traitor's kiss, but we are not told that it is given.

The expression ὑμῶν ἡ ὥρα contains an allusion to the situation of the Church and its renunciation of active resistance.

10. The Trial

The peculiar features of Luke's account are well known: there is no trial by night, Jesus spends the night in the courtyard, where the denial takes place, and he is tried by day before 'their Sanhedrin'.[3] Luke has a different idea from Mark of the legal

---

[1] D and Itala miss this point. Do the disciples see this step as the beginning of the final victory and think that two swords are sufficient because the Messiah is present? In this case v. 39 contradicts the notion, and makes it plain that it is a step κατὰ τὸ ἔθος; it is not the end of the world that is now beginning, but temptation.

[2] Here Luke seems to have access to additional information, but whether he has an accurate idea of the στρατηγοί is another matter. On the historical aspect, cf. Klostermann on xxii, 4; Schürer, II, pp. 320 ff.; Billerbeck, II, pp. 628 ff.

[3] Hirsch (II, p. 266), following Wellhausen, takes the Sanhedrin to be a place. The usage in Acts does not support this.

circumstances and of the place. He builds up his description with
motifs which are familiar elsewhere in Luke.[1]

The course of the trial has been rationalized. The examination of witnesses is omitted, for the simple reason that it is
superfluous. The fact that Jesus claimed to be the Messiah was
always public knowledge. In any case, the desired information
can be had from Jesus himself. But later Pilate is simply lied to.
It is only the 'necessity' of the Passion that is a secret. There is
no room for 'false' witnesses, for Jesus is tried on the basis of
truth. It is not the witnesses here that are the liars, but the
leaders of the people, and by their lie (xxiii, 2) they declare
their real character.[2]

xxii, 67–70

This section is sufficiently informative to be considered
separately. The train of thought is compressed and typically
Lucan. The question is formulated in two parts, which is to be
explained not by reference to any sources, but to Luke's Christological terminology, as is indicated by οὖν in v. 70. These
verses are meant to set out explicitly the fundamental identity
of the current Christological titles.[3] This passage makes it

[1] The question arises whether there is a tendency to spare Peter in the denial
scene in Luke. The fact that he makes his denial even before the beginning of the
trial might be meant to have the opposite effect. In any case, the main impression
of the scene is that it is evocative, and that it brings out the contrast between Peter
the confessor and Peter the denier (cf. v. 61a).

[2] The fact that there is no examination of witnesses should make us beware of
trying to find too many parallels in Luke. It would have been a fine reproach for
use in the story of Stephen, but Luke makes no use of it.

[3] Hirsch (II, pp. 243 f.) sees a literary connection between Luke's ἀπὸ τοῦ νῦν
(v. 69), and ἀπ' ἄρτι in Matt. xxvi, 64. But v. 69 is an unequivocally Lucan saying,
as can be seen from the eschatology it contains, which is different from Mark in
respect of the delay of the Parousia. When this is recognized v. 70 immediately
becomes intelligible. ἀπὸ τοῦ νῦν has nothing to do with Matthew's ἀπ' ἄρτι. As
regards the other alleged parallels (σὺ εἶπας and ὑμεῖς λέγετε), their function is
quite different. The course of the conversation in each case (drawn up independently
of each other) helps to explain the two phrases. σὺ εἶπας in Matthew is an
elucidation of Mark—cf. the very formulation of the question, which even in Mark
takes the form of an oath, but without Mark being aware of it. In Luke there is no
trace of all this. The answer is of an entirely different character. The question is
derived from Mark, and the answer no doubt originates there, but has been altered.
Luke makes alterations at two points. For one thing he makes clear the relation
between the titles Christ and Son of Man and the title Son of God. Then he also has
to adapt according to his eschatology. According to Mark, the Parousia will soon

impossible to decipher the Christology of Luke's writings by a statistical examination of the titles. The thing to note is that they are assimilated to one another.

Luke is familiar of course with the Jewish conception of the political Messiah. This is presupposed in Gamaliel's speech in the Acts of the Apostles. But he dissociates Jesus from this conception by the interpretation 'Son of God'. This, in spite of the statistical evidence, is the proper designation. Its real meaning is to be deduced from the Christological statements in the Gospel and Acts, not by reference to Jewish and Hellenistic religious titles, which of course are significant in their own context.

The note of political apologetic, of which so far there has been only a suggestion, comes to the fore in xxiii, 2. The verse harks back to xx, 20 ff., where, in contrast to Mark, the speakers are the same.

The accusation is thus shown to be a deliberate lie. In this way Luke is pointing out to the Roman persecutor of his own time, that the former proceedings against Jesus, on which the present proceedings against the Christians are based, were founded on Jewish slander, and have been presented in a false light ever since. Then the Roman authorities were not misled by the Jewish lie, as they now are. Luke makes it perfectly clear where the real political insurgents are—cf. Luke xxiii, 19, 25, with Mark xv, 7. Jesus was the Messiah, but that was no crime against Roman law.

Christology forms the positive completion of this apologetic.

take place; Matthew, therefore, with his ἀπ' ἄρτι shows a correct understanding. Luke, on the other hand, declares that this is not the case at all, for from now on Jesus is at the right hand of God. The Parousia has not yet taken place, therefore it is omitted from the passage. Luke cannot conceive that the Sanhedrin should see the Parousia, nor Christ seated at the right hand of God; it is the martyrs that see this. We therefore have before us a complete dialogue built up with the aid of the motif of the misunderstanding; they cannot know these things, nor can they understand the title Son of Man. In this way Luke makes out of the trial a compendium of Christology for his readers. ὑμεῖς λέγετε serves in this context to characterize the Jews who, as they often do, declare their real character. Jesus' answer is not 'evasive' (Klostermann), but a confession of himself as Son of God, as becomes clear in the end (v. 71). P. Winter (*The Treatment*) views this section quite differently, and suggests that vv. 66b–71 are a post-Lucan interpolation. Against this view we may mention the Lucan style, the continuity of the train of thought, and the Lucan character of the Christology that is set out here and above all of the eschatological outlook.

85

It is because of the kind of Messiah that Jesus is that the Jewish accusation becomes impossible. Luke's account of course is not only concerned with apologetic, but also with believers and with the dispute with the Jews.

Taylor is of the opinion (*Behind the Third Gospel*, p. 54) that in Luke there is no trial before Pilate, but there is one in v. 3, as a result of which Pilate has all the information he requires. Of course we cannot attempt to reconstruct the historical facts. Luke starts out from his own transcendental idea of kingship, whereas John is aware of the problem.

Chapter xxiii, v. 5 is a summary, which shows that from the beginning 'all Judaea' is thought of as the sphere of Jesus' ministry along with Galilee.[1]

The political theme is evident again in the connection between the episodes in vv. 2–5 and 6–16. The episode concerning Herod shows marks of Luke's political ideas.[2]

According to Luke, Jesus does not refuse to answer the Roman authorities. He gives the information they require and so enables them to arrive at the objective legal decision, which is in fact immediately done officially. The answer he gives is no fuller than in Mark, but there is no refusal to answer. On the other hand, Herod receives no answer. As a result the elucidation of the relation between Church and Empire is delayed,

[1] There is no mention of Samaria, but in this passage one cannot attach great importance to the fact. In view of what is to follow the political element is to the fore. Primarily, it is a question of establishing that Jesus has appeared in the territory of Pilate as well as of Herod. It would therefore be superfluous to mention Samaria. The formula is important, however, not so much for the way in which it is used in this particular passage, as for its own sake. It is a pre-Lucan summary, as is shown by a comparison with the other passages in Luke where Galilee, Galileans and the motif of the 'arché' appear, and in this sense it describes completely the ministry of Jesus.

[2] The meaning of the scene with Herod is expressed in v. 15. By a symbolical act Herod establishes that Jesus is politically innocent. He and Pilate serve each other's purpose—hence v. 12. Herod can no more see the hoped-for spectacle now than previously.

The history of the tradition of the scene is disputed. Whether it was created by Luke (Dibelius, *ZNW*, 1915) or was already in existence (Bultmann, p. 294) is a controversial point. There is a clear connection with the other Herod scenes, which have been considerably edited. In any case it is meant to show that the reigning Jew, as well as the Roman, can establish no political crime by Jesus. The fact that an account is given of Herod's view is the outcome of Luke's idea of the political divisions in Palestine (a procuratorial region, a dependent kingdom and the 'polis' of Jerusalem). All the courts share in the trial—and the guilt falls entirely upon the Jews of Jerusalem.

which is similar to the tendency we find throughout the Acts of
the Apostles. The affirmation of the Governor in xxiii, 4
clarifies the situation between the two. If Pilate were now to
condemn Jesus, it would be in contradiction of the verdict which
he himself has confirmed. But he does not condemn him. Jesus
does not die by the decision of the Roman judge—he is killed by
the Jews, to whom he is 'delivered' by the Roman (xxiii, 25).
We cannot dismiss the 'absence' of the verdict in Luke as
negligence, as Luke certainly read the condemnation in his
source (Mark xv, 15) and omitted it. Mark xv, 12 is also
omitted, because there Pilate appears as the one who carries out
the verdict.

Chapter xxiii, v. 22 brings out the significance of the official
confirmation of Jesus' innocence: it was pronounced 'three times'.

As regards the question of guilt, it is made clear that it is exclusively the Jews who are the actors. It is true that Herod is
involved, in that the mockery by the Roman soldiers is omitted
and replaced by something done by Herod's men. So in a sense he
occupies an intermediate position, in so far as on the other hand he
confirms Jesus' innocence, which Luke considers very important.

11. Barabbas

What is a 'sign' in Mark has a political stamp in Luke. It is
the Jews who throw the name of Barabbas into the discussion—
and again reveal their true character by declaring their solidarity with the rebels (cf. the repeated emphasis in vv. 19 and 25).
The scene is thus harder to imagine than in Mark. There, quite
apart from the question of its historicity, v. 6 provides a motif
which at least makes the course of events consistent. But how do
the Jews here come to make such a request? It seems that Luke
has created the difficulty himself, for the sake of his special
emphasis. According to his account a quite regular exchange
takes place: a substitute-criminal is offered in place of a criminal,
and Pilate finally consents to it.[1] Has Luke some kind of ritual
act in mind?

[1] The situation is far from clear. Is Luke thinking of a right of the Jews to the
release of a condemned man, but in exchange for another? Is he substituting for the
Roman celebration of the Saturnalian king a Jewish rite, although one for which
there is no historical foundation? The law and custom of antiquity give us no clue.
Is it something invented by Luke himself, who could not understand his source

In any case Jesus is not executed by the Romans; cf. xxiii, 25 with xxiii, 26, and contrast Mark xv, 15 (cf. M. Dibelius, *Botschaft und Geschichte*, I, 1953, p. 286). Pilate plays only a passive part, that of delivering the Galilean to the Jews. In place of mockery by the Romans there is repeated mockery by the Jews. Once again we see the contrast between the sources and Luke's adaptation; in the sources the soldiers are Romans and although the soldiers are still there in Luke, it is not certain where they belong. Every positive indication that they belong to Rome is removed, but it is not said where they do belong. Again we cannot go into the historicity of the details of Luke's account.[1]

12. The Crucifixion

It is well known that in xxiii, 39 Luke avoids Mark's expression 'crucified together with', but in view of v. 33 this is not of great significance.

The omission of the motif of the drink in Mark xv, 36 is probably connected with the disappearance of the Elijah typology.[2] The whole section Mark xv, 34–6 agrees neither with Luke's eschatology nor with his idea of the martyr, which is

and interpreted it in his own way? We almost get the impression of a cultic 'ransom' (ἀπολύειν). Does Pilate perhaps—again in Luke's conception—intend to use Jesus for a ritual celebration and then to set him free? The Jews however demand that Barabbas should be 'ransomed' in this way. Does Luke think of the killing of Jesus by the Jews as a ritual act? Cf. the alteration in xxii, 1 f. ('at the feast'). It is noticeable that Pilate evidently has to 'deliver' someone to them. Does the strange statement in Acts xiii, 29, that the Jews 'bury' Jesus, suggest the idea of a cultic act? It is true that this statement is pre-Lucan, and that Luke did not adopt this feature in his narrative of the burial.

[1] If the mocking in xxiii, 36 ff. is not positively designated as Jewish, neither is it designated as Roman. Wellhausen points out correctly that no Roman soldiers appear (Einleitung, p. 56). There is also the fact that Luke previously mentions the Jewish στρατηγοί in xxiii, 11. The centurion by the Cross in Mark is obviously a Gentile (Dibelius, *Formgeschichte*, p. 204), whereas in Luke he is a man moved by the martyrdom. In his adaptation Luke has not been entirely successful in removing the difficulties. The expression ἐδόξασεν τὸν θεόν proves nothing. It is true that it is used predominantly by Christians and Jews, but in Acts x, 46 it is used in a technical sense for the conversion of a Roman centurion. What is it that really overwhelms the soldier, the martyrdom as such or the miracle of the speedy death? Apart from xxiii, 44 Luke omits all chronological references, and thus gives the impression that Jesus died soon after the Crucifixion.

[2] Luke xxiii, 36 is not a rendering of Mark xv, 36, but of Mark xv, 23. There is nothing corresponding to Mark xv, 36. Luke, however, is familiar with the verse, for he borrows from it the word ὄξος.

that the martyr experiences a sense of God's nearness.[1] The
saying which he inserts in itself contains the solution to the
problem of this martyrdom, and moreover in a form which
everyone can understand, whilst Mark's version presupposes
familiarity with Biblical thought.

Chapter xxiii, v. 49 touches on the idea of the witness. ἀπὸ
μακρόθεν seems to be in harmony with the scene of the arrest.
Chapter xxiii, v. 50 again serves indirectly to characterize the
Jews: the righteous Joseph was not involved.[2] Is πόλις τῶν
'Ιουδαίων in v. 51 a piece of Lucan interpretation? Verse 52
shows another typical modification. In Mark it falls to Pilate
to confirm the surprisingly early death and he has to be officially
informed about it. In Luke, however, he has nothing to do with
the execution, therefore the passage concerned is omitted.[3]

The saying in v. 34 presents a particular problem. Does it
apply to the Jews? But can it be said of them, that they do not
know what they are doing? Or does it only apply to those who
carry out the execution, who certainly do not know? The textual
problem here is not easy to solve. Is the saying inserted, in
order to exonerate those who are mere tools, and to make it all
the more clear who are the really guilty? Jesus has told the Jews
clearly enough who he is, and it is for this very reason that they
crucify him. Or was the saying subsequently excluded because
the crucifixion was thought of as an unforgivable crime?

Verses 33 f. seem to refer only to the executioners (cf. v. 35),
but on the other hand, there is a connection with vv. 25 f. and
27–31.[4]

We shall perhaps arrive at a fuller understanding if we take
into consideration the motif of 'ignorance' which occurs elsewhere, and which is attributed to the Gentiles as well as to the
Jews (Acts iii, 17; xiii, 27; xvii, 27, 30). One might suppose
from the accusation in Acts vii, 51 that it was Luke's intention

[1] Did Luke interpret the cry in Mark as a cry of despair? See Lohmeyer, *Markus*,
pp. 345 f.
[2] The description of a man as 'a righteous man' is unusual; other examples are
in the prologue, i, 6, ii, 25, and Acts x, 22.
[3] It is possible that what remains (v. 52) has been interpolated from Matthew.
Cf. Klostermann, ad loc.
[4] Klostermann takes the saying to be a plea on behalf of the executioners, and
refers to Acts vii, 60; he interprets the saying in the passage we are considering as
an interpolation, as an insertion of this traditional motif.

to present the Jews as possessing knowledge, but there it is not
directly a question of Jesus as Messiah. The fact is rather that
although the Jews have heard Jesus' claim, they do not believe.
Therefore from the subjective point of view they are not aware
that they are killing the Messiah, for they consider Jesus to be
a false pretender. That they lie in order to reach their goal is
another matter. In Luke's opinion, it is only after the Resurrection that Jesus is proved to be the Messiah in such a way that
the fact can no longer be evaded. It is now that unbelief becomes inexcusable; this underlies the appeal to the Jews (Acts
iii, 17 f.) and that to the heathen (Acts xviii, 30), and is in
keeping with the interpretation of the event of the Resurrection
in Acts xvii. The remarks concerning ignorance to which we
have referred reveal a characteristic contrast. In Acts xiii, 27,
where Luke is following a source, ignorance is described as guilt,
which is the traditional Old Testament view. The other two
passages, on the other hand, represent Lucan interpretation, and
so give his own view, which is that ignorance is a ground for
excuse. This motif reveals itself as a typical motif in the missionary approach, for the purpose of establishing contact. We
shall consider it later in another context.

13. Luke's Treatment of the Question of Guilt

So far we have noted the tendency to put all the blame on to
the Jews. The scene at the Cross is in line with this. The people
are standing by, whilst their leaders scoff. We met this same
pattern earlier, when the people were baptized, but not their
leaders (vii, 29 f.). The execution by the Jews marks the fulfilment of the saying in xiii, 34, which adds to the saying in
xiii, 33, that the prophets must die not only in, but at the hand
of, Jerusalem. In so far as there is any suggestion that the
Romans take part, it is a survival from the sources and is not
part of the plan of Luke's account, but, rather, contradicts it.
Yet there are outside the Passion narrative sayings about guilt
for the death of Jesus, particularly in some of the formulae in
Acts, which possibly contain pre-Lucan material. What is the
relation of these to the account of the Passion?

There seems to be a discrepancy in ii, 23 which states that he
was slain διὰ χειρὸς ἀνόμων. Originally this certainly referred

to the Gentiles, as those who at any rate carried out the sentence. Next to be considered is Acts iv, 27, along with iii, 13 f. and xiii, 28. Here we have a group of formulae which trace the death of Jesus back to the combined efforts of Jews and Gentiles, including Herod. The clearest example is in iv, 27, which speaks of an event which is determined by redemptive history and is the fulfilment of Psalm 2. This same point of view no doubt also underlies the Herod episode, although this does not mean to say that the latter is based on the psalm; in fact the reverse process seems the more probable, namely, that it is an attempt to interpret an event with the aid of Scripture. In this verse iv, 27, with its context of redemptive history, there is no mention of the question of guilt, but this is not the case in iii, 13 f. and xiii, 28.

In xiii, 28, Pilate is originally thought of as the person responsible, but the verse can be easily interpreted in the sense of Luke xxiii, 25. This latter passage is similar in form to Acts xiii, 28, and was probably derived from it by Luke. In other words, Luke xxiii, 25 represents Luke's interpretation of a kerygmatic saying which originally had a quite different meaning.

Acts iii, 13 f., is more difficult to explain. ἠρνήσασθε—ἠτήσασθε could be easily interpreted as in keeping with Luke's own standpoint, but παρεδώκατε points to Pilate as the one who is responsible. Nevertheless, it is stated unequivocally where the guilt lies: ἀπεκτείνατε, with the result that παρεδώκατε might represent the event of Luke xxiii, 1 f., according to Luke's view.

It is clear that the treatment of the guilt question in the kerygma is pre-Lucan. Luke accepts this tradition, but seems to develop it with a one-sided emphasis on the guilt of the Jews, which gives rise to certain discrepancies with the source.

When we turn again to Acts ii, 23, the question arises as to what Luke means by ἄνομοι, whether he means the same as the source, or the Jews who, he subsequently says (Acts vii, 51), received the Law but did not keep it. In Luke xxii, 37, in a quotation from the LXX, ἄνομος means the criminal, not the non-Jew. In the context there is a symbolism in Jesus' execution between two criminals. Luke does not seem to be acquainted with the Jewish use of ἄνομος for the Gentiles, and he gives it a new

91

meaning. It is true that there are no further examples of the word in his writings, nevertheless there are other indications which confirm our interpretation. The most important passage for Luke's concept of νόμος is Acts vii, 53. The νόμος is essentially the moral law, not a mark of distinction between Jews and non-Jews. In Acts xxiii, 3, there is a situation similar to that at the trial of Jesus, and now the High Priest has to hear the word παρανομῶν. . . . This provides evidence that Luke interprets the word ἄνομοι which he finds in his sources, in the way in which we can see clearly here in this formulation of his own. Acts ii, 23 therefore in its present sense applies to the Jews, not to the Romans. Luke xxiv, 7 (εἰς χεῖρας ἀνθρώπων ἁμαρτωλῶν) is a further example of Luke's interpretation, which makes clear what he means by ἀνομία. Luke xiii, 27, with which Matt. vii, 23 should be compared, should also be noted for the relation between ἀνομία and ἀδικία.[1] It is significant that the theme of guilt can be combined with the theme of relative excuse, when connected with ignorance. The two themes are different in origin. The one arises from a consideration of redemptive history, and aims to show that the Passion is a Divine decree. It is then given a secondary moral application, and is used for the purpose of the polemic against Judaism. The other theme arises from the need for a connecting-link in the missionary approach. The discrepancy which results from its introduction into the text can be seen in Acts iii. In v. 17 there is a definite pardon of the Jews, which is even extended to their rulers. It is obvious from vv. 13 ff. that the source expressed a different view. This change of attitude in view of the mission is also seen in the typical language of v. 19, following upon the statement in the previous verse.

Basically, the theme is applicable only to the Gentiles, who were in fact in ignorance, but even this is hedged about with restrictions in the Areopagus speech, again for the sake of establishing the missionary link, for it is only by restricting it that the hearers can be made to realize their possibilities. Their guilt in respect of redemptive history prevents an application to

[1] Cf. 1 Macc. ii, 4 (speaking of Mattathias and his followers): καὶ ἐπάταξαν ἁμαρτωλοὺς ἐν ὀργῇ αὐτῶν καὶ ἄνδρας ἀνόμους ἐν θυμῷ αὐτῶν (i.e. Jews who had fallen away from the Law). E. Haenchen in his commentary on Acts has demonstrated the strong influence of Maccabees on Luke's language.

the Jews of the theme of ignorance, but a way of doing it is found. Conversion is possible for the individual Jew, and it is the fact of ignorance that makes this possible.

Complementary to this allowance for ignorance, there is, of course, the positive declaration that now, after the revelation, that is, after the Resurrection, there is no more excuse; the times of ignorance which God overlooked are now past (Acts xvii, 30).[1]

14. The Close of the Gospel

The most important topographical point in the remaining verses is the transfer of the Resurrection appearances to Jerusalem. The reasons for this are familiar, and have often been discussed. Chapter xxiv, v. 6, shows that Luke is deliberately giving a different picture from Mark. The journey to Galilee, of which Mark xiv, 28 and xvi, 7 speak, is replaced by a prophecy spoken in Galilee concerning what will take place in Jerusalem, and in particular by the predictions of the Passion. The verses xxiv, 8 ff., also give a different picture from Mark's account (Mark xvi, 8). Verse 11 tells of the disbelief with which the unexpected news was greeted. This has to be seen in the light of the Lucan misunderstanding.[2] Underlying the report there is

---

[1] We see that revelation here stands for the communication of correct knowledge, in the Greek, but not in the Gnostic sense. The Gnostic attitude would not be to excuse the former state of affairs and to try to establish a link, but to disclose the hopelessness of the former state. The 'atmosphere' of the two is entirely different. Whereas in the one instance the emphasis is on establishing a connection, in the other it is on 'awakening' from sleep and from death.

Corresponding to the stress on the inevitability of the decision which is now demanded as a result of the proclamation of the Resurrection, there is the fixed theme of the future Judgement, and also the possibility that is now offered of forgiveness, which is made possible by the very fact that men were hitherto in ignorance. In this connection we must bear in mind that Luke's emphasis is not on the *nearness* of the Judgement, but simply on the fact of it. He establishes the connection with the present not by means of an early expectation, but by conveying the general truth of a future resurrection to judgement, in which case it is immaterial when this event takes place. Cf. further our examination of Luke's eschatology.

[2] The significance of xxiv, 11 is that it expresses the truth that the Resurrection cannot be deduced from an idea (of Messiahship) or from the historical life of Jesus, but that it is announced as something new. It is only in retrospect that it casts light on Jesus' life, and it is not until now that the disciples understand what they should have understood long ago. Now, after the event, their misunderstanding really becomes inconceivable. That this motif cannot be explained psychologically, as we

the notion of the eye-witness in its original form, that is, in its connection with the Resurrection.

In the Emmaus story there is evidence of close acquaintance with the district. As it is a Jerusalem tradition, such acquaintance is to be expected. We cannot draw from this any direct conclusions concerning Luke's acquaintance with the district.

The specific motifs of this final passage will be discussed in another context.[1] Only the setting of the Ascension in Bethany in v. 50 directly concerns us here. This flatly contradicts the geographical reference in Acts i, 12. In view of the systematic locating of the whole course of events in Jerusalem, and in view of the consistent omission of Bethany on the one hand, and of the function of the Mount of Olives on the other, which represents 'the' mountain in the Passion, one can scarcely fail to conclude from this closing section that Luke xxiv, 50–3 is not an original part of the gospel. Luke's original account of the Ascension seems rather to be in Acts i, even if it is amplified by an interpolation.[2]

---

noted earlier, springs from the fact that the Lucan misunderstanding expresses the fundamental conviction that faith cannot be deduced, in other words, that faith is something that is possible only by faith itself. The Emmaus story shows a remarkable awareness of this problem.

[1] Cf. in particular, P. Schubert, loc. cit.

[2] Taking the longer text of the ending of Luke, which is found in most manuscripts, as the original, but, as we have said, considering the whole passage as an addition.

PART TWO

Luke's Eschatology

I. THE PROBLEM

We are not concerned with the eschatology of Jesus or with that of the primitive Christian community, but with the eschatological conceptions which Luke sets out, and which underlie his description of the life of Jesus and of the work of the Spirit in the life of the Church.[1]

If we wish to see the peculiar features of his conception, we have to reckon of course with discrepancies between the ideas in his sources and his own ideas. It is these very discrepancies that help us to understand which motifs are peculiar to Luke. For example, in the quotation from Joel in the story of Pentecost (Acts ii, 17 ff.), the Spirit is thought of as a sign of the End, in the source and also in Luke, but the interpretation is different in each case. In their original sense the 'last days' have not yet been expanded into a longer epoch, which is what happens in Luke's conception of the Spirit and of the Church, according to which the outpouring of the Spirit is no longer itself the start of the Eschaton, but the beginning of a longer epoch, the period of the Church. It is true that this is the last epoch in the course of redemptive history, but this very fact represents a change in the understanding of the 'last days'. The Spirit Himself is no longer the eschatological gift, but the substitute in the meantime for the possession of ultimate salvation; He makes it possible for

---

[1] For information concerning the eschatology of the primitive Church, reference should be made to the works of Dodd, Kümmel, Goguel, Michaelis and Bultmann. Cullmann's discussion of 'consistent eschatology' also of course deserves our close attention.

believers to exist in the continuing life of the world and in per-secution, and He gives the power for missionary endeavour and for endurance. This change in the understanding of eschatology can be seen in the way in which Luke, by his description of history, depicts the nature of the Church, its relation to the world, and the course of the mission in its progress step by step, and in the way in which he repeatedly describes the Spirit as the power behind this whole process. As far as the history of tradi-tion is concerned, this means that Luke employs for his recon-struction of history the traditional material, which is stamped with the view that the last days have already arrived.

Wellhagen traces the 'weakening' of the 'primitive escha-tological theme' through the various aspects, the view of the Church, e.g., of the Spirit, and of the ministry. Everywhere he sees as the basic theme that of the mission and of the Church, and rightly affirms that this represents a slackening of the eschatological expectation and a shift of emphasis in view of the continuance of the Church in the world. But when his investiga-tions are complete, the task of understanding the specifically Lucan form of eschatology as a phenomenon in its own context remains. For this task literary criticism and form analysis are necessary, although there is practically no analysis of the text in Wellhagen.

According to him, this 'weakening' is something which 'hap-pens' to Luke in the same way as to the Church of his time in general: in principle the early expectation is preserved, but in reality it is weakened. But this leaves unexplained the deliber-ate intention with which Luke recasts his sources, and also the fact that he does not preserve the early expectation, but elimin-ates it. We see the extent of this recasting if we make a com-prehensive comparison with the sources, particularly with the Marcan passages. Such a comparison shows that it is not an adequate explanation of Luke's alterations to see them merely as 'development', but that it is a question of a definite theo-logical attitude to the problem of eschatology. Luke in fact replaces the early expectation by a comprehensive scheme of a different kind. In Wellhagen eschatology, redemptive history and the Church are unrelated, held together merely by a view of the Church which only serves to blur the problems. The fact that these themes are ranged alongside each other, however, raises the question, whether the author was not aware of the problem of their relationship. This is primarily a question that concerns the text, but it is one that has to be asked. We shall see that a connection is in fact established between the different themes.

Luke's eschatology, compared with the original conception of the imminence of the Kingdom, is a secondary construction based on certain considerations which with the passage of time cannot be avoided. It is obvious what gives rise to these reflections—the delay of the Parousia. The original idea presupposes that what is hoped for is near, which means that the hope cannot be reconciled with a delay, as otherwise the connection with the present would be lost. The same is true of Jewish apocalyptic, for here also out of affliction there arises the hope of an early deliverance, but with the passage of time the hope necessarily becomes 'apocalyptic'. This explains the analogy between the Jewish and the Christian development. The primitive Christian hope, which at first had an immediate bearing, suffers a similar fate to its Jewish predecessor: salvation is delayed. Thus the way is open for accepting the old apocalyptic ideas.[1]

Eschatology as an imminent hope belonging to the present cannot by its very nature be handed down by tradition. It is only the ideas concerning what is hoped for, not the hope itself, that can be transmitted. It is well known that all the stages in the contrast between the beginning of eschatology and the growth of apocalyptic ideas can be found both separately and merging into one another; this is because from the outset the eschatological hope has to be expressed in concepts, and on the other hand in all the speculative development the connection with concrete reality is never lost. If we trace the 'development' from Luke's sources to his own outline, we see not so much phases in a temporal development as the basic elements in the structure of eschatological thought. Of course time itself is a factor in the development, in so far as the delay of the Parousia plays a vital part in the transformation of the hope.

[1] The explanation of the analogy as the adoption of Jewish ideas is not adequate by itself. These are certainly already there, but at the beginning of the Christian development there is a drastic reduction of them. Not until these elements emerge again can there follow the widespread readoption of the traditional ideas. The problem is not the adoption itself, but the essential conditions for it.

LUKE'S ESCHATOLOGY

II. LUKE AND THE ESCHATON

1. THE CONCEPTS θλῖψις AND μετάνοια

Evidence of the change of attitude to eschatology can be seen in the obvious change in the use of certain concepts which are found mainly in eschatological contexts. We will consider two particularly clear examples, but we must bear in mind that this cannot lead to any far-reaching conclusions, for the change such as we find here is the result of unconscious modification rather than of conscious alteration. The proof of deliberate adaptation of the account by Luke can only be furnished by the analysis of the texts.

θλῖψις [1]

In Mark's apocalypse, and also in Matthew's, this word appears as a definite eschatological term in the characteristic passage Mark xiii, 24. In Mark's source at least it signifies a strictly marked epoch in the events that are expected in the future; it is defined in v. 19, which in turn underlies v. 24.[2] The θλῖψις is the prelude to the cosmic dissolution. On both occasions Luke avoids the word, in v. 19, because the fate of the Jews does not merit this description; for Luke, θλῖψις is the fate of believers, therefore he puts in its place ἀνάγκη. Verse 24, however, disappears along with vv. 21–3. When these disappear there is of course no room for the chronology which emerges from them.

Luke viii, 13 stresses, in contrast to Mark iv, 17, that the persecution of the Church is something that will last, and renders the eschatological expression θλῖψις by the characteristically Lucan πειρασμός (N.B. ἐν καιρῷ).

In Acts the word is explicitly given a present, non-eschatological meaning. In Acts vii, 10 f., and xi, 19 it refers to

[1] Cf. the article in *TW* by Schlier.
[2] See Klostermann, ad loc., and on the Matthaen parallel. On Mark xiii, 24–7 he rightly remarks: 'Mark does not say that there is an interval between vv. 14–23 and vv. 24 ff., and Matthew prevents it by an explicit εὐθέως. It became necessary later for Christians to separate the Fall of Jerusalem (vv. 14–23), which had already taken place, from the expected end of the world (vv. 24 ff.).' We need add only that Luke is the first to see this and to carry it out, as we shall show later.

98

persecution, which in Luke is not a sign that the Eschaton is near, and in Acts xiv, 22 to the Christian life. This does not mean that Christian existence as such is thought of as θλῖψις, but only certain aspects of it (πολλαὶ θλίψεις). It is possible that this is a current expression, perhaps corresponding to the πολλὰ παθεῖν of Mark viii, 31. The whole context (N.B. ἐμμένειν τῇ πίστει) shows that it has no eschatological meaning for Luke. The same is shown in Acts xx, 23, where the word is used to describe the sufferings of Paul the confessor.[1]

μετάνοια[2]

Here again we cannot speak of a conscious new interpretation and new definition. The change comes about imperceptibly in connection with the alteration in eschatology on the one hand, and in the psychology of faith on the other.[3]

The word and its corresponding verb are found in all the strata of Luke's sources (Q, Mark, special material, Acts-sources). Sometimes the source is simply taken over, as in Luke xiii, 3, 5. Occasionally Luke omits it, as in Mark i, 15, where he interprets Jesus' message differently and distinguishes it from John's call to repentance. Mark vi, 12 is also altered, for according to Luke the task of the disciples is not to call men to repentance, but to proclaim the Gospel.

The passages Luke iii, 8; x, 13, and xi, 32 are derived from Q. In iii, 8 an alteration can be seen in the plural καρποί. The meaning of the passage is made clear by Acts xxvi, 20, which is

---

[1] We see something similar in the word ὠδῖνες, which, however, is much rarer. Mark xiii, 8 is quite understandably missing. Acts ii, 24, on the other hand, with its implications for the general resurrection, fits in with Luke's conception.

[2] Cf the article by Behm and Würthwein in *TW*.

[3] We can see the latter particularly in the regular combination with ἐπιστρέφειν. When M. Hoffer (*Metanoia*. Diss. Tüb., 1946) finds no essential difference in meaning between the two words, he overlooks the specific differences which are the point of particular interest in Luke's usage. The same is true also of Behm's article in *TW*. Luke's contribution consists firstly in the narrowing of the concept, which then requires completion by 'conversion', and secondly in the fact that repentance becomes the act of repentance. For Luke μετάνοια is not fulfilled 'in faith itself', and it is definitely not 'daily conversion', but is an act which takes place only once. One might even wonder whether it does not signify the act of confession of sin at Baptism. It is no doubt true for Mark, but not for Luke (cf. Luke xxiv, 47), that μετάνοια and ἄφεσις are synonymous. This has to be added to Lohmeyer's exposition of Mark ii, 5.

one of Luke's own formulations and is a typical expression of his viewpoint. The characteristic features are:

(*a*) The combination of μετανοιεῖν and ἐπιστρέφειν. This is certainly not to be dismissed as merely rhetorical repetition, for it shows that the word μετανοιεῖν no longer has the comprehensive meaning it originally had, when it signified the event of conversion as something complete and indivisible.

This event is now divided into a change of mind and a change of conduct, in other words into 'repentance' and 'conversion' of one's way of life.

(*b*) The works (N.B., plural in Luke iii, 8) which follow upon 'repentance' must now be emphasized separately.

Both μετανοιεῖν and ἐπιστρέφειν refer to a once-for-all event, for they are connected with the once-for-all Baptism and with the forgiveness of sins, which also can only happen once (this is the meaning of ἄφεσις throughout Luke). This can be seen from Acts ii, 38, which also makes it clear that μετάνοια is the condition of forgiveness. The connection between μετάνοια and Baptism is no longer thought of as eschatological, but primarily as psychological. It is not Baptism itself that brings about conversion, but Baptism, which does indeed bring forgiveness and the Spirit, can be granted on condition of repentance and conversion, in other words on condition of a previous change of conduct. This is the meaning of the expression μετάνοια εἰς ἄφεσιν in Luke's sense (iii, 3). (Cf. the addition of εἰς μετάνοιαν in Luke v, 32.) We find the same meaning in Luke xxiv, 47.

In Luke x, 13 καθήμενοι is added, perhaps from the act of penitence required by the Church before Baptism. Luke xi, 32 is taken verbatim from Q. The construction with εἰς is also found in Acts xx, 21. Luke xvii, 3 f. is another example of the combination with ἐπιστρέφειν.

In Acts the phrase δοῦναι μετάνοιαν occurs twice (v, 31 and xi, 18), but with μετάνοια standing for a divine gift, not a condition or an achievement. On closer inspection it shows itself to be a familiar phrase, the original meaning of which has been lost. We find it used in the same way in the Pastoral letters (2 Tim. ii, 25) and in its Latin form in Polyc. Phil. xi, 4.[1]

---

[1] The expression derives from Judaism; Sib. Or., IV, 168 f. (. . . δεὸς δώσει μετάνοιαν); cf. Wisdom of Sol. xii, 19 and xii, 10; see also 1 Clem. vii, 4; Barn.

LUKE'S ESCHATOLOGY

Acts iii, 19 provides another example of the combination, and we have already mentioned Acts xx, 21 and xxvi, 20. Finally there is Acts xvii, 30 f., from which we can see how Luke interprets the expression δοῦναι μετάνοιαν, viz., in the sense that the opportunity for repentance is given. This provides further confirmation of the view we have set out.

2. The Material contained in the Gospel (with the Exception of the Two Apocalypses)

We find evidence of the shift of emphasis right at the beginning of the Gospel, in the account of John the Baptist. The apocalyptic idea of the forerunner is eliminated. Luke tries to see John in the line of all the other prophets. He stands before Jesus as the last of the prophets, not as an authentic eschatological figure.[1]

This provides a historical perspective for the interpretation of Jesus along the lines of Luke xvi, 16; he cannot be understood by reference to the eschatological idea of the forerunner, but by reference to the long preparation for his coming in an epoch of redemptive history, that is, in the whole period of the Law and the Prophets. It is true that this period comes to its close with John, the greatest of the prophets, but his status does not carry him beyond it, for even he does not proclaim the Kingdom of God.[2] The events now taking place inaugurate the last epoch of redemptive history, but they are not themselves the final events, which are placed in the future, as the form of Luke xxi in particular makes clear. In the future there will be no 'forerunner' either. Throughout his account Luke emphasizes the 'suddenness' of these events; there can therefore be no question of an advance proclamation by a forerunner.

---

xvi, 9; Herm. Sim. VIII, vi, 1 f.; J. Behm, *TW*, IV, pp. 985 ff.; Dibelius and Conzelmann, *Die Pastoralbriefe*, 1955, pp. 85 f. (3 ed.).

[1] For further details, see pp. 18 ff. above. The outcome of this view is seen in Luke xvi, 16. Any suggestion of a connection between Elijah and John the Baptist is carefully eradicated (cf. the contrary procedure in Matthew). In Acts iii, 20 ff. we see the adaptation of the Elijah typology to Christ (cf. Bauernfeind, ad loc.).

[2] Cf. on the other hand Matt. iii, 2. The use of the word εὐαγγελίζεσθαι in Luke iii, 18, does not disprove our argument; cf. p. 23, n. 1.

LUKE'S ESCHATOLOGY

The preaching of John the Baptist (Luke iii, 10–14)

Here the eschatological call to repentance is transposed into timeless ethical exhortation. By inserting this section Luke creates a pattern of preaching which can be seen in other passages as well, and which is an exact reflection of his views: threat of judgement—challenge to repentance and conversion—exhortation. But the threat of judgement is now independent of the time when the judgement will take place, of whether it is near or far. John does not declare that judgement is near, but that the Messiah is near, whose period is still separated from the Parousia by an indeterminate length of time, or rather, by a length of time determined by God and known only by Him and by the Son.[1] The fact that John proclaims the Messiah therefore does not, as Luke sees it, mean that he proclaims that the End is near.

Before Baptism there is not only the call to repentance, but positive instruction is also given as to the manner of life that is required, and it is for this reason that ethical exhortation forms part of John's preaching. Such instruction is of course the basis for 'conversion' as Luke understands the word, as signifying a change of conduct. John's preaching as a whole provides the basis for the preaching of the 'Gospel', of the 'Kingdom of God'. This brings out both the connection and the distinction between the two epochs, one of which is now succeeding the other. The condensed phrase κηρύσσων βάπτισμα μετανοίας serves to characterize the positive aspect of John's ministry and to indicate the distance from Christian Baptism, which includes forgiveness. The question: What must we do? is used by Luke as a stereotype phrase in his pattern of conversion (cf. Acts ii, 37; xvi, 30; xxii, 10). It is this pattern which determines the interpretation of John's ministry, according to which it stands in need of the Christian completion supplied by forgiveness and the Spirit.

---

[1] John proclaims only one thing over and above the 'Law': the coming of a mightier one (but not ὀπίσω μου). John himself does not possess symbolic significance as the 'arché' of the Gospel. It is only the content of his preaching and of his ministry that is significant, in other words, the call to repentance as the appropriate preparation of men for the preaching of Jesus. In respect of John's Baptism Luke does not stress its novelty, but emphasizes its inferiority to Christian Baptism (Acts i, 5; xi, 16). He is less concerned with bringing out the element of advance upon what Israel has so far known—in fact he deliberately links John with it—than with determining the relationship with what the Church now knows, i.e. Baptism with the Spirit.

LUKE'S ESCHATOLOGY

Luke iv, 16–30

This section develops the pattern of Luke's Christology. As we shall meet it time after time, we need point out here only the eschatological motif of the Spirit, which is, of course, part of the immediate context of the Baptism and the Temptation. Even if the Spirit was originally the sign of the End, Luke has provided a historical perspective: the σήμερον of v. 21 is already thought of as belonging to past history. 'At that time', when Jesus was still living and active on earth, the fulfilment which is here described came about. We cannot conclude from the quotation which expresses and confirms the fulfilment, that Luke adhered to an early expectation.[1] It is rather in this very section that the problem of bringing eschatology within the course of history and of fitting it into the tripartite pattern of redemptive history arises.[2]

Luke viii, 10

The plural μυστήρια (cf. Matt. xiii, 11) indicates that the eschatological secrecy is now being replaced by a timeless secrecy to which there corresponds an equally timeless disclosure of the mysteries thanks to 'gnosis'. For Mark, 'the mystery' is the coming itself. But when one speaks of 'the mysteries', one is not thinking of the event of the coming, but of the transcendent nature of the Kingdom; the secrets are revealed when one 'sees the Kingdom' (Luke ix, 27).

The ethical note in vv. 11–15 corresponds closely to this

---

[1] For an analysis, see pp. 31 ff. above. That Luke is aware of the historical distance from the period of Jesus and of its different character from the present is shown by the analogous passage Luke xxii, 35 f., where the problem of this difference is considered. We can see it also in the pattern imposed upon the Spirit's activity, which is divided into three sharply distinguished epochs, the period of Israel, of Jesus and of the Church. Cf. the detailed examination in v. Baer, e.g. pp. 69 ff., 76 f.

[2] Cf. v. Baer, loc. cit. In the period of Jesus' life the Spirit is restricted exclusively to Jesus, and is later poured out on the whole Church. The period of Jesus is no longer thought of as the end of history, but as pointing forward to the further epoch of the Church. The 'acceptable year of the Lord' is not the dawn of the End, but the manifestation of the Saviour, in which the End is foreshadowed, but has not yet arrived. What is now beginning is the period of expectation, based on the knowledge of Jesus and the possession of the Spirit. In this connection we may mention a small but significant feature, the misunderstanding of the demonic motif in Luke iv, 35.

changed view of the Kingdom. Now that the main emphasis is no longer on the coming of the Kingdom but on its nature, the way into it becomes a separate problem. What matters now is ὑπομονή (v. 15), in other words, adjustment to a long period of persecution (N.B. in v. 13 the alteration of Mark's wording). Verse 12 also reflects a situation in which the Church does not envisage an early expectation.

Luke ix, 27 (in comparison with Mark ix, 1)

This verse is of central importance for determining the concept of the Kingdom and for the idea of the postponement of the Parousia. Because of this, it has recently been the subject of keen debate.[1]

Luke offers the earliest example of an exegesis of the difficult Marcan saying which takes account of the problem it presents. Even if the saying was meant originally to explain the delay of the Parousia and to make it endurable, especially in view of the death of members of the community (Bornkamm, loc. cit., n. 1), later the coming would appear unbearably near at hand. The End was in fact delayed still longer, therefore a new solution was required. If it was to be a permanent solution, it must not be jeopardized again by a further delay. Therefore it must completely omit any suggestion of a fixed time, but it must be able to offer a reason for this omission.

This is Luke's aim here. The idea of the coming of the Kingdom is replaced by a timeless conception of it. Luke rightly interprets both ἐληλυθυῖαν and ἐν δυνάμει as a realistic description of the Parousia, and therefore they are excluded. In this way the saying is made independent of any definite time. τῶν αὐτοῦ ἑστηκότων therefore means: those who are standing

---

[1] Kümmel, *Verheissung und Erfüllung*, pp. 13 ff. For the contrary view, cf. Fuchs, *Verk. und Forschung*, 1947/48, p. 76. G. Bornkamm, in the *Lohmeyer Gedenkschrift*, pp. 116 ff., rightly agrees with Kümmel that there is a suggestion of the delay of the Parousia even in Mark ix, 1 (in contrast to Dodd, *Parables*, pp. 53 f.), but for that very reason considers the saying, contrary to Kümmel, to be a community creation; similarly Fuchs, loc. cit. The usual argument, that it cannot be a community creation, as the non-fulfilment of this prophecy would give rise to difficulties (thus Kümmel, p. 15) is a strange one. The saying arose in the period when one could still hope for the arrival of the Parousia, towards the end of the first generation; cf. E. Grässer, *Parusieverzögerung*, pp. 131 ff.

by 'at the time'.[1] The interpretation of the phrase ἡ γενεὰ αὕτη in the parallel saying in Luke xxi, 32 points in the same direction.[2]

The expression 'to see the Kingdom' means that although the Kingdom cannot actually be seen, it can be perceived. The explanation of this is to be found in the interpretation of the life of Jesus as a clear manifestation of salvation in the course of redemptive history. It is from the life of Jesus that we can see what the Kingdom is like, but it is not disclosed when the Kingdom itself is to appear. Therefore the coming of the Kingdom can only be proclaimed as a future fact, without any reference to when it will happen, but the nature of it can be seen now.[3]

Luke ix, 60

Whereas this saying referred originally to the nearness of the Kingdom, now it refers to the importance of missionary work. The language is typical ('to publish abroad the Kingdom'). The three pictures of discipleship prepare the way for the Mission of the Seventy.[4]

[1] Does this mean that they will not die, but will be transformed? And only the righteous (τινες)?

[2] Cf. xxi, 32, a verse which strengthens the view that the reference is to mankind in general. The other passages containing this expression in Luke are to be interpreted similarly.

[3] Streeter, *The Four Gospels*, pp. 518 ff., thinks the omission of 'with power' means that the Kingdom is being interpreted as the Church. This interpretation, however, is not in accordance with Luke's idea of the βασιλεία. Michaelis, *Der Herr verzieht nicht*, pp. 34 ff., sees no essential difference between Mark ix, 1 and the parallel passages. Klostermann's 'until they experience the Kingdom of God' is a fundamental misunderstanding.

On the significance of αὐτοῦ, cf. Acts xviii, 19; xxi, 4; xv, 34, and the alternation with ἐκεῖ in the manuscript transmission. On the meaning of seeing, cf. Luke x, 23 f., a Q saying which, however, appears in a different form in Matthew and in Luke. Bultmann, *Syn. Trad.*, p. 114, and Klostermann take the Lucan form to be the primary one. Linguistically, however, it is Matthew's version that gives the impression of being the original one. In this case it would be Luke who introduced the reference to what is seen and heard, thus creating a link with what has gone before. What is it that the disciples see? We find the answer in vv. 21 f. on the one hand and in vv. 25 ff. on the other (what is seen now followed by what will be seen in the future). Cf. also Luke xvii, 22, Luke's interpretation of the traditional saying in vv. 23 f. (see Bultmann, p. 138). Further interpretation is provided in v. 25. The day of v. 24 belongs to the future, but it is foreshadowed in the present. Verse 22 refers to the actual period of Jesus.

[4] Klostermann points out a certain incongruity between the logia and the introductions to them. He suggests that the first has been evolved out of the saying by

105

LUKE'S ESCHATOLOGY

Luke x, 2 f.

The theme of the harvest can emphasize either the urgency in view of the imminent End or the duration of a longer period of harvesting. The passage itself does not help us to decide where the main stress lies. However, a characteristic Lucan motif appears in v. 3, although the verse is derived from tradition. In Matt. x, 16 the emphasis is on the threat to which the disciples are exposed (cf. the context, v. 14 and vv. 17 f.). In Luke, on the other hand, the emphasis is on the protection which they enjoy in the midst of danger. Whereas in Matthew the meaning appears in x, 16 b, in Luke it is in the directions which follow concerning equipment. Luke states their significance explicitly in xxii, 35: they represent the absolute peacefulness of the period of Jesus.

Verse 5 speaks of peace in the same sense. The word comes from the source, but is more strongly stressed than in Matthew.[1]

Luke, and also the third one. The second saying requires a context from the outset; there is also Luke's own interpretation.

By means of the context 'discipleship' is given a specific meaning: during Jesus' lifetime there is no other discipleship than that of sharing in Jesus' work. When Kittel says (*TW*, I, pp. 210 ff.) that there are disciples who do not follow in the physical sense, he is quite correct; but in Luke those who go about with Jesus, especially his companions on the journey to Jerusalem, are specifically distinguished from them. Among the details of Luke's language we may mention the following. Luke v, 11 has no direct source. The idea is elucidated by the addition of ἀφέντες πάντα. Cf. also v, 28, where a Marcan source is similarly amplified. In this way the literal, physical sense of discipleship is brought out more strongly. It is true that the motif of this amplification is derived from Mark (Mark x, 21, 28–Luke xviii, 22, 28) but it has been expanded by Luke. Luke vii, 9 comes from Q; Luke ix, 11 is an editorial creation, from material in the sources; Luke xxiii, 27 is also possibly editorial. Luke ix, 23 comes from Mark, but the source has been reinterpreted. In Luke ix, 49 Luke does not wish to say follow 'us', so he says 'with' us, for discipleship can only be applied to Jesus. Luke xviii, 22, 28 also show some interpretation. Verse 43 comes from Mark, but by comparison it is more charged with meaning. Luke xxii, 39 is an editorial creation, which gives Jesus a more central position in the account. Two omissions are to be noted, Mark iii, 7 and v, 24, both of which are connected with the alteration of the setting.

Matthew, however, develops a more distinctive interpretation of discipleship than Luke. This is shown by G. Bornkamm in an essay which, as regards method, is of outstanding importance: 'Die Sturmstillung im Matthäusevangelium', *Jahrb. der Theol. Schule Bethel*, 1948, pp. 49 ff. He deals with the Matthaen parallels to the passage we are considering, and shows the mutual elucidation of the Stilling of the Storm and the scenes concerning discipleship in Matthew, who links the two together (Matt. viii, 18–27).

[1] The fact that protection is stressed in Luke is a point that is nearly always missed, because the connection with xxii, 35 is overlooked. Cf. Schlatter, p. 501,

LUKE'S ESCHATOLOGY

Luke x, 11

Here we meet something which is rare in Luke, an assertion of the nearness of the Kingdom. The saying mentions the signs of its nearness. It should also be noted, that Luke emphasizes the fact of judgement.

Luke x, 18

It is clear that this is a traditional eschatological saying. But what is its meaning in Luke's context?[1] It adds support of course to the statement in v. 17, and makes possible the bestowal of authority in v. 19. But why should they not rejoice at this? Is it so that they should not think this is the end of the struggle, in other words, that they are not to mistake this event for the End?[2] The context from v. 16 to v. 20, and also vv. 21 f. and 23 f., presents a picture of the salvation that has been manifested in Jesus, but in Luke's view this does not dispose of a futurist eschatology. It is not until the Parousia that the Kingdom itself will come; what is seen now is only an image of it. In the interval the

where he draws certain literary conclusions. Klostermann, ad loc., finds no 'inner link' between the verses. Then why did Luke put them together?

For an analysis, cf. Bultmann, pp. 80, 170, 351.

In opposition to Schlatter (p. 276), who here expresses the general opinion, we may say that although to interpret this passage by reference to a supposed ideal of poverty is in keeping with a widespread notion, it cannot be deduced from the text. The authentic interpretation which Luke himself gives is normative here. What he sees in Jesus' instructions is not an Ebionite ideal, but the characterization of the period of Jesus as a period of peace within redemptive history, in the same sense as in Luke iv, 18 ff., and its differentiation from the following period of conflict (xxii, 36), a period in which the Church has continued to live but in which those who are oppressed can keep before their eyes this foretaste of peace. It is granted that there are discrepancies between tradition and Luke's adaptation, of which there are examples possibly in vv. 11 and 18 of the chapter we are considering.

[1] We cannot go into the question raised by the original meaning of the logion. There is of course a similarity with the theme of Rev. xii.

[2] Verse 19, a Q saying, does not in itself express an attitude to eschatology any different from Matt. xii, 27 f. It fits in well in Luke: the Kingdom of Satan is being attacked, the Kingdom of God is present, which means, in other words, that through Jesus those works are being wrought, the significance of which is indicated in iv, 18–21. This excludes any idea of the immanence of the Kingdom, and the same is true of xvii, 20 ff. In v. 20 ἐγώ is omitted, which gives rise to the contrast: ἐν Βεελζεβούλ—ἐν δακτύλῳ θεοῦ. Luke can interpret the saying without difficulty in line with his own eschatology: ἐφ' ὑμᾶς corresponds to ἐντὸς ὑμῶν in the other passage.

LUKE'S ESCHATOLOGY

disciples represent their Master, as we see in Acts, and here they are being prepared.[1]

Luke xii, 38 ff.

Here the delay is directly referred to, and what is more, in the pre-Lucan form (Matt. xxiv, 48).[2] Klostermann rightly states that the aim is to assert that 'it does not matter how long the delay lasts'. This is the decisive idea, which is developed by Luke into a complete scheme of the eschatological interval. He can simply take over the tradition in this passage, because it fits in smoothly with his conception. The suddenness of the thief's coming brings out the urgency of being watchful. This links up with xvii, 20 ff.[3]

---

[1] Schlatter (p. 278) correctly points out that Jesus has made his disciples invulnerable. In this we see the motif of the period of Jesus, and here we have evidence, that it is still in force. It did not cease to be effectual with the death of Jesus, but continues to determine the life of believers in the present. In what way? There are two motifs which need to be considered together:

(a) After the period of Jesus the Spirit comes and transmits its abiding redemptive benefits until the Parousia.

(b) In this passage, however, the Spirit plays no part, for it is not possible, as His ministry is strictly limited to the time after the Ascension (cf. v. Baer, loc. cit.). The coincidence of these two different motifs is of course the result of tradition. If we ask whether Luke tried to make a compromise, the answer is in the affirmative, for in Acts he makes plain the historical bases of apostolate and of witness. The office bearers are appointed not by the Spirit but by Jesus himself—cf. Luke vi, 13, and note the difference from Mark iii, 14; so now they receive suitable preparation. The Spirit belongs to a entirely different context, that of the structure of redemptive history. We must also bear in mind that the Spirit is given to all, not just to those who hold office, although they have the special power of transmitting the Spirit by the imposition of hands.

[2] Michaelis, *Der Herr verzieht nicht*, p. 9, points out that 'My Lord tarrieth' is represented as the attitude of the unfaithful servant. But the question is, how does he arrive at this attitude? Simply because the lord was long delayed. Similarly, there is Michaelis' further point, that if the sentence were of later origin, it would not announce delay, but would make it clear that the Lord would come earlier. But here delay is assumed as a fact. It is not 'announced', but assumed in such a way that 'nevertheless' one adheres to belief in the nearness of the coming. It is this very 'nevertheless' that is the new element, the proof of actual delay. Luke's solution is different, in that he does not pass over the problem, but solves it once for all.

[3] This provides an important argument in support of Fuchs and Bornkamm against Kümmel: the secret concerning the time is not original, but is connected with the delay of the Parousia.

LUKE'S ESCHATOLOGY

Luke xii, 49

We must beware of an interpretation which spiritualizes the meaning. We cannot agree here with Klostermann. Luke interprets the saying as referring to the eschatological conflagration, for he does not draw a parallel between vv. 49 and 50, but contrasts them: the End has not yet come, but instead there is the baptism of death.[1]

Luke xii, 52

The characteristically Lucan expression ἀπὸ τοῦ νῦν does not refer to the End, but to the epoch of conflict that is now beginning. The closest parallel is in xxii, 69, where Luke transforms an eschatological saying of Mark by setting it in the context of redemptive history.

Luke xii, 54 ff.

The interpretation of 'this time' is determined by the parable. The message is that one must not be led astray by the delay.

Luke xiii, 23 f.

In connection with the parallel passage Matt. vii, 13 f., Wellhausen shows that an originally eschatological Q saying has been modified. Matthew adapts it to the doctrine of the two ways. In Luke also the early expectation is eliminated. The urgency of the summons does not depend on the imminence of the End, but on the fact of a sudden, incalculable End at an unknown point of time (vv. 25 f.).

Luke xiii, 34 f.

The part played by the city of Jerusalem in the events concerning the End is a major problem. It is developed in a special

[1] On this passage, see R. Otto, *Reich Gottes*, p. 311, for a view contrary to Bultmann's, *Syn. Trad.*, pp. 165 f. Kümmel agrees with Otto that the saying is genuine (p. 40), on the ground that it contains a hint of Jesus' shrinking from suffering. The form taken by the Gethsemane tradition suggests a view contrary to that of Otto and Kümmel.

way in Luke, which we shall discuss separately later. Here we are merely concerned with the literary questions arising from this passage.

The present form and context in Luke give rise to certain difficulties, for Jesus can really only speak in this way after a ministry in Jerusalem.[1] Matthew avoids the difficulty by transferring the saying to a speech made in Jerusalem (Matt. xxiii, 37 ff.). The problem, as Luke understood it, is connected with the alteration which he makes in the acclamation at the Triumphal Entry (xix, 38). It is not likely that the prophecy refers to the Entry, in which case the saying must refer to more distant events. In other words, this passage gives an indication of the typological meaning that the Entry has for Luke.[2]

Luke xiv, 13 f.

This saying contains a pre-Lucan view of resurrection, which refers only to the resurrection of the just, whilst Luke himself assumes the resurrection of all. In Acts xxiv, 15 Luke gives his own rendering of the saying, apparently as a polemic against the restriction of the resurrection hope to the just. The general resurrection is a central motif in the call to repentance in missionary preaching, and therefore a major topic in the appeal to the Gentiles, who know nothing about it. 'Jesus and the resurrection' is the content of the message (Acts xvii, 18). Verse 31 in the same passage provides an example of how the motif is actually used. This general version of the future hope as the hope of individual resurrection is what takes the place of the collective, cosmic early expectation of the first days of the Church (cf. my articles 'Resurrection' in RGG, I Supp., pp. 695 f. (3 ed.), and 'Eschatologie', ibid., II Supp., pp. 665 ff.). The theme appears again at the centre of the dispute between Christianity and Judaism at Paul's trial (Acts xxiii, 6; xxiv, 21,

[1] Even if he is speaking prophetically, he can say this only in retrospect. On this question, cf. Bultmann, p. 20, where he raises the question whether it was a supra-historical figure, Sophia, that spoke. Luke, of course, is not aware of any identification of Jesus and Sophia. Cf. xi, 49; Sophia is pre-existent, but not Jesus. Did Luke introduce the saying in this passage as a plea to Jerusalem? Cf. Grässer, op. cit., p. 39.

[2] Klostermann raises the question, whether the saying points to the Entry or to a more distant future. The answer is connected with the textual critical aspect of the passage. In the manuscripts the reference is obviously to the Entry.

and the passage already mentioned, Acts xxiv, 15). In this passage it is therefore necessary for us to distinguish between the original meaning and Luke's meaning.[1] The emergence of the assertion concerning the resurrection in the general form of 'there is a resurrection', that is, a judgement, is a characteristic of Luke's recasting of eschatology. In this general assertion the time of the judgement is no longer of vital importance. It is not its nearness, but the fact that it is inevitable, that constitutes the summons. Thus the tense of the hope is retained, but apart from any question as to when the End will be. In this way Luke can retain the traditional conceptions, but no longer jeopardized by the delay. The event is replaced by the future state, which, it is true, begins at an 'appointed' moment, but this is of less importance than knowing that it is a fact.

Luke xiv, 15

Luke uses this beatitude to introduce a Q passage. Luke's main point, which comes out in v. 23, does not imply that the End is imminent (cf. v. 26).[2]

Luke xv, 7

Bultmann (*Syn. Trad.*, pp. 184 f.) rightly explains the wording as the result of Luke's editorial work (as also in vv. 8–10). Heavenly and earthly events are made to appear as simultaneous. This, of course, is not to be confused with eschatological parallelism, such as we see in Luke xii, 8 f., and the parallel passages.

Luke xvi, 9–13

A. Descamps makes a careful analysis of these verses, and shows that the material which Luke took and adapted had a

---

[1] On the idea of the resurrection, see Bousset-Gressmann, p. 272, and Billerbeck, IV, p. 1170. Schlatter's reference to xv, 7 is misleading (p. 341). If the source speaks of the resurrection of the just, then it is an encouragement to hope. Luke's version of the belief in the resurrection is dominated by the judgement, for which, however, the believer is prepared by forgiveness.

[2] Bultmann, *Syn. Trad.*, pp. 113 f.

thoroughly eschatological stamp. It is transformed by Luke as follows:

(a) by inserting v. 9 the hope is individualized (cf. above on Luke xiv, 13 f.);

(b) by adding vv. 11 f. the process of 'de-eschatologizing' is completed.

Luke xvi, 16

This is an important verse which we often have to consider. Here we are concerned only with the negative aspect of the demarcation: the coming of John does not mean that the Kingdom is near, but that the time for the preaching of the Kingdom has come.[1]

Luke xvi, 19–31

Luke's interpretation of the two main points in the parable can be seen on the one hand in vv. 14 f., and on the other in vv. 16–18.[2] The parable exemplifies the timeless, ethical application of the view of the hereafter which fits in well with Luke's idea.

Luke xviii, 30

This verse has links with the last passage as regards its subject-matter. The contrast between 'this' καιρός and the αἰών to come derives from Mark. Luke's interest, however, is in the light it casts on the epochs of redemptive history (xvi, 16).

The relation between eschatology and ethics can be seen in the way in which Luke links xviii, 1 ff., with the teaching in xvii, 20 ff. The theme of endurance—irrespective of duration— is characteristic.[3]

---

[1] The context also elucidates the meaning of βιάζεσθαι (in the positive sense, which is contrary to its original sense).

[2] Bultmann, *Syn. Trad.*, p. 193.

[3] On ἐν τάχει in xviii, 8, cf. Kümmel, p. 33, in contrast to Bultmann, p. 189 (but see also p. 209). On the apocalypse in ch. 17, see below.

LUKE'S ESCHATOLOGY

Luke xviii, 31 ff.

Certain editorial additions are to be noted here, among them the idea of the 'fulfilment' of Scripture. The term πάντα has a significance in this connection that has for the most part been overlooked. According to Luke, prophecy reaches as far as Christ, but not to the Eschaton. πάντα therefore is not just an empty phrase, but is meant literally. The same divisions in redemptive history are implied as in xvi, 16.

Luke xix, 11 will be discussed in the section concerning Jerusalem. By inserting this verse the editor provides an interpretation of the Parable of the Pounds which follows (v. 12: οὖν). It is interpreted as the answer to the question concerning when the End will be, but in fact this question is rejected, and instead there is a summons to be ready for a long time of waiting. This is the answer typical of Luke. The endowment of the story with allegorical features (v. 12) is in keeping with Luke's method of using a traditional passage such as this.

3. THE KINGDOM OF GOD[1]

If we are to understand this idea, we must bear in mind something which we shall discuss separately later, namely, that Luke puts historical events such as the destruction of Jerusalem in a historical setting; in other words, he deliberately removes them from the context of the End. This means that the Kingdom of God, far from being made into a historical entity, is removed into the metaphysical realm. This, of course, gives rise to the question as to what is the real connection between this entity and the Church of the present.[2]

In Matt. iii, 2 the idea of the Kingdom appears in John the Baptist's preaching. Such a thing is not possible in Luke, as he

---

[1] Cf. K. L. Schmidt's article in *TW*.
[2] English scholars in particular, such as Taylor, maintain that the idea of the Kingdom is brought within history in the sense of an immanent development, but there is little exegetical basis for this view. We shall discuss certain points connected with this view in the appropriate place. (Taylor formulates his interpretation mainly with reference to Luke's version of the Synoptic apocalypse.) Wellhagen also accepts this interpretation of the Kingdom as a historical entity, in the sense of identifying it with the Church, but again without any solid exegetical basis.

himself states in xvi, 16. It is Jesus who begins the preaching of the Kingdom.[1] Luke maintains this view consistently.[2]

Compared with Mark i, 15 there is a shift of emphasis in Luke. The declaration of the coming of the Kingdom, that it is near, is omitted, and thus the connection between the nearness of the Kingdom and repentance is severed. Instead there is the simple statement: ἐδίδασκεν, followed by Luke's programme of Jesus' saving ministry (iv, 16 ff.). What is new in Jesus' teaching, compared with John's, is not the message that the Kingdom is near, but the message of the Kingdom itself. It is true that his preaching presupposes the call to repentance, but in the sense that it is Good News it does not point primarily to the coming but to the nature of the Kingdom, which is set out in iv, 18–21. Luke is certainly familiar with the statement ἤγγικεν, but it is not part of the preaching, but only of the secret instruction of the disciples. And for the most part it is a time in the future from the point of view of which the Kingdom is near; as we see, Luke's attitude to history affects even declarations concerning the future.[3]

---

[1] See above, on xviii, 31 ff.

[2] The question whether Matt. iii, 2 belongs to the source or is editorial does not affect this statement. Matthew's aim is to draw out the parallel between John and Jesus, whereas Luke's is to emphasize the difference between them.

[3] Cf. Luke xxi, 8, 28. The meaning is clearly expressed in v. 31, where the editorial alteration compared with Mark should be noted. Here we have the key to the understanding of Luke's sayings concerning the nearness of the Kingdom. His omissions provide similar evidence. For example, he omits the section about the nearness of the Kingdom from the Q saying in Matt. x, 7, as here it is a matter of instructions concerning the preaching of the Gospel, but he retains it in Luke x, 9, as the instructions here concern the future (cf. v. 11). What Luke does is to replace the proclamation of the nearness of the Kingdom by the significant expression κηρύσσειν τὴν βασιλείαν, in which the time ₊element, which is vital for Mark and Matthew, is excluded. There are examples in ix, 2, 11, 60, and iv, 43, all of which are editorial additions. What is to come in the future is strictly speaking not the Kingdom itself but Christ; from his Parousia onwards the Kingdom will be 'seen' (Luke ix, 22, contrast Mark ix, 1). Of course Luke can also speak of the coming 'of the Kingdom' (xxii, 18), but this has to be interpreted in accordance with the other sayings. (At the same time, of course, Luke was passing judgement on the Church's preaching of his own day, and expressing the view that apocalyptic should not form part of the preaching.) Luke vi, 20 (cf. Matt. v, 3) does not contradict the view we have set out. Luke is speaking of the future Kingdom, as also in v. 23. There is another significant alteration in Luke xi, 52, when we compare it with Matt. xxiii, 13. We need to be cautious in speaking of a spiritualization of the meaning, as it is precisely because he does not think of the Kingdom in a spiritualized sense that Luke alters the source; he does so because he cannot apply the statement to the Kingdom, on account of his realist conception (in the metaphysical

LUKE'S ESCHATOLOGY

Luke vii, 28 can be taken without alteration from Q, as it contains no reference to time. Chapter viii, vv. 9 f., has been discussed above (pp. 103 f.); here the timeless mysteries of the nature of the Kingdom come to the fore; ix, 27 has also been considered (pp. 104 f.). In Mark the saying already has a note of resignation, but in Luke it is completely divorced from the immediate circumstances and refers to the vision of a state. Whose vision does it refer to? Is it the vision of the future last generation or the vision of the martyr, as in Acts vii, 56? We must not forget that persecution and the risking of one's life have just been spoken of. The actual moment is of minor importance, and is not near at hand;[1] xxii, 18 helps us to understand the meaning[2] (cf. Mark xiv, 25). What does the 'coming' in this verse refer to—the Parousia? It does not imply in Luke's opinion that it is to take place soon. The emphasis is rather on the fact that no feast will be celebrated in Heaven, so long as the Church is persecuted in the world.[3] Or does the saying refer to the coming of the Spirit? But it is impossible for Luke to identify Kingdom and Spirit. The first interpretation envisages a fairly long interval between the Passion and the Parousia.[4]

sense). For the emergence of the spatial aspects, together with the disappearance of the temporal aspects—a process which to some extent can be traced already in the sources—cf. Luke xiii, 24/Matt. vii, 13 f.; Luke xviii, 24/Mark x, 23; Luke xviii 17/Mark x, 15.

For the preaching of the Kingdom, cf. also Luke viii, 1; Acts viii, 12; xix, 8; xx, 25; xxviii, 23, 31.

We cannot draw any conclusions from Luke vi, 46, as this is not an example of an omission by Luke, but of an editorial amplification by Matthew.

[1] The interpretation 'to do violence to the Kingdom', in the bad sense, is hardly conceivable in Luke. One can lay violent hands only on the messengers of the Kingdom, not on the Kingdom itself, which belongs to Heaven. That the persecution of the messengers is spoken of in such an abbreviated way is less probable in Luke than in the other Synoptics, as it is Luke who draws a sharper distinction between the Kingdom and the message of the Kingdom. Such an interpretation is only conceivable if one refers the violence strictly to the person of Jesus, but the statement seems too general for this.

[2] On the literary question, cf. Kümmel, pp. 24 f. (vv. 15–18 are Luke's own creation). Also Dibelius, *Formg.*, pp. 211 f., von Soden, *Sakrament und Ethik*, p. 29, n. 2. Kümmel rightly points out that a considerable lapse of time is assumed; but it is not an authentic saying of Jesus.

[3] For a different view, cf. Grässer, p. 56, n. 2.

[4] This saying is often quoted as proof that Luke identifies the Kingdom with the Church, and it is therefore connected with the beginning of the community cult; this view has recently been set out again by Wellhagen, pass. Luke's conception of

LUKE'S ESCHATOLOGY

The related saying xxii, 69 (contrast Mark xiv, 62) shows that sayings of this kind refer to the incalculable period until the Parousia. Again, there is no statement concerning the time. The state which is described is beginning now, whereas Mark is speaking of an eschatological event. The modification of the source is for a definite purpose: the hearers do not see the Son of Man, therefore the corresponding Marcan declaration is omitted, and instead a permanent state is now described.[1] Luke xiii, 28, when compared with Matt. viii, 11, proves to have been edited to a considerable degree.[2] The reference to seeing has no doubt been introduced by Luke and shows plainly how concrete his conception is.

There is no reason for altering the questions about comparison in xiii, 18, 20, and so they are simply reproduced.

The following omissions should be noted:

Mark ix, 47 is missing together with the whole section. Is the reason that Luke cannot entertain the idea that one should enter the Kingdom maimed, especially in view of promises such as iv, 18 ff., according to which the Kingdom brings healing? Mark xii, 34 is presumably also not acceptable to Luke.

Luke xxiii, 51, following Mark xv, 43, speaks of the expectation of the Kingdom. We cannot be precise as to the meaning here, and there is no mention of the time when the Kingdom will come.

One passage speaks of the Kingdom of the Father, another of the Kingdom of the Son. What is the relation between the two?

As regards the Kingdom of the Father, Luke xii, 31 comes from Q; cf. Matt. xviii, 33. There is no particular emphasis in the sense of a contrast with the Son or his Kingdom.

The Kingdom of the Son appears as early as the prologue (i, 33), and also in the sayings at the Last Supper (xxii, 29 f.). What is meant in this case is the Kingdom, which the Father

the Kingdom, which is complete in itself, makes such an identification impossible. What is important for us here is the fact that this interpretation says nothing concerning the nearness of the Parousia either—a fact which Wellhagen recognizes.

[1] According to Acts vii, 56, to see the Ascended Lord before the Parousia is something reserved for the martyr. Seeing the Parousia, however, is out of the question for the present generation. On the other hand, Jesus' suffering has to be shown as the entry upon his Lordship. It is from these motifs that the Lucan form of this passage is built up. It is purely editorial.

[2] Klostermann, ad loc.

has bequeathed to the Son. The passage corresponds to a certain extent to a passage in Q (Matt. xix, 28), but it is considerably modified.[1]

This passage casts little light on what is meant by the Kingdom of the Son. The same is true of xxiii, 42, quite apart from the textual problem. Is the Kingdom of Christ the intermediate state? It does not help us much either if we turn to the sayings about Christ as King. The direct statement about Kingship (xxiii, 3) does not lend itself to any more precise interpretation.

We will briefly summarize our survey of the sayings about the Kingdom of God, before we consider more fully the Kingdom of the Son, so far as this is possible with the limited material. We have not dealt with the passages where Luke simply continues the tradition.[2] The Kingdom is not depicted any more vividly in Luke than in the other records on which he draws. The traditional images are taken over, in particular that of the feast.[3] We noted however throughout, that a change of attitude towards eschatology has taken place. This is seen in the direct statements to the effect that the End is far away and also in the characteristic terminology ('to announce the Kingdom'; cf. the sayings about seeing the Kingdom, and the avoidance of statements about its coming).

---

[1] For an analysis, cf. Klostermann; Bultmann, *Syn. Trad.*, pp. 170 f. The latter considers v. 28 to be editorial, similarly the I-form. The former stresses the lack of an article with βασιλεία, which means it is used in an abstract sense.

[2] On this aspect, cf. the article by K. L. Schmidt in *TW*. He gives information also about the earlier history of the idea.

The Kingdom as a blessing of salvation appears, for example, in Luke xii, 32 (to give the Kingdom). The presence of the Kingdom is not implied here in any other sense than in the statements about seeing. In each case it is a question of the foreshadowing of the Kingdom in the ministry of Jesus. Among further passages, cf. Luke xviii, 17; Acts xiv, 22; Luke xiii, 28 f.; xxii, 16, 30; xxiii, 42; xii, 31.

[3] This image naturally plays a special part in the sayings at the Last Supper (xxii, 30). The Supper is meant to be a foretaste of future blessedness, but this foretaste has to be understood strictly in Luke's sense: the Supper is not the guarantee of a fulfilment near at hand, but is in the interval a substitute for the salvation that is promised, in the same way as is the Spirit. It is the Spirit and the Supper that make it possible for the Church to continue in the persisting life of the world, it is they that make it possible to endure in godless surroundings and in the midst of persecution. This is brought out by the motif of the solidarity between the heavenly and the earthly community (xxii, 15 ff.). This helps to explain the connection between the Spirit and the summary accounts of the community meals in Acts. The connection between the two is quite clear. All that remains is to see how the two factors are influenced by Luke's scheme of redemptive history. For an analysis, cf. H. Schürmann (see p. 80).

LUKE'S ESCHATOLOGY

What is the position regarding the Kingdom of the Son? In view of Luke i, 33, Luke cannot think of a Kingdom of Christ as a separate entity. But as the objection might be raised, that the authenticity of these first two chapters is questionable, we have not taken into consideration the statements that are peculiar to them.

There have been three recent attempts to solve this problem, by K. L. Schmidt, O. Cullmann and J. Wellhagen.[1] Schmidt does not differentiate between the individual Synoptics and combines their statements without distinction; his findings are therefore only speculative. Cullmann does not go into the specific differences either.[2] As Wellhagen's work is not easily accessible, we will give a brief sketch of his findings.

[1] K. L. Schmidt in his article in *TW* (I, pp. 590 f.); O. Cullmann, *Königsherrschaft Christi und Kirche im NT* (see Bibliography); in addition, Kümmel in *ThR*, 1948, specially p. 123. Taylor, *Formation*, pp. 258 f. should also be mentioned.

[2] Schmidt concludes from the passages Mark xi, 10; Matt. xxi, 9; Luke xix, 38 and Mark x, 29; Matt. xix, 29; Luke xviii, 29, that 'Jesus Christ is identified with the Kingdom of Heaven'. On p. 591 he writes that the βασιλεία is repeatedly stressed 'implicitly' [*sic*] by the reference to the κύριος. It is difficult to see how a definition of the concept could be achieved in this way. There is of course no difficulty in reaching by this means the logical goal of the argument, Origen's αὐτοβασιλεία.

Against Cullman and Kümmel, loc. cit., we must note that Cullmannn's proofs do not demonstrate as far as Luke is concerned anything more than the occasional appearance of the expression, without even a hint of a closer definition. The phrase of course refers to the Kingship of Christ. Cullmann, however, does not recognize its specifically Lucan sense of a cultic kingship over Israel, which we see in the peculiar Temple-motif in Luke's account of the Passion. The following details should be noted. With reference to Cullmann, p. 12, nothing can be gathered from Acts xvii, 7 concerning the time of Christ's Kingdom. With reference to p. 14, Acts i, 11 contains nothing about the duration and termination of Christ's sovereignty. And with reference to p. 18, where is it that Satan falls to? This is questionable, to say the least. The same is true of the interpretation of Luke xi, 20.

Although Luke is familiar with the Kingdom of Christ, he does not aim to establish a systematic connection with the idea of the Kingdom of God. Despite Luke xxiii, 42, one can scarcely speak of an intermediate Kingdom, for there is insufficient material for it. Luke has certainly no thought of drawing any speculative conclusions from it. For the most part he is concerned to bring out the relation of the Kingdom of God to us. Just as it is through Christ that God enters into relationship with us, so occasionally we find alongside God's Kingdom by way of analogy the Kingdom of Christ, perhaps under the influence of views current in the Church. Luke does not go beyond this. Above all, there is certainly no identification of the Kingdom of Christ with the Church. This negative aspect is what emerges most clearly from all the sayings. How impossible it is to interpret the Kingdom of Christ as the Church is shown—although unwittingly—by Wellhagen with his apocalyptic interpretation.

LUKE'S ESCHATOLOGY

Wellhagen interprets the Kingdom of God from the historical point of view and seeks to demonstrate how the idea merges with the idea of the Church (pp. 40 ff.). It is undeniable that transcendental apocalyptic statements are still present; these may be regarded as the remains of pre-Lucan eschatology or, on the other hand, a new conception must be developed, in which the apocalyptic note can find expression. Wellhagen finds this in the conception of the Messianic Kingdom. In this sense he interprets (pp. 43 f.) Luke xxii, 28 ff.; xii, 31 f. [*sic*], xxiii, 42, and finally, Acts i, 6 (p. 31). In evidence he puts forward two arguments: the first is based on the view of the Kingdom of God that is presupposed, namely, that it has already come and is present in the Church. If this interpretation is shown to be untenable, then the inference drawn from it also falls to the ground. The second argument, however—the allusion to the interregnum of the Johannine apocalypse—holds good. It is clear that this is a case of a pure construction which is inserted where the idea of the Kingdom, interpreted historically, cannot be reconciled with the text.

Wellhagen fails to see that the Kingdom of God retains its transcendental character in Luke, in an even stronger sense. What belongs to the present is the image of the Kingdom. This does not undermine, but in fact gives added support to the fact that its realization belongs to the future. There is certainly evidence in Luke of an interpretation of the Kingdom in terms of history, as well as of the Church, but not in the primitive manner which some would attribute to him on the basis of modern ideas of the development of the Kingdom; not, that is, by linking the concept of the Kingdom with the idea of immanence, but by consistently adjusting Christian existence to the Kingdom which is still distant.[1]

[1] There is a similar misunderstanding in Taylor (*Formation*, pp. 258 f.). He sees the process whereby the Kingdom is interpreted from the historical point of view from the wrong angle. Luke does not bring the eschatological events within history. His procedure is just the opposite, for he sets them at a distance from history, which means that the eschatological element can be elaborated. For this reason he shows historical events such as the destruction of Jerusalem simply as historical events, which have nothing to do with the future Eschaton.

The fact of the separation between the Kingdom of God and the Church is not brought out enough by Schelkle, pp. 199 ff. (cf. Bibliography), although he does draw finer distinctions than the writers we have just discussed.

On the popular interpretation of Luke xxiii, 42, we may add that the verse can

LUKE'S ESCHATOLOGY

4. LUKE xvii, 20 ff.

We will now turn to the expositions of the theme of the Last Things. We shall not repeat in full the many discussions of the famous ἐντός, especially as these questions have recently been dealt with in a monograph.[1] Instead we shall consider the relation of this teaching to Luke's whole conception of eschatology, and also the special problems which Luke raises.

We have already indicated the questions which are of concern to Luke, and which prompt him to a reconsideration of the whole complex of eschatological ideas, and which also influence his particular account of the course and the nature of the Last Things.

We have noted previously distinct signs of a change of attitude to eschatology, but there is one question that has not been definitely answered: is this change a process, a part of the general development within the Church, of the problem of which Luke himself was scarcely aware? Are we therefore to form the same opinion of Luke as of his predecessor Mark, who retains the early expectation, but yet shows traces of a change of attitude, or is Luke perhaps aware of the problematic situation in which he stands? Does he lay before us a new outline, and thus provide a solution which will not demand further revision in the course of time?

The answer emerges from the fact that the problem which determines Luke's treatment of his material, which is for the most part derived from tradition, is imported by Luke himself into his material and also from the fact that this material itself is transformed in its general structure and in individual sayings

scarcely be interpreted as evidence for the idea of the Kingdom of Christ. In xxiii, 37 f., Luke has merged Mark xv, 26 and xv, 30, and inserted the title. The saying of the malefactor now stands in contrast to this. When he says 'thy' Kingdom, he is confessing what the Jews deny—that Jesus is King over Israel. The verse is therefore to be taken as being formed by way of contrast.

[1] Bent Noack, *Das Gottesreich bei Lukas* (see Bibliography); also Bauernfeind, *Th.LZ.*, 1950, Supp. p. 32. Noack gives in detail the history of the interpretation since the early Church and sums up the results. Colin H. Roberts, 'The Kingdom of Heaven', *Harv. Theol. Rev.*, 41, 1948, pp. 1–8 (ἐντός = at the disposal of . . .). On the question of the Semitic original, cf. Dalman, *Worte*, I, pp. 116 f. H. Clavier, 'L'accès au Royaume de Dieu', *Et. d'Hist. et de Ph. Rel.*, Fasc. 40, 1944. A detailed analysis also in Kümmel, *Verheissung und Erfüllung*, pp. 17–19. For the interpretation 'within', cf. Dodd, *Parables*, p. 84, n. 1.

in the light of this problem, by means of corrections and omissions.

The basic question, that concerning the time, appears on four occasions: Luke xvii, 20; xix, 11; xxi, 7, and Acts i, 6. On one occasion—Acts i, 7—it is dismissed on grounds of principle. On three occasions it is the subject of detailed teaching; in chapters xvii and xxi the apocalyptic theme is directly dealt with. Chapter xix, vv. 11 ff., gives the answer—a denial of the general supposition—in the form of a parable. Throughout, it is linked with the problem of Jerusalem. It is true that in chapter xvii this link is indicated only by the context of the report of the journey (xvii, 11), but in other passages it is stated explicitly: in xix, 11 by the editorial form of the question, in chapter xxi by the connection with the Temple theme, and in Acts i, 6 f. by the connection with the command to remain in the city (v. 4).[1] The order of the arrangement should be noted. Chapter xvii, vv. 20 ff. provides the answer to the question of the Pharisee, one which is commonly asked but which, according to Luke, is asked by a man who agrees with the Christians in acknowledging belief in the resurrection;[2] the teaching after xix, 11 is directed to the disciples in view of their special question about the relation between Jerusalem and the End; there is a corresponding situation in Acts i; and finally, Luke xxi is addressed to all according to Luke.[3] As regards the fundamental issue, there are three things that are excluded: apocalyptic calculations in general, the connection with the fate of Jerusalem, and calculations based on the Resurrection of Jesus.

The problem of the exegesis of Luke xvii, 20 ff., has been

[1] Here we must bear in mind the geographical pattern which Luke stamps upon the period spent in Jerusalem. See above, pp. 73 ff., and *ZThK*, 49, 1952, p. 18, n. 2 and p. 27.

For the moment we can leave aside the question, what is tradition and what is Luke's own adaptation in Acts i. The connection we have noted is obvious.

[2] Cf. the description of the Pharisees in Acts, especially in the account of Paul's trial.

[3] On the fact that the setting is in public, cf. *ZThK*, 49, 1952, p. 28. In the variety of the problems which we have shown there is of course a reflection of the problems of the Church down to the time of the author. It is interesting to note that the question of Jerusalem appears in two instances as a definite problem for the disciples, although of course it plays an important part also in the public statements in Luke xxi. Nevertheless one may suppose that Luke has in mind Christian circles which are drawing conclusions concerning the End from the fate of the city.

clearly stated by J. Weiss: is the Kingdom a present or a future entity? If one thinks of it as belonging entirely to the future, then what is the meaning of the statement that it is ἐντὸς ὑμῶν? If one thinks of it as present, then what is the nature of this presence supposed to be? Is it present in the person of Jesus, in the Church, in certain events, or in an immanent, organic development? The exegesis of this passage brings to light the central problem not only of the Synoptic eschatology, but also that of the eschatology of Jesus which has to be reconstructed from it. Too little consideration is given to the particular features of Luke's conception.

The futurist interpretation is as follows: it is not the Kingdom that is present, but the preliminary signs of it. The external manifestation is not disputed, but calculating when it will take place is contested. This is a correct observation, which must now be linked with the problem of the Parousia in Luke. There is of course a definite reason for the rejection of calculations, viz., the denial of the early expectation. The real problem in the passage is the juxtaposition of the statement 'ἐντὸς' and the detailed account of the course of the Last Things which follows immediately. In view of the analogous passage xix, 11, it cannot really be disputed that Luke means by the Kingdom a future entity. The spiritualizing interpretation according to which the Kingdom is present in the Spirit and in the Church is completely misleading, for Luke sets these two factors strictly within his scheme of the periods of history: during the time of Jesus' earthly life they are not yet present, but the Messianic manifestations are present and visible (iv, 18 ff.). In them salvation has come to light and has become effective. It is the message of the Kingdom that is present, which in Luke is distinguished from the Kingdom itself. He knows nothing of an immanent development on the basis of the preaching of the Kingdom.

It should not be overlooked that it is only here and in xxii, 18 that the 'coming' of the Kingdom is mentioned, and here it is not spoken of by way of positive proclamation, but in a critical attitude which brings out its limitations. The main declaration is not that the Kingdom is coming, but that the Kingdom is being preached by Jesus and made manifest in his ministry. The 'coming' itself belongs to the future, and is separated by a long interval from this manifestation. It is not that a development leading up to the Kingdom has begun with Jesus, but that in Him salvation has 'appeared', so that from now on one can see it and be assured of it.

Although this passage has to be linked with the aspect of Jesus' ministry, its specific significance can only be seen within the pattern of Christology and of redemptive history. The basis is Luke's conception of the period of Jesus as the middle epoch, described as the period of salvation within the whole course of redemptive history. This does not exclude, but includes, the future hope and the purely transcendent version of the concept of the Kingdom. The fact that the great objective description of the future follows immediately upon v. 21 is not the result of a merely accidental accumulation of traditions that have been thrown together. We see here the essence of Luke's plan: the further the Parousia recedes into the distance, the better can it be described from an objective point of view, but at the same time its connection with the present has to be brought out all the more clearly, if the expectation is not to turn into mere speculation, and become an end in itself. It is this that Luke wants to prevent. His struggle is essentially an anti-apocalyptic one. This is proved by the repeated treatment of the question of the time of the Parousia—and by the rejection of the question as such.

Turning to certain details, we may consider first the extent of the immediate context, according to Luke. The fact that Jesus is addressing a different audience in v. 22 does not signify a transition to a new theme, as though the account of the 'Kingdom' as an immanent entity was now followed by the description of the Parousia as a future occurrence, but it denotes the explanation—in secret—of what has been said. A comparison with Luke xxi, where the same teaching is given in public, shows that the fact that it is here given in secret is of no fundamental significance. It merely serves to mark what follows as interpretation. The change of audience might also be required because it helps the author to set out what follows as a continuous speech. There are of course certain passages (e.g. xviii, 1 ff.) which by their very nature can be addressed only to the disciples.

The section xviii, 1–8 provides a commentary on the petition 'Thy Kingdom come', a petition which is fulfilled at the

LUKE'S ESCHATOLOGY

Parousia. This helps us to see the structure of xvii, 24–37: vv. 26–30 show how men will behave, and vv. 31 f. show the attitude that is required. Verses 24 and 37 deal with how and where the Parousia will take place. The remaining verses serve to emphasize the teaching of the verses we have mentioned.

The image in v. 24 underlines the warning in v. 23. The lightning stands for suddenness, not, as Noack suggests, the impossibility of misunderstanding. 'Days' is a technical eschatological term. In the present context the plural indicates that the Eschaton is no longer imagined as one complete event, but as a succession of events distinct from one another. For the most part, the passage represents a deliberate compilation by Luke, in which he makes use of a variety of traditional elements.[1]

What then is the meaning of ἐντός? The answer to this question is not as important as is often supposed. Whether we take the word to mean 'intra' or 'inter', it does not vitally affect Luke's conception of eschatology. It is clear that the Kingdom itself is not an immanent, spiritual entity. It is a fundamental

[1] For an analysis, cf. Bussmann, *Syn. Studien*, II, pp. 91 f.; Bultmann, *Syn. Trad.*, pp. 24, 123, 128. Bultmann takes the saying in vv. 20 f. to be a genuine saying by Jesus couched in Lucan terminology. As regards the interpretation (p. 128), Bultmann thinks the saying refers to the future, and understands it in the sense of a sudden irruption. For the contrary view, cf. Kümmel, loc. cit. Bultmann rightly explains v. 25 as part of Luke's editorial work. Kümmel (p. 40) rejects this view. He objects that πρῶτον shows that even at the beginning it was linked with a promise of the Parousia. Against this view it should be noted that πρῶτον is a typically Lucan term, especially in eschatological contexts. It is in use before Luke as a stock term for expressing the eschatological event (Mark xiii, 10), but Luke extends its use (xxi, 9). Grässer, p. 29, n. 1, adds on this point: 'It seems to me more important than pointing out this objection to Kümmel's view that we should observe that v. 25 follows upon v. 24, the saying about the Parousia, and therefore in no sense does it meet the disciples' need for instruction concerning the death of Jesus as the presupposition for his Parousia. Verse 25 is not concerned with the death as the presupposition for the Parousia, but simply with the fact that he must suffer and be rejected. There is therefore no reason for mentioning the Resurrection.'

Loisy, ad loc., stresses the motif of the delay. Noack's argument, which is, however, foreshadowed by such as Dodd and Wellhagen, that Luke already recognizes two Parousias, in practice if not in theory, represents an important insight. The Kingdom has been seen in the earthly life of Jesus, and it will be seen again, when he comes in the future. This observation gains greater force when one remembers that according to Luke's account Satan was absent in the period between Luke iv, 13 and xxii, 3, during which time one could be secure from temptation. This brings out all the more clearly the analogy between the time of Jesus and the future time of salvation.

fact that the account of the Last Things, which is far fuller than in the sources, corresponds to the increased emphasis on its transcendence. Here we see what is for Luke the typical parallel between sayings about the nature of the Kingdom, which have no reference to time, and sayings about temporal events. He has reached the goal of his apologetic: the Kingdom has appeared in Christ, although its presence is not now immanent in the Church.

But the Church possesses a picture that can never be lost, because it possesses the account of Jesus. By virtue of this it can endure in the world. In xviii, 1–8 we see the practical aim of the teaching. From now on the time of the Parousia can no longer present to the Church a problem on which it might come to grief, for in view of the information in vv. 20 f., it becomes impossible even to ask about it.

5. LUKE xxi

We can deal briefly with the literary critical problem. The attempts of English critics in particular to reconstruct a non-Marcan source in addition to Mark, which would also provide a complete eschatological outline, cannot be considered successful.[1] They misunderstand both the extent and the individuality of Luke's revision. The divergences from Mark prove to be the result of editorial work, in which a definite plan can be traced.

The description of the setting in vv. 5–7 is definitely editorial. Luke abandons the symbolism of Mark's setting, according to which Jesus speaks from the Mount of Olives 'over against' the Temple, and transfers the speech to the Temple, before an audience which has been listening to Jesus each day. This is in keeping with Luke's scheme, according to which there are before the Last Supper only two places in which Jesus is found: in the Temple by day, and on the Mount of Olives by night (xxi, 37 f.). This scheme is part of Luke's editorial work.[2]

---

[1] Attempts at a reconstruction can be found in Taylor, *Behind the Third Gospel*, pp. 101 ff., and Manson, *Sayings*, pp. 323 ff. Both start from the Proto-Luke theory. For a discussion, see the next note. See also C. H. Dodd, 'The Fall of Jerusalem and the "Abomination of Desolation"', *J. of Rom. Stud.*, 1947, pp. 47 ff., and P. Winter, *The Treatment*.

[2] Taylor argues (p. 101) that in vv. 12–19 Mark is used, but even where they agree almost word for word, the meaning is different, therefore it is a question of

LUKE'S ESCHATOLOGY

In v. 7 the expression ταῦτα γενέσθαι, which is in contrast to Mark's συντελεῖσθαι πάντα, comes from the editor. Mark's saying has the sense of eschatological fulfilment, but Luke is concerned in what follows with events which do not belong to the Eschaton.

In v. 8 Luke avoids the word βασιλεία. Of course he cannot dispute that Jesus did in fact say that the Kingdom was near at hand, therefore he avoids the phrase and prevents a v.rong interpretation of it by replacing βασιλεία by καιρός. The references to time in v. 9, πρῶτον and οὐκ εὐθέως, and in v. 12, πρὸ δὲ τούτων, prove to be elements in a whole conception, which is based on the Marcan text. The latter is not broken up and completely re-composed, but in particular instances Luke reveals his different arrangement by corrections such as these, although as a result earlier material is not mentioned until later, and vice versa.

Mark is already using traditional material, and even in him a certain postponement of the Parousia can be traced.[1] His aim already is to correct an apocalyptic tradition which is predominantly Jewish.[2] In particular he has to transform the sayings about the fate of the Temple, which he does by deliberately placing it within the context of the Last Things.[3]

a different source with details added from Mark. This view is based on a strange methodology. According to general logic, agreement as to the wording together with difference in the meaning suggests that a source has been used but has been interpreted according to the view of the one using it. As a matter of fact the non-Marcan elements prove to be typically Lucan, and they considerably modify the meaning of the Marcan sections. Luke's interpretations presuppose merely this one source.

Taylor asks on p. 109: 'Is the substance of Luke xxi, 20–36 a non-Markan source to which Markan passages have been added, or do these passages constitute a framework to which St. Luke has attached matter peculiar to himself?' Stated in this way, the either-or is too simple. If there is no positive proof of other sources besides Mark, then what emerges from the analysis of the text is this: the fact that the non-Marcan material forms the 'framework' shows that the author has 'framed' the Marcan material, in other words, that he has taken it over and adapted it according to his own conceptions. Taylor's attempt to set out the results of his reconstruction is more impressive than his analysis (p. 113), but even this is unconvincing because it has to combine disparate material.

[1] Cf. v. 10.

[2] For an analysis, cf. Bultmann, *Syn. Trad.*, pp. 128 f.; Klostermann, ad loc. W. J. Kümmel, *Verheissung und Erfüllung*, pp. 88 ff.; W. Marxsen, op. cit., pp. 101 ff.; G. Harder, 'Das eschatologische Geschichtsbild der sog. kleiner Apokalypse Mark xiii', *Theologia Viatorum*, 4, 1952, pp. 71 ff.; Grässer, op. cit., pp. 152 ff.

[3] Klostermann rightly emphasizes this in connection with v. 4. The disciple

LUKE'S ESCHATOLOGY

In the first part of his exposition there are two references to time, οὔπω τὸ τέλος in v. 7, and ἀρχὴ ὠδίνων ταῦτα in v. 8. The first gives a clear indication of the aim which Mark is pursuing, whether it is a Jewish or a Christian expectation that he is correcting.[1] He shares the general expectation that there will be a time of war, but he makes the correction: οὔπω τὸ τέλος evidently because the idea of the Messianic war has no place in the Christian expectation, but only the supernatural advent of the Messiah. There is, however, some connection: ἀρχὴ ὠδίνων ταῦτα. The next mention of time is in v. 10, which envisages a fairly long period of missionary activity.[2]

We must now consider what use Luke makes of Mark. Once again in his great synopsis we see that the imminence of the End has ceased to play any vital part in Luke. What is merely hinted at in Mark has become in Luke a definite idea, as our analysis will show.

The new form of v. 7—after the alteration of the setting, which reveals a changed attitude to the Temple—excludes the eschatological interpretation of the fate of the Temple which is fundamental in Mark. The importance of this apparently insignificant alteration will become clear later. In v. 8 the stock phrase of the early expectation is introduced by way of amplification. Then there come the extensive, but again apparently insignificant, corrections in the chronological arrangement, of which there is a foreshadowing in v. 9. Luke does his work of amplification systematically. He inserts πρῶτον and brings out the meaning of Mark's οὔπω, but in the following passage he simply breaks down Mark's structure. Instead of the conjunctional γάρ he provides a new opening: τότε ἔλεγεν, which in this context means that up to now the principle has been stated but that now there follows a systematic exposition. This, however, cannot be achieved simply by a carefully planned construction of the description, for it is prevented by the connection with Mark's

---

have understood correctly that Jesus is speaking of the End, and they ask concerning the time, that of the whole eschatological event. If this is meant as a correction of a widespread apocalyptic tendency in the community, then v. 4 must have been formulated as such by Mark.

[1] Against Bultmann's view that it comes from a source one might ask whether v. 7 is not an interpretation. The new thing that Mark has to say is: μὴ θροεῖσθε —οὔπω τὸ τέλος. Only thus can γάρ have any meaning.

[2] Matthew transposes the verse and achieves a more compact train of thought.

127

text. Thus the events of v. 12, which Luke places before the conflict of the nations (v. 10) and the cosmic upheavals of v. 11, have to be introduced by πρὸ δὲ τούτων. Mark's statement in v. 8, ἀρχὴ ὠδίνων, must now of course disappear, as according to Luke the events of v. 12, the persecution of the Church, mark the beginning. As a consequence of the recasting, Mark xiii, 10 also disappears, with its now superfluous πρῶτον. The universal proclamation is achieved in the present, as the second part of Luke's writings shows. Luke therefore sees the persecution only as the prelude to the Last Things. It is in keeping with this that the situation in the present is described, and the word of comfort inserted in v. 18. Here again we can see the change of attitude: in v. 14 the simple 'Be not anxious' is given a psychological import, so that it becomes a conscious attitude towards oneself. It is not the Spirit Himself who speaks, but man, although of course it is given him what he is to speak. The aim, as in chapter xvii (and xviii, 1) is the exhortation to ὑπομονή, in other words, to adjustment to a long period of persecution, for such is the existence of the Church in the world.

Whereas Mark goes on to give a fuller description of the eschatological events, Luke now gives a polemical excursus about matters which are mistakenly included among the eschatological events, namely the destruction of Jerusalem and the Temple. In this way eschatology is lifted out of any historical context, and is removed from all events which take place within history. Thus the apocalyptic allusion in Mark xiii, 14 disappears, because one cannot 'read' of such a thing (N.B. Luke's concept of Scripture) and because it has nothing to do with the Eschaton.

Verses 21b, 22, 25b, 26a and 28 can be considered as examples of Lucan interpretation. The section vv. 34–6 with its 'Pauline' terminology may have been composed by Luke or taken over by him, but in any case it makes clear what is his own aim and also how he uses existing material.[1] We can see Luke's editorial activity also in the omissions: Mark xiii, 21–3, 24 are omitted, and in Bultmann's view v. 20 is altered in the light of events.

Luke recognizes that there are signs—cf. v. 11 (note, however, the alterations compared with Mark); but, as xvii, 21

[1] Bultmann, *Syn. Trad.*, p. 126.

reminds us, they do not signify that the coming is imminent, but they point to a long period which comes first. The Kingdom is announced for a long time—and then it comes like lightning. A systematic account of this preliminary period can be given. The coming itself is not included in the description. By combining the various chronological references, we arrive at the following picture:

(a) the period of persecution, with which the exhortation, i.e. vv. 14 ff., is concerned. Luke places great emphasis upon this.

Not until then do

(b) the period of political dissolution, and
(c) the period of cosmic dissolution,

follow, by which the End is gradually ushered in.

However, as it is not the sequence of events as such that is most important, but the instructions addressed to the *ecclesia pressa*, we are given a criticism of the prevailing errors. We find this already in Mark, but here it is considerably expanded, and at the same time elements which are still eschatological in Mark are excluded (cf. vv. 20 ff.).[1]

Verse 19 emphasizes more strongly than Mark that deliverance is the result of patience (Mark still thinks of the End in an immediate eschatological sense, whereas Luke introduces into the conception a preliminary period, therefore he can omit εἰς τέλος). The addition in v. 18 is in keeping with this; it is a variation of a traditional logion (Luke xii, 7/Matt. x, 30), and now points to the future resurrection as a comfort for the martyr. Verse 16 ('some shall be put to death') completes the picture. The account is transferred from an eschatological background to that of the Church. Time after time we meet the same readjustment from an immediate eschatology to martyrdom as a present fact in which the eschatological prospect provides consolation. The saying in v. 18, which in itself speaks of the general

---

[1] Even the exhortation in vv. 14 ff. has a stronger psychological colouring. What is referred to in v. 13 is not the confession of faith, which serves as 'a testimony' in the eschatological sense to the one who is addressed, but the testimony which the one who confesses receives from God. It is not necessary yet to take 'testimony' in a technical sense.

LUKE'S ESCHATOLOGY

providence of God, is now addressed to those who are killed in the persecution.

We shall omit for the time being the passage concerning Jerusalem. As these events no longer belong to the context of eschatology, a further significant theme disappears, that of the merciful shortening of the sufferings (cf. Mark xiii, 19 f.). We have already mentioned that Mark xiii, 21–3 are omitted. It is Luke's aim to relegate the Parousia to a still greater distance. The times of the Gentiles (v. 24) have not yet come; it is only the time of the Jewish dispersion, and the End will not come until after the cosmic upheaval (vv. 25 f.). In Mark the cosmic signs and the Parousia form one complex of events, but in Luke they are separated.

In v. 27 we find the last of the chronological references, in this case simply the same as in Mark, but its significance is modified by the change of context. If we summarize once again all Luke's statements, the following structure emerges: persecution, the distress of nations, cosmic signs and the end of the nations, and finally the Parousia. Verse 28 then contains instructions for the Christian, which refer especially to the period of the cosmic signs—not to the 'beginning', as in Mark—just as the teaching in vv. 14 ff. has a special reference to the epoch of persecution. Until then the important thing is not to allow oneself to be bewildered. It should be noted that the cosmic upheaval does not affect the elect; on the contrary, it brings them liberation. The present meaning of vv. 29–31 emerges from the context. As they now stand, they provide a fuller explanation of v. 28: now, in the last crisis of the world, believers can lift up their heads. It is not until now that one can rightly say 'the Kingdom is at hand'. This is the key to all Luke's sayings about the nearness of the Kingdom.[1]

Whilst the separate events before the Parousia are described in considerable detail, the description of the Parousia itself is cut down—cf. Luke xxi, 27 with Mark xiii, 26 f. It is true that the description of the appearing of the Son of Man is the same word for word, but in Luke the escort of angels is omitted. This

[1] R. Bultmann, *Das Urchristentum im Rahmen der antiken Religionen*, 1949, p. 243, n. 50, suggests that in the original logion it is the Kingdom that is drawing near, whereas in Mark and Matthew it is the Son of Man, who has just been mentioned. In this case Luke's amplification is on the right lines.

130

is in keeping with Luke's conception of angels, according to which they are subject only to God, not to the Son (Luke also omits Mark i, 13; cf. Luke ix, 26 and Mark viii, 38). At the Parousia they seem to stay in Heaven and form the background when the Son of Man sits in judgement (Luke xii, 8 f.; xv, 10; cf. the stress on τοῦ θεοῦ).[1]

In connection with the timing of the Parousia, Mark xiii, 32, is omitted, for although the Son knows the day and the hour, it is not for us to know.[2]

In v. 32 Luke omits ταῦτα, as a result of which the saying does not refer to the matters that have just been mentioned, but to the whole of the Divine plan. 'This generation' means here humanity in general, whereas in Mark it is doubtful who is meant, especially if one also considers Mark ix, 1. The saying is no longer a declaration that the End is near at hand.

Again there follows, as the climax of the account, as we have already mentioned, the practical application and exhortation. As the verses are closely linked with vv. 32 f., they too no doubt need to be seen in the light of the hortatory theme, i.e. less as promise than as warning: this generation will not escape the judgement. Here again the summons to endurance forms the climax and the conclusion, as in v. 19 above and also xviii, 1.

Summary

The main motif in the recasting to which Luke subjects his source, proves to be the delay of the Parousia, which leads to a comprehensive consideration of the nature and course of the Last Things. Whereas originally the imminence of the End was the most important factor, now other factors enter. The delay has to be explained, and this is done by means of the idea of God's plan which underlies the whole structure of Luke's

---

[1] This must be borne in mind in connection with Luke's Christology. Contrast the view expressed in Heb. i.

[2] The same view is present in Acts i, 6, where one cannot infer from harmonizing it with the Marcan passage that Jesus did not know; similarly there is no indication of any differentiation by Luke between the knowledge possessed by Jesus while on earth and that possessed by the Exalted Lord. According to Luke, Jesus has a knowledge of the Last Things while still on earth; otherwise he could not give all this instruction. For according to Luke, knowledge of the Last Things is not part of Scriptural prophecy, which extends only to the coming of the Spirit.

account.[1] Corresponding to this there is also the greater emphasis on the suddenness of the irruption. The hortatory nature of the context is obvious. As the End is still far away, the adjustment to a short time of waiting is replaced by a 'Christian life' of long duration, which requires ethical regulation and is no longer dependent upon a definite termination. The virtue of ὑπομονή comes to the fore. The appeal is no longer based on the time, but on the fact of a future Judgement. The ethical teaching is coloured by the fact that persecution now prevails. Endurance is viewed from the standpoint of martyrdom, although the specific terminology of martyrdom has not yet been developed. The longer the time of waiting, the greater the impact of suffering, which makes the expected End 'endlessly' remote.

In line with the modification we have described, there is in Luke a shift of emphasis from the imminent End to the general idea of the resurrection of the dead, independent of any fixed time.[2] In Luke xxi it is merely hinted at—because of both the theme and the source—but there is a suggestion of it. Where Luke is freely composing, it comes to the fore.

We see also how, by removing the End to a greater distance, a more reflective attitude emerges, as a result of which the individual events are separated. This development is parallel to the other development, by which the past is broken up into its separate component parts. Thus we see how the whole story of salvation, as well as the life of Jesus in particular, is now objectively set out and described according to its successive stages.

6. JERUSALEM AND THE ESCHATON

Here we find a particularly instructive example of the way in which Luke thinks of the relation between history and eschatology, or in other words, in what sense he 'interprets history'

---

[1] The Qumran sect is faced with a similar problem: 1 Q p Hab, VII, 7 ff.: 'For still the vision is for an appointed time; it hastens to the period and does not lie. This means that the last period extends over and above all that the prophets said; for the mysteries of God are marvellous.' This gives rise to the same summons as in Luke—to the 'men of truth, the doers of the law, whose hands do not grow slack from the service of the truth, when the last period is stretched out over them. For all the periods of God will come to their fixed term, as he decreed for them in the mysteries of his wisdom.' (Translation by M. Burrows, *The Dead Sea Scrolls*, 1955, p. 368.)

[2] Cf. p. 111.

The historical events are not 'interpreted' as eschatological signs, but in a non-eschatological sense.

It is a familiar fact, and one which has recently been strongly stressed, e.g. by Lohmeyer and Lightfoot, that Jerusalem is of special theological significance in Luke. Jerusalem is the place of revelations. Thus Luke establishes the link with the 'arché' of the Church. The city forms the connecting-link between the story of Jesus and the life of the Church. This ecclesiastical function of the city will be considered later. What we must note here is the parallel polemic against the city, which Luke takes over, but to which he gives a special meaning by indicating the city's fate in the Jewish war, and at the same time by definitely dissociating it from the Christian eschatological hope. We will start with the traditional lament over the city.

Luke qualifies the Q saying in Luke xiii, 34 f. by joining it to vv. 31–3, which makes it clear that the prophet must die in Jerusalem. These verses, with their description of Jerusalem as the necessary place of enmity—necessary, that is, from the point of view of redemptive history—are reminiscent of Mark. Luke employs them in the setting of the journey, which is used to set out a Christological content (cf. the first section of our study).

Such a saying and the positive ecclesiastical significance of the city, are for Luke not mutually exclusive, but inclusive. As Jerusalem is the city of revelations, the decisive phase of saving history, in which the Passion and the Resurrection are inextricably linked, takes place there. The fact that it is necessary from the point of view of saving history for the Passion to take place precisely in Jerusalem does not exonerate the Jews. The prophets do not perish merely in, but by means of, Jerusalem. We can see this in the connection—an editorial one—between v. 33 and v. 34, as a result of which the second saying also, which in itself is composed from the standpoint of Jerusalem, is brought into the context of the journey (contrast Matthew). The upshot of it all is that by its conduct the city brings destruction upon itself, as Luke xiii, 5 makes clear. By establishing this particular connection, Luke imposes a pattern on the material. The journey, the Passion, the guilt of the Jews and the resulting fate of the city form a closely linked chain. It is the fault of the Jews that Jerusalem does not fulfil its destiny. They forfeit their election by killing Jesus; admittedly it is by Divine decree, nevertheless they are guilty and lost. They have the Temple and the city in their possession, but they profane them both, therefore in the future neither can have any further redemptive function. The end of the Acts of the Apostles, the trial of Paul, shows what is, from Luke's standpoint, the last phase of the struggle for the city; Acts xxviii, 20 ff. sums up the significance of Jerusalem for Christianity, in so far as the Jews are in power there. The consequence is, firstly, that the historical judgement upon Jerusalem is deserved and, secondly, that it is an event belonging to secular history. As far as the Christian hope is concerned, the city has forfeited its function by its own conduct.

It is significant that the city plays such a prominent part in Luke's account of the Passion, which is set in the framework of sayings about Jerusalem (Luke xix, 39 ff. and xxiii, 28 ff.). Luke brings out the contrast between on the one hand the guilty people, and on the other those who weep, but who nevertheless cannot escape from their fate, for the weeping of the women is ineffectual against the actions of the men.

Luke's account is influenced by the fact that he considers the judgement has already taken place. This is evident in the passage xxi, 20 ff. It is true that this interpretation of the passage is disputed. The main argument against it is that these are sayings in the apocalyptic style, which do not refer to concrete historical events. Against this it can be argued that Mark's text can be explained in this way, but not the characteristic features of Luke's revision, and above all the function of the passage in the context of this chapter.[1]

The question arises why Luke, who otherwise never strips the image of the future of its realistic features, removes the apocalyptic terminology in this passage—and only here—and

[1] Whether apocalyptic could speak in this way is a superfluous question, as it is clear that Luke's form of the speech is a revision of a familiar source. If we see that Luke has a definite eschatological plan in mind, then it is also clear that the section about Jerusalem has no place in it, and therefore cannot be interpreted as part of the Last Things.

The argument in chapter xxi has already been foreshadowed in an earlier passage. According to Luke, Jesus himself severed the connection between Jerusalem and the End, to dispel the false notion of the disciples (cf. xix, 11, which is unquestionably editorial, and therefore reflects Luke's own view). The political element appears in v. 22, where the destruction is spoken of as a punishment. The fate of the other nations has clearly nothing to do with this event.

replaces it by a historical account. This can only be explained by relating the passage to the historical events. In vv. 20 f. we see the change of style almost word for word; in place of the eschatological abomination there is the destruction of the city (cf. Klostermann, ad loc.). Verse 20b clearly expresses the meaning of these events. This verse, together with v. 22, is a warning against the mistaken idea that the End is near.[1]

That 'all things which are written' are here being fulfilled is not contradicted, but confirmed by this interpretation. The real 'Last Things' according to Luke are not 'written', but proclaimed by Jesus.

The thought in xix, 11 and the consequent meaning of the following parable show that Luke is aware he is contradicting a part of Christian tradition.[2]

7. Conclusion

If Luke has definitely abandoned belief in the early expectation, what does he offer on the positive side as an adequate solution of the problem? An outline of the successive stages in redemptive history according to God's plan. But what practical bearing has this? The basic factors in the existence of the Church are Christ and the Spirit; but the question arises, what can these mean to the Church, now that its relation to them can no longer depend on the imminence of the End? Now, as we complete our analysis of the concept of eschatology, we touch on the question

---

[1] If Jerusalem is meant in v. 21 (and not Judæa—cf. Klostermann), then there is still time for flight from the city; this is a further difference from eschatological happenings, for one cannot escape from them. Is there here possibly a reflection of events in the Jewish war from the Christian viewpoint, or is it perhaps that disputes have been caused within the Christian community about the behaviour of Christians in view of the threatening siege?

The interpretation from the historical point of view can be seen also in v. 23, where 'this people' means the Jews. The reference to the creation disappears, as it is not relevant in this passage. Similarly the theme of the shortening of the sufferings no longer has any meaning, still less the reference to the elect (Mark xiii, 20). Instead there is a realistic description of the fate of Jerusalem and of the Jewish people; their fate persists into the present, in the fact of their dispersion, which will also continue into the future—until the times of the Gentiles are fulfilled. In other words, in the course of history the Jews will never again be gathered together, for they have attained their final state as far as history is concerned.

[2] Even the source is aware of the delay, but by adding v. 11 Luke makes it the main point of the story.

of Christology and the doctrine of the Church, and thus on the phenomenon of the Spirit. Luke carefully sets out the relation of the Spirit to eschatology at the beginning of his second volume, in the first place simply by the way he describes the events, and then by a detailed explanation in Acts i, 4 ff. The negative statement 'It is not for you to know' is supplemented by the reference to God's plan, and further by the reference to the Spirit, who appears as a substitute (N.B. ἀλλά) for knowledge of the Last Things and makes it unnecessary to know when they will take place. Luke is the first to make this deliberate appeal to the phenomenon of the Spirit as a solution of the problem of the Parousia.[1] Instead of possessing such knowledge, the disciples are called to be witnesses before the world, a task for which they are enabled by Divine power. These are the two themes we must now consider—Christ and Christian existence in the world.

[1] It cannot be held that even in Paul, indeed right from the beginning, the Spirit in fact makes it possible to deal with the delay of the Parousia. This would mean that the problem was already solved at the beginning, and was therefore of secondary importance. What we are concerned with is when this solution was realized and when it was thought out theologically. It cannot be said that this was done by Paul or by any other writer before Luke.

PART THREE

God and Redemptive History

I. INTRODUCTION: THE SITUATION OF THE CHURCH IN THE WORLD

As the life of the world continues, there arise certain problems concerning the relation of the Church to its environment, which had remained hidden at the beginning because of the belief that the End was imminent. It is a question mainly of the relationship of the Church with Judaism and with the Empire, and it is significant how Luke deals with these problems. He engages in apologetic. In itself, of course, this does not amount to a positive theological answer to the problems, but Luke does achieve this by the fact that he lays as the foundation of his defence of the Church a comprehensive consideration of its general position in the world; he fixes its position in respect of redemptive history and deduces from this the rules for its attitude to the world. This is an original achievement.

We will begin with the apologetic he offers with the Roman state in mind. It cannot be disputed that Luke's apologetic aims are political, but there is room for variety of opinion concerning their exact nature and purpose.[1]

[1] We will give a few examples. Harnack and Wendt in particular question whether there is any apologetic purpose at all. Loisy is representative of one type of interpretation (*Naissance*, p. 56): 'The anti-Jewish polemic, which can be traced in all the Gospels, is particularly pronounced here, for the author sets out to show that Christianity is the most authentic form of Judaism, and that by virtue of this it has a right to enjoy from the Roman authorities the same tolerance as does official Judaism.' A similar view is expressed by Goguel, *Naissance*, p. 115. For other views, cf. Dibelius, *Aufsätze*, p. 180; Cadbury, *Beginnings*, 5, pp. 297 ff. (Roman law and the trial of Paul); Sahlin attempts to revive without success the thesis that Acts in its present form is a written defence for use at Paul's trial. Streeter, p. 551, puts forward the somewhat different view that it is an apology for Paul, but after his death.

137

GOD AND REDEMPTIVE HISTORY

1. The Political Apologetic

Does Luke wish to recommend Christianity to the Romans by emphasizing its distinction from Judaism and showing it as an entity in its own right or, on the contrary, by showing it to be the legitimate form of Judaism, in order to win for Christians also the protection of those Roman laws by which the Jews are protected? The controversy concerning this problem suffers from the fact that on both sides the arguments are based on isolated statements. What is required is that we should examine the whole material from this one angle.

The apologetic aim can be seen most clearly in the account of the Passion and in certain sections of the missionary journeys, but there are more or less latent traces of it in the whole Gospel. If we can take it that Theophilus was a Gentile, then we can see it even in the preface. The legal terminology, which recurs in the account of the trial in Acts, supports the idea.[1] This makes superfluous the thesis that what we have before us is a special written defence for Paul. Wherever we find apologetic in Luke's writings, it is not meant for any particular circumstance, but is something basic. It has to reckon with the fact that the State is here to stay, and thus it marks a stage beyond that of the early expectation. Whereas in the original eschatological perspective it was felt that the State had to be withstood, now the attempt is made to enter into conversation with it, in order to achieve a permanent settlement.

In the account of John the Baptist's preaching, which Luke himself has compiled,[2] he selects two examples of ethical instruction, those directed at the organs of the State, the military and the government. They are instructed in good morals, in which loyalty to the State is implicit.

Luke iii, 19 specifies a non-political reason for the imprisonment of John.[3]

---

[1] For a detailed account, cf. Cadbury, *Beginnings*, 2, pp. 489 ff.

[2] Bultmann, *Syn. Trad.*, p. 155.

[3] It is interesting that along with this the other aspect of the state can be found; cf. iv, 6, which is one of Luke's own creations. It shows the other side of the same coin. We can see the same structure in the sayings as in eschatology; it is the result of the growth of a more objective view, of the transition to a closer examination of the facts.

GOD AND REDEMPTIVE HISTORY

The Messianic programme in iv, 18 ff. represents Jesus' career as a non-political one. The significance of this account from the point of view of apologetic is seen in the Passion, where the non-political sense of the royal title is taken for granted and therefore not discussed.[1]

The arrival of Herod in Jerusalem is foreshadowed in two passages. In ix, 7 ff. he wishes to 'see' Jesus, which provides indirect confirmation of Jesus' innocence from the political point of view, for to 'see' refers to miracles and Herod's interest in them; xxiii, 8 harks back to this statement, and again the upshot is that Jesus is innocent. The passage xiii, 31 ff. shows the death of Jesus to be that of a prophet and—according to Luke—non-political, and vv. 34 ff. reject, on account of Jerusalem's position in redemptive history, the idea of any political meaning in the 'journey', for it is something decreed by God (δεῖ).

The acclamation at the Entry loses all political significance in Luke; the concept of the Davidic Lordship is replaced by the simple title of King, the non-political sense of which is preserved (xix, 38). Accordingly the Temple is the only goal of the Entry, and the only place of Jesus' activity.[2]

Chapter xx, v. 20, compared with Mark xii, 13, brings out the dispute with the Roman authorities in particular. Verse 26 expressly confirms the failure of the plot. Here Luke is preparing the way for his later account, and in fact in xxiii, 1 ff., he takes up this point and makes it the main accusation before Pilate. He thus shows that it is not a matter of questions before the Roman authorities concerning the application of religious legislation in respect of the Jews, but that the political supremacy of Rome is the sole point at issue. The whole account presented in Acts confirms this finding.

Luke certainly leaves no doubt about the demand of loyalty, as seen in the confession that is required before kings and rulers (xii, 11), but he also speaks of a 'wisdom' which the latter cannot withstand (xxi, 15). He makes plain in connection with Pilate, Gallio, Felix and Festus what attitude should be taken towards the State, and what the State must take note of if it does not wish to sacrifice its own legal position. Luke emphasizes

---

[1] Cf., on the other hand, John xviii, 33 ff.   [2] See above, pp. 75 ff.

that to confess oneself to be a Christian implies no crime against Roman law.

The reverse side of this emphasis on loyalty—first that of Jesus himself, then that of Christians—is the demonstration that the Jews are lying in their accusations. Again the Passion provides the model: the accusation in xxiii, 1 f. is represented in xx, 20 ff. as a deliberate lie (in Luke it is the same people that are involved). What is more, by means of this lie they are disguising their own seditious sentiments: xxiii, 18 ff. underline their solidarity with the political insurgent—in contrast with Mark. Thus the impossibility of their proceedings, which rest on false accusations by the Jews, is made plain to the Romans (in Acts there is no instance of Roman intervention without previous Jewish agitation). The Jews have raised the question, whether one should pay taxes to the Emperor, and they declare their true character by the accusation that follows.

Three times the Imperial representative confirms the innocence of Jesus (xxiii, 22), and he refuses to condemn.[1]

The apologetic motifs prove to be part of Luke's editorial composition. The material itself is derived almost exclusively from Mark and the apologetic remarks are found in sections which undoubtedly come from Mark (even if one posits further sources for 'Luke's' account of the Passion).

There are thus two themes side by side in the account of the Passion, the dogmatic theme of the necessity of the suffering and the 'historical' theme of the guilt of the Jews and of the innocence of the Empire, which appreciates the non-political character of the Gospel and of Jesus' Kingship.[2]

Corresponding to this conscious attitude to the Empire there is also the attitude to the Jews. This again is developed mainly in Acts, but it underlies the account of the Passion. It can be seen in the trial before the Sanhedrin, which simply serves to set out in summary form the Christological factors that are

[1] See pp. 85 ff. Luke does not report any condemnation of Jesus by Pilate. Pilate merely 'delivers' Jesus to the Jews, who themselves put him to death. It is Jerusalem that kills the prophets. Thus Luke takes the kerygmatic formulae in Acts literally and turns them into narrative. We might accuse Luke of obscurity if we did not know his source, but as we do know it, we can prove that his account is a deliberate modification.

[2] Does the strange passage about the two swords perhaps belong to tnis context?

involved (xxii, 67–70). The title Messiah is here interpreted as synonymous with the title Son of God, in other words, contrary to the Jewish understanding of it, in a non-political sense. Thus a threefold demonstration of the facts of the case is given to the Jews—who now must tell lies; to the Empire, which objectively defines the legal position; and to the ruler owing allegiance to Rome, who agrees with the findings of the Roman representative.

The evidence of Acts

The first convert from paganism is a Roman centurion (Acts x).

Acts xiii, 6 ff. presents the exemplary conduct of the Roman official, who seeks to know the facts (v. 7). The stereotype motif of Jewish intrigue appears, and at the same time the miraculous defeat of it is told, a demonstration which is for the benefit of the Roman as well.

The crossing to Europe provides a further typical example (xvi, 11 ff.). This is the first time that Luke mentions Paul's Roman citizenship—not, as one would assume from the theory of such as Loisy, the irreproachable character of his Judaism. Roman law acts as a saviour in need, but not without the loyalty of the Christian citizen being underlined.

Chapter xvii, v. 7 makes it quite clear what the political problem is. The reader of course immediately understands the situation.

In the passages already referred to the apologetic aim is implicit, but it is not yet the main emphasis in the accounts. It is a different matter in the passages to which we now turn, where the apologetic aim is part of the underlying idea.

The appearance of the words ἀπολογεῖν and ἀπολογία is in each case an indication by the author of the purpose of his account. The noun occurs in Acts xxv, 16, where the question is that of determining the legal position. Significantly, there is no mention of the relation to Judaism, and reference is made only to the Roman procedure. The problem is not that of the relationship between Christianity and Judaism. It has for the most part been overlooked that in Acts this relationship is dealt with only in the presence of Jews, e.g. by Paul for the benefit of the Pharisees (xxiii, 6 ff.) and of Agrippa (xxvi, 1 ff.). The noun occurs also in the introduction to a 'defence' (xxii, 1 ff.). Verse 25 shows very clearly how the method of argument changes as soon as it is a Roman that is being addressed; now Paul does not speak of his Judaism, but of his civil rights; the protection of which he claims for himself. We can see the same change between xxv, 23 ff. and xxvi, 32.

We see here, and shall see later, that the relationship of the Church to Israel belongs to an entirely different category than that of political apologetic. It is never used in argument with the Romans. It belongs to the dispute of the Church with Israel, and only there. Whenever Luke refers to it, he has a two-fold aim: to prove the legitimacy of the Church's claim in respect of redemptive history, and to call the Jews to repentance. This argument, based upon redemptive history, is never confused at any point with the arguments used in dealings with the State. In connection with the State only political and legal arguments are used.

We find the verb in Acts xxvi, 1 f., 24; xix, 33; xxiv, 10. This last verse should be considered along with xxv, 8, where the following pattern is clearly set out:

$$οὔτε\ εἰς\ τὸν\ νόμον\ τῶν\ ’Ιουδαίων$$
$$οὔτε\ εἰς\ τὸ\ ἱερὸν$$
$$οὔτε\ εἰς\ Καίσαρά\ τι\ ἥμαρτον.$$

We must note that in this passage Paul is raising the question of the Jewish Law before the Roman authorities. His purpose in doing so is to withstand his Jewish accusers and show that they are liars. Even with respect to their own Law (which is not the concern of the Roman State itself—cf. xviii, 14 f.; xxv, 18–20) their charges cannot stand.[1]

The concept of Law appears a number of times in interesting contexts. We will consider first the classical treatment of it in the scene with Gallio (Acts xviii, 12 ff.).

This scene is meant to stand as a picture of the ideal conduct of the organs of the State. The official should see how weak the Jewish charges are, and then no trial is necessary. The State can declare that it has no interest in the controversy between Jews and Christians, for its Law is not affected by it. It is therefore not

[1] Here the question arises, whether Luke is aware of the protection of the Temple under Roman Law. There is no reference to it elsewhere.

a question of the Christians being recognized as legitimate Jews. Gallio is not interested in either. The real point at issue, however, is a finer one. The gist of the Jews' accusation is : παρὰ τὸν νόμον (v. 13). It is usually debated in exegesis whether this refers to Roman or Jewish Law.[1] To state the alternatives in this way is the result of attempting to reconstruct history and of taking the wrong approach of asking what the Jews meant in the actual historical circumstances. But if we concern ourselves not with the actual facts, but with the record of it and with the author's intention, then the interpretation is plain, and is confirmed by other passages.

The main point is that Luke makes the Jews deliberately present their accusation ambiguously. They want to deceive Gallio, but he sees what they are doing and rejects the accusation. This interpretation finds support in the fact that Gallio declares the affair to be an internal Jewish one, and therefore he is not prepared to recognize a case of 'Law' as he understands it, although at first he cannot take the accusation to be anything other than a complaint about a breach of Roman Law. Employing technical legal terms, he makes clear the position: ἀδικία ἢ ῥᾳδιούργημα.

It is true that this does not amount to an acquittal, but neither does it give grounds for a trial. This is obviously what Luke wants to show to be the actual case. The problem of Jew and Christian is not taken up in relation to the State, but, on the contrary, is deliberately excluded. This is in agreement with the picture presented by the account of the Passion.

A comparison with other passages shows how deliberately Luke employs the concept of law. In Acts xxi, 28 it is a question of the Jewish Law, but the complaint is only raised amongst Jews. A different approach is made to the Roman, as in xxiv, 5 f., where they speak of causing political unrest and public scandal. Paul, however, in his defence takes up the concept of law and clarifies it in every respect (xxv, 8), and in this way the Roman is presented with the facts, but the Jews are foiled in

---

[1] Roman: Zahn, Preuschen, *Beginnings of Christianity*. Jewish: Loisy, Goguel, Wendt, Haenchen. There is a clear connection with the theory sometimes met concerning the nature of the apologetic. Jacquier, *Actes*, p. 552, agrees with our interpretation when he speaks of a 'deliberate ambiguity in the meaning of the word "law" '.

GOD AND REDEMPTIVE HISTORY

their intrigues. And in the background there is always the fact that it is the Jews who are continually causing public disturbances. It is they who need to be watched by the authorities, not the Christians.

The remaining passages in Acts fit without difficulty into our picture; xxi, 38 presents the familiar Roman attitude as a purely political one. The speech of Tertullus assumes the same point of view in the Roman to whom it is addressed.[1] Paul also takes it for granted, for he never appeals before the Romans to the law which affords protection to Jews, but to his Roman civil rights. In similar vein Lysias, from the point of view of the representative of the State, sends his report to Caesarea (xxiii, 26 ff.).

Luke now has to explain of course why Paul in spite of everything is not set free, and he does so in xxv, 9. The following verses again make it plain, that there is no question of guilt either from the Roman or from the Jewish standpoint. The same meaning is conveyed by the scene in xxv, 23–6. Festus is even deprived of the excuse that he is making a concession to the Jews, for if Paul is kept under arrest, it would be against the judicial findings of the Romans (xxv, 18; cf. Pilate's declarations).

The only passage in which Paul expounds the relation between Judaism and Christianity before a Roman (xxiv, 14 ff.) has the purpose of separating this problem from the issues involved in the trial, therefore it does not represent a positive argument. And the governor is not 'perplexed' (xxv, 20) on account of the findings of religious law, but because of Jewish pressure. The analogy with the trial of Jesus is quite obvious.

When Festus outlines his own attitude, he speaks exclusively from the point of view of Roman criminal procedure (xxv, 14 ff.). He would gladly hand over the proceedings to the Jews, but is not able to do so. In the end it is confidence in the justice of the Emperor that forms the great climax of the narrative. There is no suggestion whatever of any weakening of this confidence.

---

[1] On the speech of Tertullus, see Lösch, *Theol. Quartalschrift*, 1931, pp. 295 ff. He shows in particular the official nature of the terminology. This does not of course prove the 'genuineness' of the speech, but it does provide evidence of Luke's plan. See also Dibelius, *Aufsätze*, p. 147.

GOD AND REDEMPTIVE HISTORY

2. THE CHURCH AND JUDAISM

The Jewish war had no noticeable effects on the general position of Jews in the Roman Empire, and Luke does not suggest any peculiarity in their legal position. When Luke is describing the Jews for the benefit of the Romans, he does not emphasize any specific characteristic, such as that of their religion, but simply describes them as notorious disturbers of the peace. Therefore once again it is not a question of special legal issues, but of the application of normal legislation.

Luke creates a basis for the direct discussion of the dispute between the Church and the Jews by his grasp of the principles involved in the problem. It is only against this background that his statements can be fully understood.[1]

In the very usage of 'Ιουδαῖος we can trace a certain hardening.[2] Here two motifs are joined—the collective polemic and the fact that the starting-point of the mission is always in the synagogue. There is a link between the two. That the starting-point is in the synagogue is of course required by redemptive history (cf. Acts xiii, 46: ἀναγκαῖον). On the other hand there is at the same time a reference to the cutting off of the Jews from redemptive history (ibid., πρῶτον). We can say that the Jews are now called to make good their claim to be 'Israel'. If they fail to do this, then they become 'the Jews'. For the individual the way of salvation is open, now as always. The polemic is at the same time a call to repentance; the continual reminder that the Church is grounded in redemptive history prevents the connection with Israel from ever being forgotten.

The combination of condemnation and call to repentance can be effectively seen in Peter's speeches with their statements of

---

[1] Both the outline of the attitude of the Jews to the Christian mission and also the thesis of Luke xxi, that the judgement of history has fallen upon the Jews, are based on an understanding of the principles involved in the problem of the Jews.

[2] Cf. Gutbrod's article in *TW*. Alongside each other we find the use of the word as a simple designation and also its use in a sharply polemical sense. We can see the change from the one to the other in Acts xiv, from v. 1, through v. 2 to v. 4, where the Jews are made to stand out as such, but it is clear from this passage that it is not the Jew as an individual who is rejected. The possibility of addressing the Jews is not removed, nor the possibility of the individual Jew's attaining faith. 'The Jews' in the pointed sense are those who have rejected the Gospel, and who are now presented as the typical enemies of the Church. For the development in the usage of the term, cf. xviii, 5–12 and xviii, 14–19, also xvii, 1–5 and xvii, 10–17.

guilt leading up to an appeal.[1] This same pattern in the dispute is set out by Luke also in the narrative.

He now has to give an explanation from redemptive history of the way in which the Jews have behaved, and draw out the consequences for the Church. On the one hand he establishes the guilt of the Jews, but for the purpose of retaining a point of contact he concedes that they acted from ignorance (iii, 7). This provides him with a link with the fact that it was an event decreed by God—which does not remove the guilt, but does make it possible to keep the point of contact (iii, 18). On the other hand he distinguishes between the people and its leaders, a distinction which he indicates as early as in the story of John the Baptist.[2] Because of John's baptism a split runs through the Jewish people, separating the penitent from the impenitent.[3]

It is from the plan of redemptive history that we can understand the juxtaposition of the two statements:

(*a*) that Jews and Christians are in fact not distinguished;[4]
(*b*) that they are sharply opposed to one another.

Both statements are simply the outcome of the same conception of Israel and the Church. Thus the extreme sharpness of polemic becomes possible, but at the same time the avoidance of a summary Christian anti-Semitism.[5] Both statements are the outcome of the view that the Church represents the continuity of redemptive history, and to this degree is 'Israel'.[6]

There is one fact which can make the dispute more difficult for the Christians. From the angle from which he views redemptive history Luke employs the reproach, that the Jews themselves do not keep the Law,[7] but as a matter of principle the

[1] Acts ii, 23 and ii, 36, 38; iii, 13 ff., 17 ff.; clear examples in xiii, 27 ff., 32, 38, 40 f.
[2] The significance of the fact that in Luke iii, 7 it is only the people, but the whole people, that is baptized, is made plain by the distinction brought out in Luke vii, 29 f.
[3] The part played by the leaders in the Passion fits in with this, and helps us to understand the account given in Acts of the friendliness of the people and the hostility of the leaders.
[4] The Sadducees of course are an exception, for they deny the resurrection (Acts xxiii, 6; xxviii, 20), and therefore are not genuine Jews.
[5] In this Luke is sharply distinguished from the developments of early Catholicism which are soon to begin.
[6] Luke of course does not create the term 'true Israel'.
[7] Acts vii, 53; xxiii, 3. The reproach of ἀνομία in ii, 23 (in Luke's sense) no doubt applies here as well.

GOD AND REDEMPTIVE HISTORY

Jews do in fact adhere to the Law, whilst it is given up on principle by the Church (Acts xv, 28 f.). Luke gives an answer of fundamental importance by his account of the course of redemptive history within the Church itself since its 'arché' in Jerusalem. This means that the beginning as such becomes a specially important problem of which an account needs to be given. Luke supplies this by writing his second book.

The critical attitude to the Jews and this examination of the principles involved in the problem of the Law belong together. The latter presents itself as the problem of a historical development, which means for Luke something determined by redemptive history. In this respect Luke differs from the Apostolic Fathers in their attempts at a non-historical solution.

The period of the Church's beginning is characterized by universal adherence to the Law. Therefore the community's link with the Temple is set down in summaries which give the main gist of the narratives (Acts ii, 46; v, 12, 42). In its attitude to the Temple we see the community taking over its inheritance of redemptive history. We must remember that Jesus himself went into the Temple.

However, the question still remains, how it is that the Gentile Christian Church does not keep the Law and yet stands within the continuity of redemptive history. The answer is provided on the one hand in the Cornelius story, and on the other hand in the description of the Apostolic Council. The Apostolic decree sums up the Law as pointing to a permanent separation. The actual separation of the Church from the Temple and the Law is here shown to be possible and even in accordance with Scripture (xv, 16 f.). Adherence to the Law is associated with a definite phase in the Church's development, during which it is strictly observed. Of course Paul also has to be fitted into this pattern (xxi, 18 ff., also the personal testimony in his defence, summarized in xxv, 8 and xxvi, 5).[1]

The question of the Law cannot really be used as a point of contact with the Jews, precisely because of the existence of a community that does not observe the Law. Good reasons could no doubt be given for the freedom from the Law, but it did not

---

[1] There is an example in Acts xvi, 3 of the use of the Law as a point of contact. This account of Paul's behaviour makes it clear that the accusations of the Jews are patently untrue.

GOD AND REDEMPTIVE HISTORY

provide any positive link. Luke creates this by emphasizing the agreement about one central dogma, the doctrine of a general resurrection (Acts xxiii, 6; xxvi, 5 ff.).[1]

3. Conclusion

We will attempt to see in conjunction the attitude to the Jews and to the Romans.

The solidarity of the Church with Israel derives from redemptive history. Externally their unity can be seen in that both possess the Scriptures. The important thing is that they should be interpreted correctly, and the way has been shown by the Risen Lord (Luke xxiv, 25 ff.).[2] The inner unity lies in the fact that both believe in a resurrection, of the general kind we have described.

It is in relation to the Jews that the Church is confirmed in its own status as part of redemptive history, but this aspect is of no help in determining its relation to the Empire or in political apologetic.[3] We can see how different the approach is in the fact that the axiom, that one must obey God rather than men, is used only in dealings with the Jews (Acts v, 29; cf. iv, 19). It is true that Luke requires this confession when confronted by the Empire—Luke xii, 11 and xxi, 12 ff. leave us in no doubt about this—but in presenting Christianity to the State, the alternative which we have noted is not expressly stated. The incident of the tribute money shows how this alternative works out in relation to the Roman Empire. In Luke's opinion there is no real conflict between God and Caesar.[4]

We can sum up Luke's political attitude as follows:

(a) towards the Jews: one must obey God rather than men;
(b) towards the Empire: one should render to Caesar what is Caesar's, and to God what is God's.

[1] We must of course distinguish between Pharisees and Sadducees. In the light of this doctrine it becomes impossible for the Sadducees to represent the people of God—and the Pharisees are inconsistent, if they do not become Christians.

[2] We shall consider this in detail later. We must bear in mind not only the systematic treatment of the problem of Scriptural interpretation in the preaching in the synagogues (Acts xvii, 11), but also the Christological summaries from Scripture of the type of Acts xvii, 3.

[3] These contrasting attitudes cannot be deduced from the text, but are the result of reflecting on what was presumably the historical situation.

[4] There is no trace of any conflict arising from the cult of the Emperor.

148

GOD AND REDEMPTIVE HISTORY

Luke knows that this does not in fact avoid a clash, because Rome does not accept this alternative. This can be seen in his statements about persecution and his emphasis in the ethical instruction on endurance in persecution, but—and this is what we must note here—he does not say this to the State, because he is pursuing an apologetic aim.

We can be certain that Luke's apologetic does not represent a merely incidental element, a practical adjustment to the world. It is based on an examination of the principles from the angle of redemptive history. The fact that the End is no longer thought of as imminent, and the subsequent attempt to achieve a long-term agreement as to the Church's relation to the world show how closely related this question is to the central motifs in Luke's whole plan. We shall now go on to consider the fundamental question of God and the world, as it manifests itself in the interpretation of redemptive history.

II. THE RULE OF GOD IN REDEMPTIVE HISTORY

1. The Pattern of Thought Concerning Redemptive History

It is not our purpose to consider sayings concerning God and His rule in general, for they are part of the normal belief of the Church.[1] We shall turn rather to the related ideas which are elaborated in the context of redemptive history, ideas concerning God's plan, will and providence. In addition there are certain motifs which develop out of the missionary approach. We must consider what is the connection between these two groups of motifs. No doctrine of God is expounded in its own right, for there is no theological necessity for it.

God's control of redemptive history is described under two aspects. The framework is formed by general statements concerning the redemptive rule of God, which rest upon the

---

[1] We see this, for example, in the idea of praying to God, of His miracles, and of His special providence, and we can see the same in the titles. He is Creator and Ruler in a general sense (this is brought out in the two speeches in Acts xiv, 15 ff. and xvii, 22 ff.).

conception of a systematic execution of the Divine plan, the real content of which is seen in the special event of the revelation in Christ in the centre of history.

We will set out in advance the main stages that are marked. Although Luke gives no explicit description of the structure, his whole account is based on a definite conception. The pattern that emerges is as follows:[1]

The basis is the idea of God's plan. Its beginning is marked by the Creation, which, however, is not thought of as an 'epoch', but represents the limit of reflection concerning redemptive history. There is no speculative development of the idea of the Creation. Wherever the Creation is mentioned (Acts xiv and xvii), it is with reference solely to the Word of God that is to be proclaimed, to God's commands and to the offer of salvation.

The corresponding limit at the other extreme is the Parousia. Again speculation is strictly avoided, more strictly than in the rest of the New Testament—including Paul. No account is given of the Parousia itself, and no statement is made as to what follows it. Only the course of events up to it is described.

Between these limits history runs its course in three phases:

The period of Israel, of the Law and the Prophets.

The period of Jesus, which gives a foretaste of future salvation.

The period between the coming of Jesus and his Parousia, in other words, the period of the Church and of the Spirit. This is the last age. We are not told that it will be short.

There is a continuity linking the three periods, and the essence of the one is carried through into the next. The call to repentance as found in the Old Testament is not abandoned, but assumed by Jesus as well as by the Church. It is prophecy in particular that creates the continuity. In the first period it is directed to Christ, and in the second period Jesus' prophecy extends to the Kingdom of God. Just as Israel could make sure of its promise, so the Church also will be able to do, for in it the benefits of the period of Jesus remain operative. This is shown by the fact of the Spirit.

[1] On the threefold scheme, cf. v. Baer, passim, e.g. p. 77.

GOD AND REDEMPTIVE HISTORY

The position of Jesus in the centre is of course the most significant element in the description. The fact that another period has intervened between Jesus and the present gives rise to a problem, for because of this the 'centre' of history itself is now an ascertainable historical fact. Another consequence of this intervening period is that the beginnings of the Church also have become something that can be observed as historical fact, and from such observation one's own position can be determined. In this way any speculation about getting nearer to the End is avoided. In this respect Luke says nothing beyond a clear warning against any calculation.

It should be noted that Luke's view of the world and the corresponding ideas have no special features.

2. GOD'S PLAN

The idea of God's plan is expressed even in the terminology, of which a striking example is provided by the many compounds with πρό. The fact that they are so numerous is symptomatic for Luke.[1] A number of passages speak of God's βουλή. On two occasions the word is used to signify that Jesus' death was according to plan, and in one instance it serves to sum up the whole message.[2] The word gains its special significance when it denotes the plan of salvation, by being linked with the verbs ὁρίζω and προορίζω,[3] which have a more definite meaning.

[1] We will refer here to the articles in *TW* for the concepts we shall be considering. Compounds with πρό –: πρόγνωσις (Acts ii, 23), προκαταγγέλλω (iii, 18; vii, 52), προκηρύσσω (xiii, 24), προορίζω (see above), προχειρίζω (iii, 20; xxii,14; xxvi, 16).

[2] The word is rare in the New Testament. Outside Luke's writings it occurs only three times, and in two of these passages the reference is similarly to the plan of salvation (Eph. i, 11 and Heb. vi, 17). Of course we also find in Luke the general use of the word, e.g. in reference to human counsels (Acts xxvii, 12, 42). In Luke vii, 30 it is used for the 'will' of God. Of the three passages which concern us here, in Acts xx, 27 the word is used as a brief summary, and we cannot of course deduce from this passage all that this plan involves. Verse 21 gives a fuller account. The nature of revelation as the communication of knowledge comes out particularly clearly here. It is a question of knowing the events in God's saving activity, up to the limit which is set for man (Acts i, 7). In Acts ii, 23 it is found—perhaps as an interpretation—in the context of a kerygmatic formula, where it denotes the 'necessity' of the death of Christ. The same idea is present in the prayer in Acts iv, 24 ff. (cf. v. 28). Those who brought about the death are seen as instruments in the plan of salvation—but this does not excuse them.

[3] The simple verb is found in Rom. i, 4 in connection with the familiar Christological formula, and also in Heb. iv, 7, again with reference to the plan of

151

GOD AND REDEMPTIVE HISTORY

God's 'ordaining' covers both the past, in particular the fate of Christ, and also the future, for Acts x, 42 speaks of Christ's being ordained as Judge. There is no speculation here, for it is only the fact of judgement that is established and confirmed. The passage receives its particular stamp from the citation of witnesses—who also are 'ordained'—and from the appeal to the prophets. Thus the 'whole plan of God' is brought into view. There is a parallel in Acts xvii, 31. The usage is stretched to its farthest point in xvii, 26, where world history in general is included. However, it is not a question of unfolding a theory of history but of laying the foundation for the call to repentance which follows and which is based on the motif of judgement, in other words, it is a question of missionary propaganda.

The Christological reference in the statements we have mentioned, whether they refer to the Passion that has already taken place or to the future Judgement, is there from the beginning. The idea of the plan of God in itself is of course an old one, but now it is taken up by Christians for the purposes of argument on the point which is most pressing in the dispute with the Jews: it can be used to explain the fate of Jesus. From this original purpose the sayings then extend to cover past and future. This can be seen in the fact, not that on the basis of this idea the broad course of future history can be constructed, but that the sayings concentrate on the one point in the future which is directly implied in the original Christological reference—the coming of the Judge. In Acts i, 7 the thought of predetermination is used specifically to prevent apocalyptic speculation. Because God alone ordains, the course of events is hidden from us, but on the other hand for the very same reason we can be certain that the plan will be carried through. We receive, not knowledge, but assurance, through the sending of the Spirit (v. 8) and through fulfilling one's calling as a witness. The contradiction with xx, 27 is only apparent, for in the one passage it is a question of God's transcendent rule, and in the other of what He has been willing to reveal. The extent of this revelation

salvation. In Acts xi, 29 it is used of a human resolve. On the passage Acts xvii, 26, cf. especially Dibelius, 'Paulus auf dem Areopag', *Aufsätze*, pp. 29 ff. The compound occurs a few times in the Pauline epistles, where it is used exclusively of God.

See the previous note for the passages ii, 23 and iv, 28. The same idea is found in Luke xxii, 22.

is determined not by speculation but by soteriology. Plan and promise correspond (Acts iii, 18), for the latter is made possible only by the former. This means that fulfilment is certain.

The function of Scripture in this context is determined by the fact that the point at issue is not the general question as to whether there is a rule of providence, for Jews and Christians are in agreement about this. Acts xvii suggests that one might reach agreement about it even with the Greeks. It is a question rather of proving that this particular event has been brought about by God as in a special sense the saving event. It is for this reason that the kerygmatic proclamation points to the evidence of Scripture.

The most important indication as regards the whole complex of ideas is the use of the significant word δεῖ. It is again in the defence of the Passion that the word is particularly used,[1] already in pre-Lucan tradition of course.[2] In Luke, however, the 'necessity' of the Passion is fully brought out.[3]

[1] There are clear parallels to the usage of the LXX: for the will of God revealed in the Law, cf. Luke xi, 42; xiii, 14; xxii, 7; Acts xv, 5; for the will of God in general, cf. Luke xv, 32; xviii, 11; Acts v, 29; xx, 35, inter alia. Concerning Scripture, cf. Luke xxii, 37; xxiv, 44.

[2] Mark viii, 31 and parallel passage. The word does not occur in the second and third prophecy of the Passion. Luke puts in its place the fulfilment of Scripture. δεῖ is really only the shorthand sign for this. In Mark ix, 11 the Jewish eschatological element appears, according to which it is necessary that Elijah should first come. This passage is omitted in Luke, as he entirely eradicates the expectation of Elijah. Cf. with Mark ix, 11, also Mark xiii, 7, 10, 14, and xiv, 31. The statistical evidence shows that in Mark δεῖ is used in only two contexts, in connection with the traditional eschatology and with the Passion of Jesus. On this point, cf. Grundmann's article in *TW*, and E. Fascher, 'Theologische Beobachtungen zu δεῖ', *Neutest. Studien für R. Bultmann*, 1954, pp. 228 ff.

[3] Cf. Luke xvii, 25. Although the context is eschatological, the word δεῖ is used not in connection with the future, but with the Passion. In xxiv, 7 it is a question of a subsequent proof that the Passion was part of God's plan, by means of a reference back to one of Jesus' own statements. A comparison with xxii, 37 shows the harmony between Scripture and Jesus' own statement. In Luke xxiv, 26 the demonstration of the necessity of the Passion is made the climax of the Resurrection story; cf. v. 27 and v. 44, where the circle is completed by the fact that Jesus quotes the Scriptural proof and refers to his earlier sayings. In Luke xxiv, 46 ἔδει is probably a secondary reading. On the other hand we find again in Acts xvii, 3 a formula of the same type as in Luke 24. Taken together, these passages point to a usage that is already stereotyped, and to a fixed pattern of argument: it is from Scripture that the correct idea of the Messiah as a suffering Messiah is derived. The fulfilment is then confirmed in the historical Jesus.

Grundmann stresses the eschatological character of δεῖ. For Luke, however, this has to be modified, for it is in the very passages where the word occurs that the change from eschatology to redemptive history is obvious. The conclusion that

GOD AND REDEMPTIVE HISTORY

The usage spreads from here to other events in the course of redemptive history. Not only the death, but the whole ministry of Jesus is implicit in the kerygmatic proclamation, in so far as the Resurrection casts light not only on Jesus' death, but also on his deeds and on his whole being. Luke deliberately indicates this in his account of the Resurrection.[1]

God's plan is primarily concerned with the saving events as a whole, not with the individual man and his destiny. According to it redemptive history leads up to Christ, and then on to the Last Judgement. The predestination of the individual has not yet come to expression in the conception of the plan. We can see this from the abstract way in which the motif of 'election' is expressed.

3. ELECTION

Luke is not familiar with the idea of a fixed number of elect.[2] On the whole the group of words ἐκλέγειν, etc. is relatively

because πρῶτον δεῖ is an eschatological term and is applied to the Passion, the latter should be understood as an 'eschatological happening' is not based on sufficient evidence and completely misrepresents Luke's interpretation.

The word is also used in a general sense (Matt. xxiii, 33/Luke xi, 42), and in a secular sense (Luke xv, 32; xxii, 7; xiii, 14, 16).

[1] In the prologue the necessity of a visit to the Temple is raised (Luke ii, 49). According to Luke iv, 43, he 'must' preach the good tidings. Underlying this is the idea of the progress of the Gospel according to plan. This can be found already in Mark, but Luke defines it more precisely by making it clear that the plan can be seen also in the whole course of Jesus' life. He brings it out by the way he arranges the Gospel. The similar systematic progress in the course of Church history is described in Acts. Luke xiii, 3 shows the three necessary stages in Jesus' ministry. According to Luke xii, 12, the Spirit teaches what one must say in order to make a correct statement when called upon to declare one's faith. Chapter xviii, v. 1 speaks of what is required in the Christian way of life, and xix, 5 of a fixed intention. The evidence of Acts is the same; iii, 21 contains one of the Christological sayings. Then in iv, 12 we find the change to a soteriological reference in conjunction with the ὄνομα idea. The connection with Scripture can be seen in i, 16, and with the appointment of a witness in i, 22. Chapter v, 21 is concerned with the Christian life, ix, 16 and xiv, 22 with the lot of Christians. A traditional motif is obviously present here, as is shown by a comparison with 1 Thess. iii, 3 f., but what is significant is Luke's use of the word δεῖ.

We must also note the use of the word with reference to the fact that Paul's missionary activities are all according to plan, and in particular that he 'must' see Rome (Acts xix, 21; xxiii, 11). It is significant that sayings of this kind occur most frequently in the later chapters of Acts, where the marks of Luke's composition can most clearly be seen.

[2] The only evidence to the contrary is in Acts xiii, 48, which probably contains a current expression to which we cannot attach much weight. Other passages prove

154

GOD AND REDEMPTIVE HISTORY

rare. This is surprising when one considers the number of sayings about the predetermining rule of God. When we try to understand this surprising fact, we cannot avoid the explanation that to a large extent the language of 'predetermining' replaces that of 'election', and that so far as Luke is concerned the saving events as a whole are more important than the individual aspect of election. The latter aspect is covered by other ideas, those of repentance and conversion. The same applies to the group of words, καλεῖν, etc.[1]

without question that Luke is not aware that this passage implies predestination. The participle used as a noun does not mean that God's plan allows for only a fixed number of elect in the world; in fact the word is used as an ordinary designation for Christians (as in Luke xviii, 7, for suffering Christians).

The verb is used as follows:

(*a*) In the secular sense: Luke x, 42; xiv, 7.

(*b*) In connection with Christ: Luke ix, 35 (with reference to his being divinely appointed as 'Son'; in xxiii, 35 we hear the same word on the lips of his enemies).

(*c*) In connection with the call to a ministry in the Church, where besides the present call there is also the fact of being foreordained, e.g., Acts xxvi, 16. Luke vi, 13 shows marks of Luke's editorial work. The expression in Acts xv, 7 is more forceful.

(*d*) In connection with the patriarchs: Acts xiii, 17.

(*e*) In an eschatological context. In the other Synoptics the word is used only in an eschatological sense, so here we can note a marked difference in Luke. It is true that he takes over the eschatological usage—from Mark—but he does not extend it. He omits Mark xiii, 20 either because he rejects the theory of a shortening of the days or does not require it. Mark xiii, 27 similarly disappears, as in Luke's view these matters have nothing to do with the End. Mark x, 40 is missing, together with the whole section. In the corresponding passage Luke xxii, 24–30 there is no mention of election. One cannot, however, say that it has been 'omitted', as it is possible that Luke is reproducing not Mark, but a variant. In Acts ix, 15 the noun is used in a Semitic turn of phrase for appointment to a commission within the Church. The passage agrees basically with xxvi, 16.

[1] K. L. Schmidt suggests in his article in *TW* that the word is found in Luke because it is in common use, but the use of it in Luke is no more extensive than in Matthew, for example, not to speak of Paul. When the word is found in the Gospel it is generally derived from the sources. As regards the meaning, investigation brings to light the connection with Luke's non-eschatological form of the idea of election. The following examples should be noted:

Mark i, 20: for this passage Luke has a variant without καλεῖν. In the analogous scene of the call of the Twelve Luke uses ἐκλέγειν, his technical term for the call to a ministry within the Church. Luke v, 32 is derived from Mark and shows the change of meaning. In Mark the word has the pregnant sense of the 'call' of Jesus. Luke defines it further as a call to repentance, and therefore no longer sees its Messianic significance. Mark iii, 31 has been transposed by Luke. καλεῖν is missing, in keeping with the altered sense of the section (see p. 48). Chapter vii, v. 39 provides an example of a typically Lucan use, the invitation to a meal. This same situation prevails in chapter xiv: vv. 7 f., 12 f., 16 f., 24; vv. 16 f. come from Q, but Luke has repeated the word. (On the other hand, it is missing in Luke's parallel

GOD AND REDEMPTIVE HISTORY

Neither an anthropological nor a cosmological theory can be developed from the ideas concerning election and no more can a doctrine of predestination. Yet the idea of God's plan of salvation and the fact that the idea of election is applied to redemptive history as a whole brings to the fore the problem of the past and its interpretation. This is the next main problem we must consider.

4. THE ADVERSARY

We will consider briefly in passing the role played by Satan in Luke's plan. His role is a subordinate one; he is not taken into consideration in the statements concerning either God's plan or His act in Christ, or in those statements with a wider historical reference. Satan does not enter as a factor in the saving events. In fact the only part he plays is the negative one of being excluded from the period of Jesus' ministry. Between the 'Temptation' and the Passion he is absent, then he reappears (Luke xxii, 3) and the 'temptations' are back again; but it is not explicitly stated that he is responsible for the Passion. In the preaching about Christ's sufferings he is not mentioned either.

The statements are in fact in line with the tradition. Some small changes of emphasis can be noted. In two passages the range of his power is more precisely defined. According to Luke iv, 6 the worldly powers are at his disposal; but this

to Matt. xxii, 8 f.). Luke is of course aware of the symbolism of the banquet setting and employs it allegorically in xiv, 24; xix, 13 is derived from Q. It refers to a call to a commission. Acts iv, 18 and xxiv, 2 provide examples of a secular, legal usage. The upshot of all this is that the evidence is lacking for Schmidt's assertion.

There are the following compounds:

ἐπικαλεῖσθαι (Acts ii, 21), contained in a quotation, in the familiar technical, cultic sense. This is particularly plain in Acts vii, 59, where we find the word without an object. This is not so in the quotation in xv, 17. προσκαλεῖσθαι occurs in Acts ii, 39, again in a quotation. Luke uses the word for being commissioned to a task by God (Acts xvi, 10), and by the Spirit (xiii, 2). The comparison is instructive for the relationship of God and the Spirit as regards their practical functions. The eschatological meaning of the quotation in ii, 39 has been transformed by Luke into the 'call' in the Church's sense. Cf. also Acts xviii, 16. κλῆσις and κλητός are not found in Luke.

The use of the words κλῆρος and λαγχάνω reveals nothing special in Luke's conception.

authority has been 'delivered' to him, which indicates his limitations. Further, according to Luke xxii, 31, he has 'asked to have' the disciples, which again indicates his dependence.

The connection between Satan and the evil spirits becomes clear when we compare Luke xiii, 11 and xiii, 16. In Luke his activity is described more from the psychological angle than in the source; cf. Luke viii, 12 with Mark iv, 15, and also Acts v, 3. In Acts x, 38 he is the oppressor, which is the traditional conception. Acts xxvi, 18 speaks of his power, but the passage does not refer to redemptive history as a whole, but to the event of conversion as it concerns the individual. Throughout it is clear that the statement, that man is under his power, does not serve to lessen man's responsibility but to underline the call to repentance.[1]

III. THE PAST

1. SCRIPTURE

The actual relationship to the past is determined by two factors, by Scripture and by the connection with Israel, which are of course inseparable. On the one hand there is the task of giving positive evidence of promise and fulfilment, whilst on the other hand the argument with the Jews has to be conducted on the basis of Scripture, and it has to be proved that the Jews are no longer a factor in redemptive history, that they are no longer 'Israel'.

In his own way Luke has given a foreshadowing in the life of Jesus of the function of Scripture in the Church. During his lifetime Jesus employs the proof from Scripture—Luke xxiv, 44 provides evidence of this—and also after his Resurrection (Luke xxiv, 27). These passages set out the principle of exegesis which is later frequently employed in the Acts of the Apostles. The continuity between the ancient promise and Jesus becomes clear when he is described as 'prophet', whatever elements this idea might contain, as in Luke xxiv, 19.

[1] This has to be affirmed against the trend of Catholic theology. An exegetical analysis is given by Schelkle, p. 18.

GOD AND REDEMPTIVE HISTORY

The introductory formula for quotations, ἐν βίβλῳ, is peculiar to Luke (Luke iii, 4; xx, 42; Acts i, 20; vii, 42; cf. Klostermann on Luke iii, 4). Besides this he takes over the traditional terms, 'Scripture' and 'the law and the prophets', to which is added on one occasion (Luke xxiv, 44) 'and the psalms'.[1]

We will consider Luke's terminology first. The word γραφή in Luke iv, 21 signifies a definite passage (ἡ γραφὴ αὕτη). This is in keeping with the use of the plural (Luke xxiv, 27—cf. also vv. 32, 45).[2] The word as used here does not yet stand for the whole of the canon, but it is possible to see a suggestion of this use in Acts viii, 32 (ἡ περιοχὴ τῆς γραφῆς). Yet we cannot be certain.[3] The evidence seems to be that in Luke we do not find the fixed usage of 'the Scripture' such as we find in other New Testament writings, especially in John (cf. however, John v, 39), but for the most part he is in agreement with the other Synoptics. His usage is along the lines of the expression γέγραπται.[4]

The verb is taken over by Luke from his sources.[5] In xxii, 22 he replaces Mark's καθὼς γέγραπται (Mark xiv, 21) by κατὰ τὸ ὡρισμένον. In other words, he interprets the meaning in a way which reflects his own understanding of Scripture, based on the idea of God's plan which emerges from redemptive history.

In Luke's view one cannot interpret the 'law' solely as commandment, or 'the prophets' solely as prophecy. This emerges clearly from Luke xxiv, 44 and Acts xxiv, 14. The truth is rather that law and prophets together form on the one hand the

---

[1] Luke evidently has a predilection for the Psalms. We also find that David appears primarily not just as a great figure from Israel's past, but as a prophet (Acts ii, 25 ff.). The difference between Luke xx, 42 and Mark xii, 36 is very significant.

[2] Acts xvii, 2, 11; xviii, 24, 28.

[3] A little later v. 35 speaks again of 'this' scripture.

[4] Cf. Mark xii, 10 and Luke xx, 17. In a few passages Luke has no parallel to Mark; cf. Mark xii, 24; xiv, 49; xiv, 27 (where the proof from Scripture is missing in Luke). We cannot be sure of the reason for the omission, as 'fulfilment' plays as important a part in Luke as in Mark; he also shares the view of Mark xii, 24, that ignorance of the Scriptures incurs blame (cf. Acts xiii, 27).

[5] Luke iv, 4, 8, 10 come from Q; vii, 27 from a variant of Q; iii, 4 and xix, 49 from Mark.

basis of the call to repentance and on the other hand the basis of the proof from prophecy.[1]

The concepts νόμος and ἐντολή are not used to describe the Christian faith. This fact needs to be noted, for by the turn of the first century Christianity is coming to be viewed and spoken of as the 'new law'. In this respect Luke clearly follows a different line from the early Catholic development. In Luke these concepts indicate the historical relation of faith to that on which it rests, the past redemptive history of Israel and the story of the primitive community, which did in fact adhere to the Law; but now the Church has been freed from the Law by the apostolic decree.

Two aspects are intertwined here. First there is that concerning the principles involved in redemptive history, which sees the problem of the Law against the background of Scripture. Then there is the immediate apologetic aspect of the problem, under which Luke develops two distinct motifs.

He stresses the difference from Roman and Jewish Law, as we saw earlier, and he contrasts the strict way in which the

---

[1] For the 'legal' sense of νόμος, cf. Luke xvi, 17 (from Q) and Luke x, 26. Here of course we must mention the idea that the primitive Church was tied to the Law as a matter of principle; but the seeds of later development are already present, for according to Luke this adherence is not binding for all time, but is linked with a particular phase in the history of the Church.

The prophetic function of the Law is clearly expressed in Luke xxiv, 44. Thus Moses is mentioned in connection with the proof from prophecy (Luke xxiv, 27). It is significant that the prophetic character of the Law comes out most strongly in the prologue. On the prophets, cf. Luke xxiv, 25; Acts iii, 25; x, 43; xxvi, 27. The law and the prophets are linked in two respects, for they both prophesy and they both command. The prophets' call to repentance, in fact, helps to prepare for the coming of Jesus; this we can see in the ministry of the last and greatest of them. The inclusion of John the Baptist among the prophets shows that prophecy is not thought of in a narrow biblicist sense as being confined to a fixed canon. Alongside Scripture there is the fact that God continues to speak through the mouth of prophets, and since the time of Jesus on the new basis of Christian prophecy by the Spirit. This view is fully set out in the story of Pentecost on the basis of a Scriptural prophecy.

The continuity linking the epochs of saving history does not rest solely on the evidence of promise and fulfilment, but also on the fact that the former call to repentance is still valid in the Christian dispensation as the constant basis for the proclamation of the Gospel of the Kingdom of God. We can see this in the speeches in Acts, both in the speeches to the Jews, which lead up to the call to repentance, and also in the appeal to the Greeks, where the call is made with the same force. The doctrine of the Resurrection serves as a fixed motif in the call to repentance. In this way the preaching of repentance is continued and at the same time superseded, for forgiveness is now granted.

primitive community keeps the Law with the Jewish breach of it.[1]

The idea of the Law is not developed into a theological concept. There is only a slight hint of Pauline teaching in the statement in Acts xiii, 38, that there is no 'justification' through the Law. Here it is a question of employing a familiar expression in setting down one of Paul's speeches. In any case no doctrine of justification is built up on the basis of the concept of the Law. Luke understands this statement rather from the standpoint of his view of the Law as an intolerable burden (Acts xv, 5—cf. v. 10, also xxi, 20), which is thoroughly un-Pauline. What Luke is interested in is in setting out the course of redemptive history and in making it clear that the primitive community— including Paul—keeps the Law without exception. Thus the Apostolic Council does not deal with the problem of the Law in Pauline fashion as a matter of principle but promulgates an ecclesiastical regulation, which now draws a distinction within the Church itself between two historical phases, but at the same time maintains the continuity.

The fact that the primitive community keeps the Law (Acts xix, 39; xxi, 24; xxiii, 3, 12; xxiv, 14—cf. also the description of its life in the narratives and summaries in the earlier part of Acts) is proof that it is bound up with Israel. The Law prepares the way for the Gospel just as Israel does for the Church and her mission.[2] It is an element belonging to redemptive history, not something timeless. This is emphatically expressed in Luke xvi, 16, where the connection of the two aspects becomes clear, that of the Law as an epoch, and of the Law as a component part of Scripture (see also Acts xiii, 15). Luke xvi, 17 then goes on to express the 'permanence' of the Law, the fact that its position

[1] The word ἐντολή does not play a large part in Luke (especially in comparison with Matthew, and also John with his special conception). A few Marcan passages are missing in Luke: Mark vii, 8 f. disappears as part of the great omission. x, 5 is missing together with the whole section. Luke has a very different version of Mark xii, 28, 31 in x, 25 ff., with νόμος instead of ἐντολή. On the whole we find the normal usage, e.g. in Luke xxiii, 56, one of Luke's own compilations. It is also used in the secular sense (Luke xv, 29; Acts xvii, 15). The verb is rare. It occurs in a quotation in Luke iv, 10; in Acts xiii, 47 it introduces one, and in Acts i, 2 the Risen Lord 'commands' through the Spirit.

[2] The course of events in Acts depicts this; the Gospel prepares the ground, to the extent that Jesus remains strictly within Jewish territory. The message to Israel and the message to the world follow as historical stages.

is one of principle. In other words, the epochs are separate, but there is no break between them, for the elements in the former one persist into the next.

Luke's whole account of the primitive community and the Law proves to be something composed in the light of redemptive history, and not a historical record in the modern sense.

On this basis the concept of the Law can be used for apologetic purposes. The transgression of the Jews is clearly set out in contrast to the attitude of the primitive community: they are ἄνομοι (Acts ii, 23[1]). The same point is made very boldly in vii, 53. The usual accusation of the Jews against the Christians can therefore be rejected.[2]

What practical use does Luke make of Scripture? Above all, what is the importance of Scriptural prophecy? Scripture points to Christ, to the dawn of salvation. This is made clear right at the beginning. In iii, 4 ff. Luke alters and expands the quotation in Mark i, 2 f. The laying low of the mountains is seen as a saving event. In the world at present they are the lonely place of manifestation, but one day everything will be openly revealed. The completion of the quotation beyond what Mark gives introduces a universal note (cf. Luke ii, 30 f., and especially Acts xviii, 28). There is a correspondence between the beginning and the end of the whole work, Scripture providing the theme. The Eschaton and the Judgement, however, do not seem to come within the range of Scriptural prophecy. This seems to be expressed in Luke xvi, 16, but can it be substantiated?

John the Baptist, according to Luke, does not proclaim the Kingdom of God, and Luke xvi, 16 shows why: it is not yet possible for him to know anything about it. Only Jesus possesses this knowledge, for it is the message of the Kingdom of God that constitutes the new element in the present epoch of salvation, in contrast to the old epoch whose last representative was John the Baptist. The horizon of Old Testament prophecy is therefore limited; it reaches as far as the coming of the Spirit (Luke xxiv, 49) and the dawn of the Eschaton (Acts ii, 16 ff.), but not as far as the Kingdom of God. Only Jesus' prophecy touches on this.[3]

---

[1] Luke interprets the passage as referring to the Jews (cf. xxiii, 3).
[2] Acts vi, 13; xxi, 28; xxv, 8.
[3] The 'Habakkuk Commentary', I Q p Hab. IV, 1 ff. (cf. p. 132) offers an instructive parallel to this realization that a knowledge of eschatology is revealed

The individuality of Luke's view of Scripture can be seen in another detail. We have seen that the Jews are accused of not knowing Scripture (Acts xiii, 27) but on the other hand, Luke xxiv assumes that one can only understand it in the light of the Resurrection, and the failure of the disciples themselves to understand runs right through the Gospel narrative. Luke now indicates a compromise. He concedes to the Jews that their ignorance to some extent excuses them (Acts iii, 17 f.).[1]

Now, however, as a result of the Resurrection, the truth has been inescapably disclosed. For whoever now hears the message and does not obey it, there is no more excuse, but only the Judgement. It is this view that underlies the structure of the speeches in Acts with their fixed sequence of motifs. The Resurrection is the turning-point, since which time one can no longer make the excuse of ignorance, nor can the Jew any longer put forward as an excuse his non-Christian understanding of Scripture. If he does this, then he forfeits Scripture—and again the Church appears as the legitimate heir of Israel; Scripture belongs to the Church, for she is in possession of the correct interpretation.

2. ISRAEL

Evidence of the relation of the Church to past redemptive history is to be found in the taking over of the traditional terminology of the 'people', which we can see particularly in the

only to the elect in the last epoch of history: 'And God told Habakkuk to write the things that were to come upon the last generation, but the consummation of the period he did not make known to him. And as for what it says, that he may run who reads it, this means the teacher of righteousness, to whom God made known all the mysteries of the words of his servants the prophets.' (Translation by M. Burrows, op. cit., pp. 367 f.)

[1] The theme of ignorance is found also in the argument with the Greeks, where it is even laid down as a principle (Acts xvii, 30). Up to now was the time of ignorance, which God allows as an excuse—He 'overlooks' it. This passage shows with particular clarity how the proclamation 'in the present' of the Resurrection and the Judgement to come creates for the hearer a situation from which he cannot escape. The same is true of the preaching to the Jews. The difference is that there the fact of their guilt stands in the foreground as the starting-point of the argument. Acts iii, 17 f., shows how Luke modifies what is primarily an assertion of guilt from the point of view of redemptive history by a motif which is typical of the missionary approach. Lohmeyer, *Gottesknecht und Davidssohn*, p. 17, does not distinguish between the different motifs, and therefore arrives at untenable conclusions.

speeches in the earlier part of Acts. The concepts which indicate Israel's position within redemptive history are now applied to the Church. By this means the nature of the Church is brought out, and at the same time the polemical controversy with Judaism is implied.[1] We will select a few characteristic passages.

'Israel' appears in a stereotype form of address in Acts ii, 22; iii, 12; v, 35; xiii, 16. More important for our purpose are the passages in which something of the original Jewish-Christian character of the speeches still remains. In Acts ii, 36 'all the house of Israel' is to know. This is possibly an example of a stylistic adjustment by Luke to fit the situation, but it might also simply be an example of the original horizon of a Jewish-Christian source (cf. iv, 10). Luke is able to reproduce such sayings without difficulty, in view of the fact that he equates the Church with Israel. Acts xiii, 23 f. speaks of a Saviour of 'Israel'. The non-Lucan context suggests it comes from a source. The universalist note is expressed in v. 38, and in v. 39 in language of a Pauline colouring. Verse 38 gives Luke's interpretation of the traditional expression.

Acts i, 6 speaks of the Kingdom being restored to Israel. It is not the hope of this that is rejected, but only the attempt to calculate when it will happen. Verse 8 makes clear what Luke has in mind. Right at the end of Acts Luke puts into Paul's mouth words concerning the hope of Israel, and as Paul says that it is because of this that he is in prison, it must be the Christian message in its connection with the ancient promise, in other words as the fulfilment of it, that is meant. The emphatic passage, xxviii, 28, which comes a little later, shows who now shares in this hope: salvation is passing to the Gentiles, which is something that is proclaimed by Scripture itself (cf. xxviii, 26 f. and v. 28 itself). The same idea is set out in xiii, 17 ff. From these two passages we can see quite clearly how Luke thinks of the Christians, according to plan, taking over the privileges of the Jews as one epoch is succeeded by the next.

The concepts which described first Israel and then the Church as a 'people' in the fullest sense ($\lambda\alpha\acute{o}\varsigma$, $\ddot{o}\chi\lambda o\varsigma$, $\ddot{\epsilon}\theta\nu o\varsigma$), are particularly frequent in the first part of Acts. These concepts are

---

[1] We can pass over here the problems of literary criticism and the history of tradition connected with the speeches, which still remain unsolved. All we need to note at this point is the fact that Luke adopts these ideas and this terminology.

part and parcel of the scheme of redemptive history. Luke does
not develop any new concept, and does not need to define afresh
the traditional terms, for he can employ them for his purpose
just as he finds them. Therefore we cannot speak of any special
'Lucan' use of these terms, but their use is of course facilitated
by Luke's obvious liking for Biblical phraseology.[1]

The principal item from the history of Israel which continues
into the Christian period is the Temple.[2] It is to the Temple that
Jesus makes his way. It is there that he delivers his final teaching, which is dominated by two themes, questions concerning
the Law and the doctrine of the Last Things; there, according
to Luke, Jesus makes his important statement concerning the
future significance of the city of Jerusalem (Luke xxi, 20 ff.).
The vital significance of the time spent by Jesus in the Temple
is suggested by the strict adherence to the geographical scheme
while Jesus is in the city (Luke xxi, 37 f.).

The primitive community remains loyal to the Temple; this
information is given not only by the narrative, but also by the
summary accounts of its life. In other words, this fact has the
importance of a matter of principle (Acts ii, 46; v, 42). It
is the story of Stephen that finally comes to terms with the

[1] The three concepts we have mentioned alternate, but Luke's favourite expression is certainly λαός. In the Gospel he often inserts it in passages from sources,
e.g. Luke vi, 17; viii, 47; xviii, 43; xix, 47; xx, 9, 19, 26; xxi, 38; xxiii, 35. It
is generally used for the common people; cf. Luke i, 21; iii, 15; iii, 18; vii, 1;
viii, 47; xx, 1; ix, 45, etc.

For the alternation with ὄχλος, cf. Luke vii, 29 and vii, 24; viii, 47 and viii,
42, 45; ix, 13, and ix, 12.

The phrase πᾶς ὁ ὄχλος sometimes means all those who are present. The story
of John the Baptist is an exception. According to Luke's account 'all the people'
were baptized, but the leaders remain apart. This is assumed in Luke vii, 29 f. In
this way Luke creates two groups in his description of redemptive history. The
leaders place themselves outside the saving events, that is, outside of 'Israel'.
Their future actions, above all their proceedings against Jesus—and later against
the Church—are determined by this fact, and the same applies to the whole Jewish
people, in so far as they identify themselves with their leaders. Luke is thus able
to distinguish between the Jews and the people of God on the basis of quite
definite evidence, and in Acts xv, 14 he uses a deliberately paradoxical phrase to
describe the state of affairs: ἐξ ἐθνῶν λαός.

λαός stands for Israel in Acts xxi, 28; xxviii, 17; x, 2, etc., and for the Christian
community in Acts xv, 14; xviii, 10. The identity of the community with Israel
is therefore assumed and accepted in practice, even if it is not expressed in theory.
For the general use of the concepts reference should be made in each case to the
relevant articles in *TW*.

[2] Cf. the articles in *TW* by Schrenk on ἱερόν and by Michel on ναός.

problem of the Temple, which is already foreshadowed in the Gospel.

As is well known, the statement of which Stephen is accused in Acts vi, 14 is found in Mark xiv, 58, as one of Jesus' sayings. In the latter passage, however, Luke has omitted it, and in the story of Stephen he describes the accusation as false witness. How is this to be explained? There are in Luke two motifs in the controversy concerning the Temple. On the one hand there is the typical argument of Acts vii, 48, which in this case is addressed to the Jews, as in xvii, 24 it is addressed to the Greeks. On the other hand the primitive community continues in the Temple, and the Jews are told of the judgement on the Temple not because reverence for the Temple is wrong, as Acts vii, 48 might seem to suggest, but because since Jesus' occupation of the Temple they have no right to possess it. Thus it has been profaned, and the judgement that comes upon it is a profane one, and has nothing to do with redemptive history. The end of the Temple in Luke has therefore to be distinguished from its eschatological destruction in Mark.

The question arises whether these two motifs in Luke are entirely unconnected. They are both typically Lucan, and the first one in particular is unmistakably so (Acts vii, 48 and xvii, 24). The other one, the judgement upon the Temple, is part of the tradition, but Luke has given it his own historical perspective. The two coincide in the fact that they provide justification for Christian worship apart from the Temple. There is a certain inconsistency in the fact that Stephen presupposes circumstances which arise later, although he argues his case at a time when, according to Luke's scheme of things, the Christians are still going to the Temple. In other words there is a conflict here between tradition, which has the 'primitive community' in mind, and the need to account for the actual circumstances of the present.

It is plain that the debate concerning the Jewish cultus does not belong to the present, but is a matter of history. It is set out by means of historical reflection on the 'beginning' of the community, not in an actual struggle concerning the present relationship of the Church to the Temple and the Law. The solution —freedom from the Law and the Temple—is already before Luke as an accomplished fact. Thus Luke is the first writer who deliberately describes the past of the community as 'the past'.

GOD AND REDEMPTIVE HISTORY

In contrast to the Temple, definite figures and events from Old Testament history are not included in Luke's historical scheme. The fact that Abraham is more prominent in Luke than in Mark is a result of the sources.[1] No line of redemptive history is drawn descending from Jacob.[2] Luke's use of Scripture is different and his plan of redemptive history does not follow in every detail the separate events which constitute the history of Israel, nor does he trace its inner continuity. The only instance where this is done is in the strange speech of Stephen. Apart from this it is Israel as a whole that is envisaged, without any distinctions being drawn within the course of her history. We saw this earlier in the way in which the law and the prophets are thought of as one entity.

The same is true of the two figures, who seem to lend themselves most readily to typology or to the elucidation of redemptive history—Moses and Elijah. Moses appears as a prophet in Luke xvi, 29 ff.; xx, 28; xxiv, 27, 44; Acts iii, 22; vii, 37; xxvi, 22; xxviii, 23. This is part of tradition. In Luke the background for this is provided by the fact that the Law has so definite a prophetic function.[3] Despite Moses' connection with

[1] Luke xiii, 28 appears to be an editorial compilation from Q material, referring not to redemptive history, but to eschatology. The judgement of Israel is traditional, and as regards the patriarchs there is nothing to note that is peculiar to Luke, but the distinction between the patriarchs and the Jews as a whole seems to be more sharply stressed. Luke xvi, 22 ff. is part of the special material. The passage shows that Abraham has no redemptive significance (cf. J. Jeremias' article on Abraham in *TW*). What is essential is the message, in other words Moses and the prophets, rather than figures who bear a redemptive meaning in themselves. This latter aspect is brought out in Luke least of all the New Testament writers. Cf. xiii, 16 and xix, 9.

[2] He appears in Luke xx, 37 and Acts iii, 13 in a compilation from Ex. iii, 2, 6. The idea of the descendants of the three patriarchs as the sons of the Kingdom is not present in Luke. He is not familiar with the original meaning, and therefore he alters the quotation for the purposes of argument and adds the concluding remark. The train of thought is as follows: (*a*) he calls God the 'Lord'; (*b*) He is the God of the living; (*c*) in the intermediate state they are with Him. This is an indication also of their future resurrection, which is to be distinguished from their present state. Against Odeberg in his article in *TW* we must point out that the meaning is not that just as resurrection is certain for them, so it is also for their children. The point is that God indicates through the Word that they are 'in Heaven'. This is not the conclusion, but the premiss. The important thing is that God is the God of the living.

[3] Moses appears in Acts vii, 17 ff. as one who suffered. This comes from the source. Apart from this passage Luke draws no significant conclusion from such a view. There are echoes of the theme of suffering in Luke ix, 31 (cf. Luke xxiv, 27,

the Law, no special significance attaches to his figure as such. In the case of Elijah we can go so far as to note the deliberate elimination of any significance attaching to the figure as such. Moses and Elijah are treated by Luke in the same way as John the Baptist, whose message remains valid but who, as a person, belongs entirely to the past epoch of redemptive history.[1]

It is characteristic of Luke's interpretation of history that it is only the idea of the people of God as such that is a determining factor, not the details of Israel's history. Even the Old Testament's own interpretation of history, according to which history follows a regular pattern of election—apostasy—disaster—turning back to God—new deliverance—is not taken over. The idea of tradition is applied to Israel only in the general sense, that the Church is now the people of God. In the way in which the idea of redemptive history is developed it becomes clear that Luke's attitude to history represents something entirely new compared with that of Judaism.

3. WORLD HISTORY

We can deal with this aspect only in passing. For Luke's attitude to world history reference is usually made to the

---

44; Acts xxvi, 22 f.), but we must stress that in Luke's form of the story of the Transfiguration there is no suggestion of any typology between Jesus and Moses or Elijah, for they both appear exclusively as messengers. If we relate Deut. xviii, 15, 18 to Christ (Acts iii, 22 f.; vii, 37), then there is admittedly a suggestion of typology; but Luke has simply taken it over from the tradition without reflecting on it.

The story of the Transfiguration in itself is reminiscent of Moses' ascent of the mountain of God. It is true that Luke has effectively employed the mountain—symbolism (cf. *ZThK*, 49, 1952, pp. 16 ff.); it is therefore all the more remarkable that he does not do this in association with a Moses typology, but in connection with his own development of the symbolism of the lake. And if the story of the Feeding of the Five Thousand was meant to reveal Jesus as the new Moses (cf. J. Jeremias in *TW*), then Luke was not aware of it, as his setting of the story in Bethsaida shows.

[1] The following traditional motifs can be traced in Luke: Luke ix, 7 f., where it is Jesus' miracles that seem to give rise to the identification, and Luke vii, 27, with the alternation of 'my' and 'thy' in the quotation. Luke's aim, however, does not lead him to accept the tradition, but to reject it. There is no 'forerunner' in the special sense either before the coming of Jesus or before the future Parousia. The Parousia comes 'suddenly'. Although John announces the coming of Jesus, he has no essentially higher status than the other prophets. This also affects the conception of Elijah. Cf. in particular the exclusion from Mark ix, 11 f., of the idea that Elijah must come first. His eschatological function, that of ἀποκατάστασις, is also excluded by Luke. On this point, cf. especially Bauernfeind, on Acts iii, 20 ff. and Acts i, 6.

167

statement in Luke iii, 1, but we must beware of reading too much into this verse. It is true that a synchronism of world history is given, by means of which Jesus is allotted a definite point in time, but there is no suggestion of a particular conception of this point as an exceptional 'hour' in the history of the world. There is no trace of a 'theology of history' as a comprehensive view of world history as a whole. This allotting of Jesus to a definite point in time is in harmony with the fact that the 'today' of Luke iv, 18 ff. belongs to the past and is now described as a historical phenomenon. There is no other view of history in iii, 1 than that implicit in the view of redemptive history which prevails throughout Luke.[1]

On the other hand, there is one passage, the Areopagus speech, which takes world history as one of its themes. Here Luke is concerned not only with the past of the Church; the horizon reaches right back to the Creation and includes all nations,[2] but his survey is strictly related to the missionary situation. Luke provides the basis for the missionary appeal with the ideas of the Creation (the past), of God's dominion over the world (the present) and of the Judgement (the future). There is no question of a speculative development. No concept of world history is developed, nor are the periods into which it is divided set out. Of itself it does not imply salvation or disaster. Jesus' place in it is not one that can be demonstrated as part of a

---

[1] As N. A. Dahl correctly points out, 'It is not historical circumstances, but the creative Word, that effects the continuity of history.' (*Th.R.*, N.F. 22, 1954, pp. 35 f.)

[2] For the interpretation, particularly of the philosophica lcontext, cf. the comprehensive analysis by Dibelius, 'Paulus auf dem Areopag', now included in *Aufsätze*, pp. 29 ff.

Since the first edition the following have appeared: W. Eltester, 'Gott und die Natur in der Areopagrede', *Ntl. Studien für Bultmann*, 1954, pp. 202 ff.; ibid., 'Schöpfungsoffenbarung und natürliche Theologie im frühen Christentum', *NTSt*, 3, 1957, pp. 93 ff.; B. Gärtner, *The Areopagus Speech and Natural Revelation*, 1955; W. Nauck, 'Die Tradition und Komposition der Areopagrede', *ZThK*, 53, 1956, pp. 11 ff.; H. Hommel, 'Neue Forschungen zur Areopagrede act 17', *ZNW*, 46, 1955, pp. 145 ff.; E. Schweizer, 'Zu den Reden der AG', *ThZ*, 13, 1957, pp. 1 ff.; F. Mussner, 'Einige Parallelen aus den Qumrantexten zur Areopagrede (Apg. xvii, 23–31)', *Bibl. Zeitschr.*, N.F. 1, 1957, pp. 125 ff.; H. Conzelmann, 'Die Rede des Paulus auf dem Areopag', *Gymnasium Helveticum*, 12, 1958, pp. 18 ff. In view of my demonstration that the Speech does not contain any division of world history into periods, I cannot understand how W. Eltester can assert that I trace in it a 'threefold historical pattern' (*Ntl. Studien für Bultmann*, p. 205, n. 6). On this matter, cf. Nauck, op. cit., p. 30.

system, but is a 'chance' one, as and when it pleases God. The fact of Jesus is not deduced, but proclaimed, and the reference to history serves to underline the summons and the proof, that now the time of ignorance is past and the will of God has been irrevocably declared, in a way that can be understood. Beyond this the theme of world history is not developed.

PART FOUR

The Centre of History

I. INTRODUCTION

Luke's Christology is set out as he unfolds the position of Christ in the centre of the story of salvation, a period which is described in Luke iv, 13 and xxii, 3 as one free from the activity of Satan. In it there occur the events, the significance of which is described in passages such as Luke iv, 18 ff. and xxii, 35 f. This 'centre' divides the first epoch, that of Israel, from the third and last epoch, that of the Church.

Of course the period of Jesus was considered before the time of Luke as in a special sense a time of salvation. Behind Luke iv, 18 ff. there stands an older tradition (cf. Mark ii, 19a, where a connection with the delay of the Parousia can already be traced). It is Luke, however, who sets the motif in its historical perspective. He deliberately takes the 'today' which is expressed in this passage as belonging to the past, and builds up the picture of Jesus' whole career on the basis of this historical interpretation.

II. GOD AND JESUS CHRIST

1. THE CHRISTOLOGICAL TITLES

We cannot deal with these at length, for the special elements in Luke's Christology cannot be set out by a statistical analysis of the titles applied to Jesus. It is characteristic of Luke that although he develops a Christology of his own, he is no longer aware of the original peculiarities of titles such as 'Son of Man', etc. He has taken them over from the tradition and interprets them according to his own conceptions. On one occasion he explicitly reflects on the way in which the meanings of the main terms contained in tradition are related (Luke xxii, 67–70). The train of thought here, in contrast to Mark, is such that the identity of meaning is made plain to the reader.[1]

In the main part of the Gospel and Acts the titles which are found most frequently are κύριος and χριστός. In Luke the latter preserves—or regains—to a considerable extent its character as a title. At the same time we should not read any cosmological reference into the title κύριος, such as there is, for example, in the hymn in Phil. ii, 6 ff. It is true that Jesus is Lord over the evil spirits, and over every power of the enemy, even in his life-time (Luke x, 18 ff.) but we are not to speculate on this position —cf. x, 20. From the isolated statement in Acts x, 36, which expresses a cosmological position, Luke himself draws no infer-ences. It is strange that in Luke the angels are not subject to the authority of Christ (see below). Here we see a significant dis-tinction between Father and Son, which implies the latter's subordination.[2]

---

[1] The promiscuous use of the titles does not of course mean that Luke has no preference for certain terms, but we should not place too great emphasis upon this when trying to ascertain his views. His tendency is to use the normal terminology of the Church.

[2] Among the details, we may mention that the use of 'Son of Man' is largely determined by the source (Mark). In Acts it occurs only once as a title, in vii, 56, where there is a close similarity with Luke xxii, 69, but in this latter passage we can note the difference from Mark. It is not possible to prove anything either for or against a specific 'Son of Man' Christology.

As is well known, the title 'Christ' is prominent in Acts, cf., e.g., Acts ii, 31, 36; iii, 18, 20; iv, 26; v, 42; viii, 5; ix, 22; xiii, 5, 28. A survey of these passages shows that one cannot trace this usage back to sources, but must ascribe it to Luke. Essentially this title does not represent the relationship between God and Jesus, but rather the connection between promise and fulfilment. We find it in a charac-teristic group of passages which provide the Scriptural proof for the suffering of the 'Messiah' (Acts xvii, 3; Luke xxiv, 26, 45 f. Cf. also Acts xxvi, 22 f., and finally Acts xviii, 5). This is evidently a fixed type of argument (cf. above, p. 153, n. 3). First of all the basic idea of the Messiah as such in Scripture is given, without any reference to the historical Jesus, the 'necessity' of his sufferings appearing as the main element in the idea. In the interpretation of this title, therefore, suffering plays a major part. The course of the argument therefore is that on the basis of this Scriptural evidence the similarity with the destiny of Jesus can be demon-strated, which proves the latter—precisely because of his Passion—to be the Messiah.

The other element contained in this title is seen in the important declaration, that God 'anointed' Jesus. There is evidence again of subordination, but the idea

THE CENTRE OF HISTORY

Luke takes over, either from tradition or from the language of the LXX, certain designations, which by their number constitute a special feature of his terminology: Jesus the prophet, the holy one, the righteous one, the παῖς. We can leave on one side the question, what Christological conception was originally expressed when these titles were applied to Jesus. In Luke they have already become traditional, and in his view they have the same meaning as the other titles, Christ and Lord. They might be of assistance in reconstructing the early stages in the development of Christology, but the fact that they occur in Luke only bears witness to his preference for Biblical and traditional terminology. We must not forget, however, that Luke interprets them in the light of his own conception.

The introductory chapters of the Gospel present a special problem. It is strange that the characteristic features they contain do not occur again either in the Gospel or in Acts. In certain passages there is a direct contradiction, as for example in the analogy between the Baptist and Jesus, which is emphasized in the early chapters, but deliberately avoided in the rest of the Gospel. Special motifs in these chapters, apart from the typology of John, are the part played by Mary and the virgin conception, the Davidic descent and Bethlehem. On the other hand there is agreement in the fact that the idea of pre-existence is missing.[1]

---

is not developed. The same idea is present, of course, in the story of the Baptism; cf. Acts iv, 27; x, 38; Luke iv, 18.

It is remarkable that 'Son of God' occurs only once in Acts (ix, 20, and viii, 37 var.); that this title, however, in spite of the statistical evidence, is of outstanding importance, is shown not only by the stories of the Baptism and of the Transfiguration, but also by the argument in Luke xxii, 67–70, where the train of thought reaches its climax with this title.

[1] Mary disappears to a greater extent in Luke than in Mark and Matthew. On Luke viii, 19 ff., see above, pp. 48 f. A polemical note is perceptible here. It is difficult to avoid the suspicion that Acts i, 14 is an interpolation. Mary and the birth play no part in the kerygma, nor does Acts i, 1 f., which defines the scope of the historical record, make any reference to them. Neither Luke xxii, 70 nor Acts xiii, 33 makes any mention of a connection between Jesus' status and his birth. Cf. on the other hand the emphasis on διό in Luke i, 35. No conclusions are drawn in the Gospel according to the genealogy from the Davidic descent. Luke xviii, 38 reproduces a title from Mark without drawing any inference from it. Luke xx, 41 is probably also taken by Luke in a polemical sense. The following references to David in Acts should be noted: i, 16 and ii, 25 f., where he appears in the function of a 'prophet' (this is in keeping with Luke's preference for the Psalms); in iv, 25, which contains a related idea, David is father, but of the whole people. Further passages are vii, 45; xiii, 34, 36; xv, 16. In ii, 25 ff., and xiii, 23

THE CENTRE OF HISTORY

2. FATHER, SON AND SPIRIT

The essential relation of Father and Son is not a subject that is explicitly considered, therefore there are no direct statements concerning it.[1] There is, however, a definite conception of it implied and assumed in Luke's account, which we have to deduce from indirect references.

It is taken for granted in the tradition that God the Father has a position of superiority, and because of this the fact is not explicitly stated. There are functions which are attributed only to God. Only He appears as Creator (Acts iv, 24; xiv, 15; xvii, 24). There is no mention of the co-operation of a pre-existent 'Son', for the idea of pre-existence is completely lacking—an aspect of Luke's subordinationism. The plan of salvation is exclusively God's plan, as Acts i, 7 makes plain, and Jesus' function within it is that of an instrument.[2] God's pre-eminence can be seen in the curious fact that He alone has dominion over the angels.[3]

he is described as the forefather of Jesus, but without going beyond the traditional phrases. Luke does not link this idea with his own theological conceptions, although it is a theme which would have provided a most apt illustration of the continuity of redemptive history. We see here the same restraint that we noted earlier· where a question of principle is concerned, Luke refers only to Israel as such, not to individual figures in Biblical history. Where they appear, the reference is to their sayings, which are more important than their existence as persons.

[1] The negative reason is that the traditional idea of God is adopted without question, and Luke's affection for the Bible, and the extent to which he is influenced by the LXX, only serve to strengthen this. The positive reason is that the scheme of redemptive history also presupposes this subordinationism.

[2] The result of this is the special modification of the relationship in accordance with the pattern of redemptive history.

[3] The angel 'of the Lord' in Acts (v, 19; viii, 26; xii, 7 ff.) is always the angel of God (as in Luke xii, 8 f., and xv, 10). As indications of this we may note that, according to Luke iv, 10, the angels guard Jesus at God's command; this saying comes from Q, but Luke changes its significance, because he goes on to alter Mark i, 13: according to Luke the angels do not 'serve' Jesus. ($\delta\iota\alpha\kappa\sigma\nu\epsilon\hat{\iota}\nu$ is not used in Luke of supernatural subjects.) In any case, during his earthly life their 'service' is not necessary, because Satan is absent. After his return (xxii, 3), an angel appears (xxii, 43—assuming the longer text to be the original); but it appears 'from heaven' and is exclusively in God's service. Cf. Luke ix, 26 with Mark viii, 38: the Son possesses 'glory', but the angels belong to God alone. Cf. also Luke xii, 9 and Matt. x, 33. Mark xiii, 27 is omitted, for it is not Christ who has command of the angels. The angels do not 'come', but only Christ, as Luke ix, 26 shows; he comes in the glory of the angels, who remain with God in heaven, therefore there is no question of a rule of Christ over the heavenly powers even after his Ascension.

THE CENTRE OF HISTORY

The part played by Jesus in redemptive history and his status have no metaphysical basis, but are entirely the gift of God. God proclaimed or 'anointed' him as Son at the Baptism.[1] If the Son can baptize with the Spirit (Luke iii, 16) or, to be more exact, can pour out the Spirit (Luke xxiv, 49)—after his exaltation and not before—it is only because he has received the Spirit from the Father for this very purpose (Acts ii, 33).[2] The famous verse Acts ii, 36 in any case expresses a clear subordinationism, whatever may be the relation of Luke's interpretation of the saying to its original meaning.[3] All the three principal Christological titles, Christ, Lord and Son, signify in this respect the same facts. Whichever of them is used to express Jesus' position, his office appears as something conferred on him by God.

The same meaning is implied on the two occasions when Jesus is described as the Chosen One. This expression fits in particularly well with Luke's view of God's saving activity and shows how this view and the idea of subordination hang together.[4]

---

[1] Cf. above, p. 171, n. 2. We know from the absence of the idea of pre-existence that there is no idea of a physical divine nature in the title of 'Son'. Luke does not think in such categories at all. We can see this particularly in the story of the Baptism, which leads up to this title as its climax; the relationship is not thought of in physical categories, but in the light of the bestowal of the Spirit. In this respect Luke does not correct his source. In the analogous story of the Transfiguration he underlines the fact that the awareness of suffering is linked with Sonship, and in this way he harmonizes it with the sayings about suffering, which in other passages are set out in connection with the idea of Christ (see the note already referred to). On the special case of the Birth story, cf. Dibelius, *Jungfrauensohn und Krippenkind*, e.g., pp. 41 f.

[2] Cf. Acts v, 32, where the act of outpouring is described as an act of God. We shall consider later this alternation of statements about the rule of God and of Christ.

[3] On the question as to the original meaning of the sentence, cf. on the one hand Bauernfeind, *Apostelgeschichte*, p. 51, and on the other Kümmel, *Kirchenbegriff*, p. 11. Before excluding, on the basis of literary analysis, one of the two titles from the original text, one must bear in mind that the combination 'Lord and Christ' is derived from Scripture (Ps. ii, 1 f. LXX). Luke is aware of this connection, as Acts iv, 26 shows. It is clear that in Luke's sense the phrase includes the Messianic character of Jesus' earthly life. The wording does not allow us to distinguish in Luke's interpretation between Jesus' appointment as 'Christ' and as 'Lord' as between two different acts, as the use of the title Kyrios even in Jesus' lifetime shows. In the passage as it stands only the fact of the appointment is stressed, and nothing is said about the time of it (despite vv. 34 f., for v. 36 states the facts quite generally; the mention of the Resurrection and Ascension is connected not only with the preceding account of the kerygma, but also with the motif that from this time onwards the status of Jesus is inescapably manifest. See p. 177 below).

[4] In the first instance Jesus is described as 'Chosen One' in connection with the title of Son, and in the second instance with that of Christ. We see again the

The motif of Jesus at prayer, which has been stereotyped by Luke also indicates his subordinate position, an outstanding example being the scene in 'Gethsemane'. This will be more fully discussed later.[1]

The raising of Jesus from the dead is clearly not characterized as a 'resurrection', but as an act of 'being raised'.[2] The familiar kerygmatic formulae in Acts present the saving events in the form of a direct account of God's deeds; a striking example of this is in Acts ii, 22. The use of the passive in passages where Jesus appears as the subject of the sentence (e.g. ii, 33) is in keeping with this. Yet there is another turn of phrase to be noted, also in a kerygmatic context, in which the deeds of Jesus are described as such and considered as relatively autonomous.[3] We must look into the significance of this juxtaposition.

These two ways of speaking, according to which now God and now Jesus appears as the subject of the sayings, or as the actor, belong to a definite stage of development. Whereas at first, in the most primitive form of the kerygma, everything that took place through Christ was seen from the standpoint of God's intervention, in the course of development Jesus himself comes

promiscuous way the titles are used. We cannot go into the history of the tradition of the concept here.

Subordination is of course implied in the description of Jesus as παῖς; cf. Acts iii, 13, 26; iv, 27, 30. In iv, 27 the word is linked with the anointing, in iv, 30 it is used in connection with the deeds which God performs 'through the name of his holy Servant'; iii, 26 refers to the sending of Christ, and iii, 13 to his glorification. Besides revealing subordination, these passages also reveal the positive purpose and status of Jesus as a factor in the saving events. The two aspects of course correspond, and cannot be separated from one another, for the whole account of Christology is not based on abstract considerations, but is a description of the actual saving events.

The connection with the Servant of the Lord in Second Isaiah is not brought out; in particular, there is no suggestion of 'substitution' in this title, as Cadbury rightly affirms (*Beginnings*, 5, p. 366). It is not even present where Luke quotes Isaiah 53.

[1] Prayer is closely connected with the Spirit, and reveals the same relationship of subordination and distinction as the latter. See below.

[2] Here we can simply refer to the essay by H. Braun: 'Zur Terminologie der Acta von der Auferstehung Jesu', *ThLZ*, 77, 1952, pp. 533–6. He stresses that the usual Christian term 'to rise' is rare in Luke. We can go further than this, and point out that in the passages of a kerygmatic nature it is not found at all. Braun's conclusion is that 'It is in the careful use of the verbs that we can find the subordinationist implications of ἀνάστασις brought out.'

[3] Cf. ii, 22 with x, 38. Luke brings out the gist of the latter passage by developing his account into a systematic description of the 'life of Jesus' in its various stages.

to be seen and described as a figure in his own right, as a phenomenon in redemptive history. At the same time the style of the summary reports naturally changes. The expansion of the kerygma and the separate stories about Jesus into a Gospel and ultimately the growth of the Gospel from Mark to Luke belong to this same development. Yet even where Jesus is the subject of a sentence, the subordination remains; a clear example can be seen in the connection between Acts x, 38a and 38b.

From this we see that the status of Jesus is something that is bestowed upon him entirely by God. It expresses on the one hand his subjection to God, and on the other hand his special pre-eminence in relation to the world. From whichever angle the figure of Jesus is considered, there emerge two series of sayings, the juxtaposition of which is at first sight surprising. In the first we see the distinction between God and Christ, whereas in the second the two appear, as far as their activity is concerned, practically identical. On closer inspection both types of sayings are seen to spring from the same basic conception. The idea of the the distinction between God and Christ has not necessarily been thought out and developed, but there is the beginning of a process of development immediately the function of Jesus in God's saving work is defined. It was inevitable that this definition should take place. The longer the period of the Church in the world lasts, the greater becomes the need of a positive understanding of Jesus' ministry. And the longer the period lasts, the more clearly do the two elements in the description stand out: the ministry of the historical Jesus and the present ministry of the Ascended Lord, or in other words, the stronger does the tendency become to understand his past ministry by analogy with his ministry in the present.

For Luke Jesus is already on earth Christ, Son and Lord. In the use of the titles he makes no distinction between the historical figure and the Exalted Lord. What, then, is the meaning of 'exaltation'? The answer is found in the description of his rule in the present, and by reference to his future role as Judge.

It has often been pointed out that no real function of the Exalted Lord is expressed in Luke. The only relevant saying is the one to the effect that he is seated at the right hand of God and will one day appear as Judge. In fact, if we compare Luke and Paul, we see some radical differences. If, according to Paul, God has delegated to Christ the status of Lord, this means that Christ now exercises to the full extent the function of ruler. The idea of delegation helps to solve the problem which is so difficult for the Jew, as to how Jesus can be described and revered as 'Lord'. Luke, on the other hand, is not aware of this problem. It presents no difficulty to him to describe both God and Christ as 'Lord'. But is it not implied in this double use of the term, that in Luke also the Exalted Christ is active, even though in Luke's version it might present a different picture than in Paul's?

Luke gives definite sayings about the past, in so far as it is discernible, and about the future, in so far as it is known by prophecy; the subject on which he writes, in other words, is the past of Jesus and that of the Church. Sayings about the present can be found only in an indirect form. The Church of the present is conceived primarily in terms of the Spirit as an element belonging to redemptive history. The idea of the Spirit is not developed, but His activity is constantly in evidence. Similarly, no picture is given of the present ministry of the Exalted Lord, such as is possible—and is given by Luke—in the case of the historical Jesus; but again his activity appears constantly. It is presupposed when the community prays to him (as it is in Acts vii, 59), and above all when it acts 'in the name' of Christ.

The fact that redemptive history falls into certain clear divisions does not mean that the community of believers has no living contact with Christ in the present, and that it has instead merely a historically mediated knowledge of his past and future ministry. From the standpoint of the community, the Exalted Lord stands immediately by the side of God (the image of the session at the right hand of God has a real significance in regard to faith). It is the Exalted Lord who heals (Acts ix, 34), and he appears from Heaven to Paul. This is not considered by Luke as analogous to the Easter appearances, for it could happen again at any time.

As we have already pointed out, Christ shares with God the title of Lord, but at the same time his subordinate position is maintained as a matter of principle. This is made possible by the development of the idea of 'the name', which in Luke virtually replaces the traditional idea of the 'intercession' of the Exalted

177

Lord on our behalf.[1] The acts performed by virtue of the name are in conformity with what is recorded of the ministry of the historical Jesus, for it was this that set the pattern for the future. We can go so far as to say that to speak of the efficacy of the name is the specifically Lucan way of describing the presence of Christ.[2] In this name there is salvation (Acts iv, 12).The name effects healing (iii, 16). Therefore it is not without meaning to evoke it and to use it as a formula. When this formula is used God acts.[3] The whole content of the Christian message can be summed up as 'the Kingdom of God and the name of Jesus Christ' (viii, 12). It is necessary to be loyal to the name and to be ready to suffer for it (ix, 16; xv, 26). These sayings refer exclusively to salvation. There are no sayings about a general rule of Christ over the world, for this is reserved for God (Acts xvii, 22 ff.).

The deeds of God therefore are divided into two groups, those He does alone and directly, and those He performs through Christ. The first group includes His universal sovereignty and the execution of His plan of salvation. The second group includes the activities which concern the life of the Church, and which are delegated to Christ as Mediator. Among them are the deeds performed by virtue of the name, which have already been mentioned, and the sending of the Spirit. In connection with this latter event the relation becomes particularly clear if we place

[1] This is, of course, a basic theme in the Epistle to the Hebrews, but it is firmly established before this: Rom. v, 1; viii, 34. Cf. E. Fuchs, *Freiheit des Glaubens*, pp. 116 ff.

[2] In Luke the presence cannot be represented by the Spirit, for as a factor in redemptive history the Spirit is allotted a definite place. One cannot, of course, infer the presence of the 'person' of Christ. It is precisely because the person is in Heaven that mediation by the name is necessary. Similarly, the relationship with Christ is not a mystical one; it is determined by confession of faith (Acts iv, 12), the invocation of the name and acting by the power of the name (cf. the whole context of Acts iii and iv). On the conception of the Spirit, cf. now, in addition to Barrett, the important article '$\pi\nu\epsilon\hat{\upsilon}\mu\alpha$' by E. Schweizer in TW, VI, pp. 387 ff.

[3] Among the consequences are the following: miracles (Acts iii, 6; iv, 7, 10, 30), deliverance (iv, 12), forgiveness (x, 43), and exorcism (xix, 13). If we add to these iii, 16 and the passages about confession of faith and suffering (ix, 16, 27; xv, 26; xxi, 13; viii, 12) we see that the whole realization of faith is linked with the conception of the name. The account in Acts xix, 11 ff. shows how magical ideas are deliberately avoided. Acts iv, 30 shows how carefully the Christological considerations are thought out in this connection: the one who ultimately effects these deeds is God. But He acts 'through the name'. It is in the light of the part played by the idea of the name that the present function of Christ is to be defined.

THE CENTRE OF HISTORY

ii, 33 and v, 32 side by side. As the community derives its understanding of Christ from the impressions it receives in its own
experience, from this point of view God and Christ are so close
together that the statements about the part played by the one
and by the other are not sharply distinguished, for it would
serve no purpose to do so.

We have already remarked that in the use of titles Luke
makes no distinction between the historical and the Exalted
Christ.[1] Yet such a distinction is worked out in respect of the relationship of Christ to the Spirit before and after his exaltation.[2]

The complex of events, Resurrection—Ascension—Pentecost,
forms a clear division between two epochs. Before his exaltation
Christ is the only bearer of the Spirit, but in a special sense, for
he is not under the Spirit, as we shall see. His endowment with
the Spirit is differentiated from the later outpouring upon the
community by the very manner in which the Spirit appears: He
comes to him in 'bodily form'. Jesus is not baptized 'with fire',
as is the community. On the other hand, he is not yet empowered
to bestow the Spirit during his lifetime.[3]

[1] Nor does Luke seem to suggest that there is any difference in Jesus' knowledge of ultimate things before and after the Resurrection or the Ascension. There
is no mention in Luke of limitations such as in Mark xiii, 32. Acts i, 7 shows the
significance of this omission. It is worth noting that in this context there is an
indication of the difference between Jesus and the Father: it is He who has ordered
the event, but the Son has knowledge of it. This is implied in the way in which
Jesus answers. Above all, a knowledge of eschatology is assumed in the whole
apocalyptic teaching (Luke xvii, 22 ff.; Luke xxi). Luke has to explain why, on
the one hand, Jesus taught so much about the Last Things and, on the other hand,
remained silent concerning the time. Here we see again the connection with the
problem facing the Church.

If we consider Acts i, 7 together with the omission of Mark xiii, 32, we see
that in this respect Luke does not bring out any difference between Jesus' earlier
knowledge and the knowledge he has now. It is worth noting the significance
which Luke xxi, 32 gains by virtue of the omission.

[2] In this connection mention should be made of the account by v. Baer, who
brings out the difference between the two epochs of salvation by reference to the
theme of the Spirit. The relationship of Jesus to the Spirit in particular is com-
prehensively set out by Barrett (see Bibliography), to whose study we shall make
repeated reference in the following section.

[3] I owe an interesting suggestion in this connection to G. Bornkamm. He points
out the curious position of the logion in Luke xii, 10 in the context (i.e. following
upon vv. 8 f.—cf. Mark and Matthew), and asks whether it might not be that
blasphemy against the Son is forgivable according to Luke because it is not until
Pentecost that it is plainly revealed who he is. This fits in well with the motif
discussed earlier (pp. 139 ff.), that of the time of ignorance, as a ground for
excuse.

179

THE CENTRE OF HISTORY

Luke gives his own stamp to the story of the Baptism. The Spirit comes in answer to prayer. How far removed this is from John's baptism is emphasized more than in Mark. It is well known how large a part is played by the motif of prayer in Luke. The three scenes which mark the main stages in Jesus' ministry —the Baptism, the Transfiguration and the Agony in the Garden—are assimilated to one another. On each of the three occasions a heavenly revelation is depicted as the answer to prayer. In the passage we are considering the motif of the Spirit and that of prayer are linked together and both indicate the same two-fold relationship of Jesus to God and to the world, that of subordination and pre-eminence.

It is made plain time after time that Jesus is a bearer of the Spirit. It is true that the statement that he is 'full of the Spirit' does not of itself set him apart from believers,[1] but the actual description which Luke gives does make a very emphatic distinction. If we compare Luke iv, 1 and iv, 14 with Mark i, 12 we see that any suggestion which might be understood to mean that Christ is subordinate to the Spirit is avoided.[2] If immediately afterwards in iv, 18 ff. in his account of the Messianic programme Luke refers back to the 'anointing', it is because the Spirit is considered to be the essential presupposition for the special Messianic ministry (cf. Acts x, 38).

In the description of Jesus as bearer of the Spirit there is implied his relation to the powers of the world. It is not accidental that it is in the story of the Temptation that Luke emphasizes the relationship between Jesus and the Spirit. It is in the encounter with Satan that the endowment with the Spirit is made manifest, and Satan has to yield. At the same time we see what constitutes the redemptive character of that period free from Satan which is now beginning.

---

[1] Barrett, p. 101: 'It is important to observe that Luke describes Jesus in the same terms as the apostles, whom he portrays as inspired teachers and miracle-workers.' Cf. Luke iv, 1 with Acts vi, 3, 5; vii, 55; xi, 24. However, we must not overlook the qualitative distinction. For one thing, Jesus is in his time the only bearer of the Spirit. He has received the Spirit in a different way from the community. It is said only of him that he was 'anointed' (Acts x, 38; iv, 27; Luke iv, 18). Finally, the phrase 'in the power of the Spirit' is used only of him (Luke iv, 14; x, 21). It should be noted also that in xx, 42, where in Mark the phrase is used in connection with David, Luke replaces it by a reference to Scripture. He is evidently conscious of the difference between Jesus' inspired words and the statements of Scripture.

[2] Barrett (p. 101) stresses the fundamental significance of Luke iv, 14.

THE CENTRE OF HISTORY

The position of Jesus, as indicated by the Spirit, comes out clearly in the sayings concerning his ἐξουσία and δύναμις. The latter idea is expressly linked in Luke with the idea of the Spirit, whilst on the other hand ἐξουσία and δύναμις are closely connected. Barrett in particular has investigated these connections.[1]

We shall not go into the origins and different shades of meaning of these two ideas, but shall attempt to bring out the distinctiveness of Luke's usage. We can start from the formal distinction, that δύναμις stands primarily for actual, and ἐξουσία for potential power.[2] There is the additional nuance, that ἐξουσία stands for delegated authority.[3] We see this in Luke's particular usage. Apart from the occasional use in a secular sense, Mark and Matthew speak only of the authority of Jesus; for them the idea has a positive redemptive meaning.[4] In Luke on the contrary we find a more formal use. Only he speaks of the ἐξουσία of the adversary (Luke xii, 5).[5] In Luke xxii, 53 we read of the 'power of darkness',[6] and in Acts xxvi, 18 of the power of Satan.[7] In all these passages we can see the special nuance in Luke's doctrine of Satan: he makes it quite clear that Satan has been granted his power for a certain period, and in this sense he describes it as limited.[8] He gives an indication of this in the story of the Temptation,[9] where ἐξουσία signifies Satan's power over the world, but it is added that he does not possess it

[1] Especially pp. 69 ff. [2] Barrett, p. 78.
[3] We can see this in passages where the word is used in a secular sense, particularly in Luke vii, 8/Matt. vIii, 9 (from Q); for further examples of a secular use, cf. Mark xiii, 34; Luke xii, 11; xix, 17; xx, 20; xxiii, 7.
[4] In other words, they start from the positive account of the authority which God granted to Jesus in order that he might accomplish his saving work: Luke—in keeping with his subordinationism—thinks rather of a formal delegation. We have already shown the practical consequences of this.
[5] A comparison with Matt. x, 28 reveals the wider use of the word, which is characteristic of Luke.
[6] On the connection of this Lucan form with the particular motifs in his account of the Passion, cf. Dibelius, *Formgeschichte*, p. 202. All we are concerned with here is the special expression of Luke's doctrine of Satan, in that he ascribes an ἐξουσία to Satan as well, which Mark and Matthew avoid doing on principle.
[7] This passage has to be understood in connection with Luke's psychology of conversion. There are no cosmological implications.
[8] On Luke x, 19 where, it is true, δύναμις is referred to (see above), Barrett comments (p. 74): 'This is the power temporarily allowed by God to Satan.' He also refers to Luke iv, 6 and xxii, 53.
[9] Luke iv, 6. Its position between v. 1 and v. 14 should be noted.

181

in his own right. Therefore it is possible to escape from his power (Acts xxvi, 18). This sense is present also in Luke xxii, 53; this hour is Satan's only because it is granted to him, for in the last resort even he is only an instrument in God's plan, of which the Passion forms a part.

When we compare Mark vi, 7 and Luke ix, 1, we find that Luke has added the second concept and thus created one of his rhetorical duplications. What is the real relation between the two? In this particular verse they are used practically synonymously. The same is true of other passages, e.g. Luke iv, 36 (cf. Mark i, 27).[1] The similar passage Luke x, 19 also shows how closely the two words are associated. At first sight it seems that there is a distinction, in so far as the 'authority' which Jesus possesses and can impart seems to be superior to the 'power' of the enemy. This superiority is a fact, but it is not implied in the difference in meaning between these two concepts, for as we have seen, Luke speaks without hesitation also of the ἐξουσία of Satan.

If the two words partly overlap in Luke, the difference must nevertheless not be overlooked.[2] δύναμις stands for miraculous power[3] and for miracle itself.[4] From our point of view the most

[1] We see what is characteristically Lucan if we consider v. 32. Mark speaks of the power of the teaching itself, but Luke has a formal use of λόγος; the special nature of Jesus' word is purposely described in order to distinguish it from the usual word.

[2] For a detailed discussion of the various meanings, cf. Barrett, loc. cit.

[3] Luke adopts from Mark the conception of δύναμις as an inherent, constant possession of power: Mark v, 30/Luke viii, 46. On this idea, cf. Barrett, p. 75. Luke vi, 19, where it is introduced independently, shows how well it fits in with Luke's thought. For the whole conception we must compare the familiar passages Acts v, 15 and xix, 11 f., but here the word δύναμις is not used in this specific sense, as xix, 11 f. clearly shows. Here δύναμις is the deed, not the power to do the deed. (Cf. the next note.) The passages from Luke's Gospel which we have mentioned, e.g., ix, 1, have to be seen in their individual meaning; in this particular case it is not a transference of power as in viii, 46, but a delegation of definite functions. It should be noted that there is no account of any rite of transference, in particular no laying on of hands.

[4] Barrett thinks that Luke obviously avoids the use of δύναμις in the sense of miraculous deed (pp. 71 f.). The evidence he brings forward is not enough to confirm this. He points out that in Luke x, 13–15 the word occurs only once, whereas in the parallel passage Matt. xi, 20–3, it occurs three times. But v. 20 is an editorial creation by Matthew, and the same applies to vv. 23b and 24 (Klostermann, Lagrange). The passage shows therefore that Matthew extends the use of the word, not that Luke restricts it. Matt. vii, 22, as against Luke xiii, 26 f., is secondary (Bultmann, *Syn. Trad.*, p. 123). Mark vi, 2, 5 do not prove anything,

THE CENTRE OF HISTORY

important factor which differentiates the two words is the connection which is established between δύναμις and spirit. Here again we can see Luke's adaptation of tradition in the light of his conception of redemptive history. Barrett points out the eschatological context in which the word is found in Mark (Mark ix, 1; xiii, 26).[1] In Luke on the other hand—and only in Luke—the concept is linked with the Spirit (Luke iv, 14) and therefore no longer has an eschatological reference, but is associated with the historical ministry of Jesus and the present life of the Church.[2] Barrett correctly points out: 'that is, the third Evangelist seems to have regarded "power" as the energy of the Spirit, while the characteristic connotation of δύναμις in Mark is eschatological' (p. 77). We must bear in mind, however, the position of the Spirit in the historical scheme. We can see that Luke is thinking of the succession of epochs in his scheme when he places this Spirit-power combination at two special junctures: at the transition from the Temptation to the ministry (Luke iv, 14), and particularly at the transition from the Gospel to the Acts of the Apostles. Luke xxiv, 49 points forward to the events with which the second book opens, in particular to the story of Pentecost.[3]

as Luke is not reproducing Mark at this point. It is true that Mark ix, 39 does not correspond to Luke ix, 50. The reason, however, does not lie in the use of δύναμις, but in the whole trend of thought that is expressed here. The same is true of Mark vi, 14/Luke ix, 7. Luke xix, 37—which Barrett considers an exception—shows that the difficulty does not lie in the use of δύναμις in the sense of miracle. The verse is an editorial creation by Luke in a prominent passage, the scene of manifestation which opens the third section of Jesus' course. In the background is Luke's idea that with the transition to the Temple Jesus' miracles cease, therefore it is possible to look back to 'all the mighty works'. D and Syriac fail to see this and alter it so that the 'seeing' refers to the event that is now taking place. Barrett fails to take into account particularly the linguistic usage of Acts (ii, 22; viii, 13; xix, 11). He correctly points out that Luke no longer takes δύναμις as a paraphrase for the Divine name (cf. Luke xxii, 69 with Mark xiv, 62).

[1] p. 73. Mark ix, 1 has been altered in Luke ix, 27 on account of its eschatological statement. Luke could accept Mark xiii, 26, but in the following verse had to omit the statement about the angels. The account of the Ascension in Acts i, 9, 11, where the analogy between the Ascension and the Parousia is clearly expressed, explains why he changes clouds to the singular.

[2] The two passages in the prologue, Luke i, 17 and i, 35, represent a special case of the use of 'Spirit' and 'power'. Here the two are practically identical. Cf. Barrett, p. 76. One could come to the same conclusion by comparing Luke iv, 18 with Luke v, 17. Barrett (loc. cit.) points out the danger, however, of pressing this too far.

[3] The reference back to Luke xxiv, 49 in Acts i, 8 and the linking of both

183

The conception of the Spirit therefore contains on the one hand a definition of the relationship of Jesus to the Father;[1] even more, however, it serves to describe his position in the world, or, to be more precise, in redemptive history, which includes his relationship with the Church. Here again the period of Jesus appears as a redemptive epoch of a unique kind, in which the Spirit rests upon one person only.[2] This uniqueness is underlined still more by the fact that between the Ascension and Pentecost there is an interval without the Spirit (see Baer, pp. 77 ff.). Thus the Spirit enables us to see on the one hand the individuality of Jesus, his position in the centre of redemptive history, and on the other hand the continuity between him and the Church, or in other words the positive link with the present.

In conclusion, we may say that there is no systematic consideration of the ontological relationship of Father and Son. We find a clear subordinationism, which derives from tradition and is in harmony with Luke's view of history. Jesus is the instrument of God, who alone determines the plan of salvation. From the point of view of the community, however, the work of Jesus seems completely identical with that of the Father, therefore both can be designated as 'Lord' and can be represented as the instigator of the saving events which the community now experiences. In so far as there is need of a working compromise, it is met by the concept of the name. Luke finds the latter already in use, but he develops it in his own way.

The relationship of Father and Son also is seen primarily from the standpoint of the sequence of redemptive history, as are all the central themes in Luke's thought. It is this that gives the various concepts their unity. The position of Jesus is differentiated according to the stages of his life right up to his present session at the right hand of God and his future coming as Judge.

passages with the teaching about Jerusalem shows how consciously the literary continuity of the two books is achieved. The general overlapping of the specifically Lucan motifs from the end of the Gospel to the beginning of Acts is quite intentional.

[1] Cf. also Luke xix, 37, the praise of the Father for the δυνάμεις.

[2] We must also mention the linking of δύναμις with the motif of the Messianic protection, which Luke has in mind when Jesus sends out his disciples without equipment, i.e., in the section from Luke ix, 1 to x, 20.

III. THE CENTRE OF HISTORY

1. THE PLACE OF JESUS IN HISTORY

One negative fact must be borne in mind from the first, that the place of Jesus in the course of redemptive history does not depend on any idea of pre-existence. On the other hand, the apocalyptic categories (e.g. that of the eschatological precursor) are excluded. In the foreground stands the definition of the relation to Israel and, of course, to the subsequent period of the Church.

According to Luke the whole of Jesus' ministry takes place within the region of Israel.[1] The continuity is maintained by a strict geographical pattern, which is entirely Luke's own creation. As John the Baptist appears only in the role of a prophet, there is a direct encounter between Jesus and Israel (Luke xvi, 16).[2] Jesus' ministry is a type of salvation (Luke iv, 18 ff.), but it has a temporal as well as an eternal meaning. The appearance of Jesus in Israel is on the one hand a typical foreshadowing of the future mission of the Church, and on the other hand also the historical basis of it.[3] Jesus is at one and the same time a particular historical figure and an eternal type. The historical continuity is seen in the fact that he builds on the foundation of the old call to repentance and then goes beyond it in his message of the Kingdom. Alongside this historical connection there is the typical one, according to which he appears as the supra-temporal 'fulfilment' and gives in his ministry a foretaste of the future Kingdom.[4]

[1] Lohmeyer, *Galiläa und Jerusalem*, pp. 42 ff. Cf. the detailed evidence given in Part I above.

[2] It is not through John that this encounter takes place. He does not represent the 'arrival' of the new age, but serves to bring out the comparison between the old age and the new one which has come with Jesus.

[3] Cf. the analogies between the Gospel and Acts, which bring out the constant relationship between the two. On the other hand it is systematically brought out that the Church engages in missionary activity only in regions where Jesus did not work. This is how the relationship was interpreted historically.

[4] The addition to the requirements of the old Law does not consist in a 'new Law' or in evangelical counsels, but solely in the message of the Kingdom. So far as the call to repentance is concerned, the old law—rightly understood—is accepted. It remains valid, and is adequate (Luke xvi, 17—note the context). Cf. also the down-to-earth preaching of John the Baptist.

THE CENTRE OF HISTORY

Corresponding to the relation of Jesus to Israel is that of Israel to Jesus. Even John the Baptist's call to repentance leads to a split (Luke vii, 29 f.). It becomes clear that it is not simply the people as such that is the recipient of promise. The period of Jesus makes manifest the continuity and at the same time the split between the Jews and the people of God. The crisis comes to its climax in the Passion, to which God provides the answer of the Resurrection. Thus against the background of the ancient story of salvation the factors of the new period come to light, to which from now on the eyes of Jew and Gentile alike are directed—the Spirit and forgiveness.

2. The Life of Jesus as a Fact of History

As one no longer thinks of oneself as awaiting an imminent Parousia, but is aware of a future judgement as an indisputable fact, the figure of Jesus comes to be seen as belonging to past history. Both the Parousia and the life of Jesus are connected with the present, but a modification has clearly taken place as regards the early expectation. The connection of the Parousia with the present does not consist in the fact that it is near at hand, but in the fact that, whenever it takes place it will be of decisive importance one day in the future for everyone. But how is Jesus' connection with the present thought of?

The problem is, what did he leave behind when he went to Heaven? The answer in the first place is that the Spirit was poured forth. But to this we must add the transmission of his words and deeds. Therefore Jesus is present in a twofold way: as the living Lord in Heaven, and as a figure from the past by means of the picture of him presented by tradition.

According to this conception, the life of the community rests not only upon the acts of the Spirit, but also upon the acts of Jesus during his lifetime and upon his words. Because they are known, the latter continue to exert their influence in the present. This knowledge brings to light a present relationship as well as the historical one, in so far as one turns to his words, for they are a permanent norm, independent of time.[1] In the same way,

[1] We must note the different structure in two kinds of sayings, those which are occasional and those which are permanently valid. The meaning of the former is historically mediated, but the meaning of the latter is immediate. The difference

however, 'seeing' his acts and his fate has an 'immediate' impact upon the belief of the present. The first impulse to the development of Christology comes when the life of Jesus is looked at as a fact of history. We must consider also its connection with the Church of the present.

The fact that the meaning of Jesus' life is that it is an account of salvation results in a systematic unfolding of the account. The important thing is no longer simply to interpret the life of Jesus as one indivisible event, but to set out a series of happenings in a definite period of time. Thus Luke builds up the picture of the three stages through which the course of Jesus' life leads to the goal set by God's plan of salvation. Tradition supplies the material, but the structure is Luke's own creation. Corresponding to these three stages there are three aspects of Christology.

IV. THE LIFE OF JESUS

1. JESUS AND THE WORLD

If we wish to understand Luke's view of Jesus' relation to the world, we must draw the following distinctions, in accordance with the scheme of redemptive history:

(*a*) his position over the world today, seated at the right hand of God;
(*b*) the position he took up himself during his earthly life;
(*c*) his future position as Judge.

The account of his present position results from the unfolding of the actual faith which the community possesses, and the account of his future position is provided by eschatology. What

is partly expressed by the fact that in Luke's account the former are spoken privately, whereas the latter are spoken publicly.

Luke is able to reproduce the ethical sayings without alteration, but he has to adapt the eschatological sayings to the present outlook. He interprets the instructions to the disciples, which refer to the situation prevailing at the time, as historical, as, e.g., in Luke xxii, 35 f., where a new instruction, which replaces the old, is given for the age that is now dawning. This gives the old instruction a typological meaning.

The account of the events is based on a different process of interpretation. The alteration is that these events are now thought of as taking place at a time in the past. The classical example is the 'today' of Luke iv, 21.

THE CENTRE OF HISTORY

we must now consider is the position which, according to Luke's account, he himself assumed during his lifetime. His two-fold position as Lord of the Church and Lord of 'the world' is not explicitly worked out, but it is seen indirectly in the actual position which Jesus adopted over against the powers of the world, and it can be traced in the corresponding pattern of private and public statements.[1]

Jesus is Lord over the evil spirits.[2] His position as regards Satan has been described.[3] The latter is successfully repulsed in the Temptation and disappears for the period of the ministry.[4] The existing worldly powers, Romans and Jews, come into the foreground of the story, particularly in the Passion.[5] In both cases there is a combination of submission and sovereignty. Jesus submits to the Law—and thus provides a norm for his followers after his death—and accepts the political supremacy of the Emperor.[6] On the other hand, he describes himself as King before the representative of the Empire, and over against Israel claims the supremacy as Christ—Son of man—Son of God.[7]

---

[1] On this pattern, cf. *ZThK*, 1952, p. 24, n. 2.

[2] It should be noted, that Jesus confers power over evil spirits on the disciples before the outpouring of the Spirit (Luke x, 17–20).

[3] We noted earlier the constant motif, that Satan is shown as dependent. Jesus' relation to him has of course to be distinguished from his dependent relation to God.

[4] Therefore passages such as Luke xi, 17–23 do not mean that there is a constant conflict with Satan during Jesus' ministry; they have a symbolic meaning and are meant primarily to be a comfort to the Church of Luke's time, which knows that since the Passion of Jesus it is again subject to the attacks of Satan.

[5] We have shown in Part I how Luke recasts his sources to bring out the issues involved. Cf. also the account of his apologetic in Part III.

[6] For obedience to the Law, cf. xvi, 17 and xxi, 33. For submission to Caesar, cf. xx, 20 ff., where Luke follows Mark, but in xxiii, 2 he develops the motif further by making it a ground of accusation.

[7] Luke xxii, 67 ff. It should be noted that in the Passion Jesus' political relationship to the Empire is not explicitly discussed (cf. on the other hand John xviii, 33 ff.); the non-political character of his Kingship is tacitly assumed. The fact that Christians realize Christ's Lordship over the 'world' in no other way than by confessing it, is exactly in keeping with this (Luke xii, 11 f.; xxi, 12 ff.). We saw in Part III that Luke deliberately avoids a direct opposition to the Empire. As for the future, then of course in the times of the Gentiles (xxi, 24) the fate of the Empire too is sealed, but this does not affect the present dispute. Here there is a significant difference between Luke's approach and the fundamental attitude of apocalyptic, which makes what is to be said about the State from the point of view of the Parousia into a simple statement about it in the present. The underlying principle, which forms the background of Luke's thought, is also seen in the interesting passage iv, 6b.

THE CENTRE OF HISTORY

The explanation of this difference is to be found in the fact that his Kingship becomes manifest in his supremacy over the Temple of which he takes possession; he exercises his supremacy by teaching, firstly about the Law, but also about his future position at the Parousia. Thus his Kingship does not stand opposed to the Empire on the political plane, yet it implies the claim to supremacy over the world, a claim which is made by the proclamation of the Kingdom of God. His sovereignty is not in contradiction with his submission to God's law, but represents the fulfilment of it.

In the nature of the case the relationship with Israel plays a greater part than that with Rome. We must bear in mind the fact already mentioned more than once, that as a matter of principle Jesus restricts his ministry to the sphere of his own people.[1] This limitation has of course to be considered along with the universalist tendency in the Acts of the Apostles. It is a result of dividing the story of salvation into successive stages and represents a deliberate plan running through the account. This limitation which we find in the Gospel is the presupposition for the universalism of the period after the Ascension. Thus Israel is the model for the universal Church. This is seen again in the course of the mission, which starts from Jerusalem,[2] spreads out via Samaria and extends right to the ends of the world. It is also seen in the fact that the synagogue is the regular starting-point in the Pauline mission. This pattern Israel-Church is therefore already present in the life of Jesus.

Although Jesus restricts himself to Jewish territory, he covers it all from the beginning of his ministry.[3]

---

[1] Cf. Lohmeyer, *Galiläa und Jerusalem*, pp. 42 ff., and the evidence in Part I and in *ZThK*, loc. cit.

[2] When Luke speaks of the 'arché' in Jerusalem (Luke xxiv, 47; Acts i, 4–8), it has not just a historical significance, but concerns basic principles.

[3] Luke iv, 44. For the justification of the reading 'Judæa', see pp. 40 f. above. In connection with this pattern linking geography and redemptive history, Lohmeyer correctly points out that in Acts Galilee practically disappears. There is no report of any activity there. But Lohmeyer fails to see the implications of his observation, because he mistakenly transposes the 'journey' to Samaria. The account is quite consistent: where Jesus has ministered cannot afterwards be a region for missionary activity. This is the case with Galilee. Jesus did not preach in Samaria, therefore the Church can engage in missionary work there. If the 'journey' were in Samaria, not only would the account in Acts be thrown into confusion but also that in the Gospel, for the restriction of Jesus to Jewish territory would then be broken down.

Jesus' relation to the synagogue also belongs to this pattern. His appearances in the synagogue are set out more systematically than in Mark.[1] A further type is thereby created for the Christian mission. Jesus' relation to Scripture is presented in a similar way.[2] The climax of the dispute with the Jews comes of course with his entry into the Temple.

Whereas this brings out the continuity between Jesus and Israel, it is the Passion which causes the break, not of course as a summary rejection of all Jews, but so as to face every individual with the question whether he will belong in the future to the true or the false Israel. In so far as Israel does not believe, she forfeits her redemptive vocation. It is not until this point in the course of events that the step beyond Judaism is taken; but the dispute is repeated at every place to which the mission extends.[3]

2. Jesus' Life and Teaching

It is significant how Luke on the one hand and Matthew on the other adapt their source—Mark—at the beginning of their respective Gospels. Matthew deliberately places first the basic teaching of Jesus, and it is preceded only by those events which provide the necessary foundation for the account of Jesus' teaching ministry. It is true that Luke also places at the beginning an introductory sermon, yet he does not give any details, but a brief summary of the ministry. Then, before the first call and before any detailed teaching, there follows the miracle which demonstrates his authority. In the account in Luke iv, 16 ff., and also in the rest of the narrative, it is Jesus' deeds which prove that Scripture is being fulfilled.[4]

What is described in Matthew (vii, 28; viii, 1) as the result of preaching, is in Luke the result of Jesus' coming, which

---

[1] Luke iv, 16: 'as his custom was'.

[2] In the 'programme' in iv, 18 ff. Jesus takes Scripture and applies it to himself. The Risen Lord quotes proofs from Scripture (xxiv, 25 ff.). We must also bear in mind the actual part played by Scripture in Luke.

[3] Cf. Acts xiii, 46; xviii, 6; xxviii, 28, where the 'last word' is spoken to the Jews.

[4] It is to the deeds that the people of Nazareth will react in the future (Luke iv, 23).

THE CENTRE OF HISTORY

manifests itself by deeds.[1] He gives the first report of success in iv, 37, after a miracle. Although the wording is the same as in Mark, the significance of it is different in Luke, for he has altered the position of the preceding scene, Mark i, 16–20, which in Mark serves to demonstrate the mighty effect of the word.

Whereas in Mark the call of the Twelve is the beginning, which prepares the way for Jesus' public appearance, and Jesus needs no credentials because his word has power, Luke recounts the calls in passages which are preceded by the evidence of miracles. Before the first call (v, 1–11) comes a definite miracle of revelation, and the second one follows after the ministry of Jesus has already become widely known. Here again, therefore, the call is the outcome of the ministry. It is the two together that prepare the way for the Sermon on the Plain, the position of which, when compared with the position of the Sermon in Matthew, reveals how great is the difference in the underlying conception.

In a later passage, vii, 18–23, we find the characteristic Lucan form of the report of John the Baptist's question. Whereas in Matthew it follows the mission charge, in Luke it is preceded by two miracles, in which there appears a characteristic variation in Luke's interpretation of miracle. In the one case the miracle has demonstrative power (vii, 16 f.), but in the other it is received by faith (vii, 9). When signs are demanded, they are refused (see below). Both aspects are to be found in the passage vii, 18–23, and one of them derives from Q: the former of the two, however, is introduced by Luke (v. 21). In this editorial verse Jesus, according to Luke, performs miracles as a proof.[2] By means of this interpolation Luke provides an illustration of the programme set out in iv, 18 ff.; the two passages contain echoes of one another and Luke makes the most of this comparison.[3] The purpose of the miraculous proof is that of

[1] Thus the traditional expression ποιεῖν καὶ διδάσκειν (Mark vi, 30; Matt. v, 19) gains its special significance in Luke: Jesus is δυνατὸς ἐν ἔργῳ καὶ λόγῳ (Luke xxiv, 19—note the order; cf. Acts vii, 22, where we find the reverse order: ἐν λόγῳ καὶ ἔργῳ, but this time referring to Moses). It is put even more sharply in Acts ii, 22.

[2] In other words, Jesus answers John's question positively.

[3] The mention of raising from the dead, which comes from the tradition, contains an echo of course of the preceding narrative.

191

vindication.[1] In v. 22 we find the phrase 'what you have seen and heard', but according to v. 21 they have only seen. The explanation is that the tradition here mentions the good tidings for the poor, in harmony with iv, 18 ff. Besides, the combination of seeing and hearing sounds like a stock phrase. We should beware of attaching too much importance to such phrases, nor should we deduce too much from the fact that seeing is placed first (the reverse in Matthew), particularly as in Acts viii, 6 we find the reverse order (and on the other hand in Matt. xiii, 16 seeing comes first, and also of course in the tradition). Nevertheless, there are in Luke passages which show that he does consider seeing more important than hearing, which corresponds exactly to the relative importance he attaches to Jesus' words and deeds.[2]

The part played by miracle in Luke is not adequately explained by reference to a 'seeking for wonders'. It is true that this is a feature of the age, which Luke shares, but we must not overlook the fact that he seeks to include the Christological aspect of miracle within the framework of his general conception. Jesus' deeds are for Luke the evidence of the time of salvation, which has 'arrived' with Christ. At the same time he points out the dangers of an unbridled seeking for wonders. The curiosity which wishes to 'see' Jesus (cf. Herod, Luke ix, 9, whose desire is fulfilled in xxiii, 8, and Jesus' relatives, iiiv, 19 ff.) is not satisfied. This sense of 'seeing', which is peculiar to Luke, must also be borne in mind. When one demands signs, the only answer one receives is the preaching of repentance (Luke x2 9 ff.).[3]

---

[1] But it has clear limitations; Luke also reproduces in v. 23 the word of warning about the 'skandalon'.

[2] The same phrase as in Luke vii, 22 occurs also in Acts ii, 33 and iv, 20. It is strange that in Acts ii, 33 Kittel finds hearing 'almost' given the priority over seeing (*TW*, I, p. 216). It is true, as we have said, that we cannot draw conclusions as to the meaning merely from the order of the words, but there are sufficient indications in Luke that for him seeing comes first. In Acts xxii, 14 f., the order is of real significance and in Acts xiii, 12 seeing and believing are vitally linked. Cf. the results, as set out in Acts ii, 7, iii, 12 and iv, 13. Cf. also the passages which speak only of seeing: Luke x, 23; xix, 37; Acts viii, 13 (following on v. 6); xiv, 11; xxvi, 16.

In this connection we must bear in mind Luke's idea of the Kingdom of God and the relation of Jesus' ministry to it: in Jesus' deeds we see an image of salvation. In his teaching the Kingdom is proclaimed, in other words, the nature of what he does is interpreted. This again means that what he does comes first. The sayings about 'seeing the Kingdom' are a proof of this.

[3] It should be noted that it is in Luke's version that we find this. Barrett, p. 90.

THE CENTRE OF HISTORY

What emerges is as follows: the sign is given—it cannot be demanded. Its purpose is to bear witness and to prove—but it is misunderstood.[1] In particular, the distinction between Jesus and the Church is carefully brought out.[2]

3. JESUS' MINISTRY

It is well known, and needs no further proof at this point, that Luke divides the ministry of Jesus into three phases.[3] He adds to the temporal scheme a geographical scheme, which at the same time has an underlying Christological significance.[4] The scene of manifestation, which introduces each phase, Baptism—Transfiguration—Entry into Jerusalem, is fundamental for the understanding of the three phases.[5]

---

[1] Barrett, pp. 88 ff., brings this out very well. P. 89: '. . . the miracles are understandable and ought to be understood, and yet are misunderstood.' In this connection Barrett points to the story of the Temptation (p. 91): 'It is enough here to say, as is obvious enough, that the response of Jesus to Satan is quite in harmony with his later refusal to produce signs on request, and to point out that such a request for signs is regarded in the Gospel tradition as of a diabolical origin.' Finally he refers to the warning in Luke x, 20.

[2] The idea of miracle is of course no different, and at important points miracles take place in the Church as well, but then they have not the outstanding importance of being characteristic of a whole 'period'. It should be borne in mind that since the Resurrection it is miracles that corroborate the message, but even this gives them only a secondary importance. This has to be taken into account when considering passages such as Acts v, 15 and xix, 11 f. Of course we cannot dispute Luke's 'seeking for wonders', which produces results such as Acts xxviii, 6. But it has to be understood against the background of his general conception, in which there are elements which keep such things under control. On the view of miracles in the ancient world, cf. R. M. Grant, *Miracle and Natural Law in Graeco-Roman and Early Christian Thought*, 1952; G. Delling, 'Zur Beurteilung des Wunders durch die Antike,' Wissenschaftliche Zeitschrift der Ernst Moritz Arndt-Universität, Greifswald', Gesellschafts-und sprachwissenschaftliche Reihe, V, 1955/56, pp. 221 ff.

[3] In this section reference should be made to the detailed discussion in Part I.

[4] In Part I we attempted to show that the course of the 'journey' is through the same regions as the earlier 'travels', i.e. through Galilee and Judæa, and that what is new about the journey is not the change of place, but the manner in which Jesus proceeds, that is, conscious of Jerusalem as the goal, or in other words, conscious of the suffering that awaits him. This consciousness of suffering appears as something implicit in the 'journeying'. It is easy for Luke to use this kind of symbolism, of course, as he has no personal knowledge of Palestine (the attempts to prove the opposite have all been unsuccessful).

[5] We can only mention in passing that in the present structure the birth story is inserted before the account of the Baptism, and as regards its significance it is in fact a doublet. In the structure as it stands the birth story does not introduce one

193

THE CENTRE OF HISTORY

The Baptism reveals Jesus to the reader as 'Son of God'. As the importance of the Baptism itself has been reduced by Luke, the voice from Heaven which makes the proclamation stands out all the more. In this way the meaning of the travels in Galilee and Judæa which follow is indicated. Right at the beginning, the episode in Luke iv, 16 ff. sums up the purpose of the travels and unfolds the Messianic programme in which the significance of the underlying theme of the story of the Baptism is brought out by the mention of the 'anointing'. The factor of the 'Spirit' has already come into play, for He is the condition for the repulse of the Tempter. As Luke thus immediately links the Temptation with the Passion, a wider prospect opens right at the beginning.

It is with this sign that Jesus' course 'begins'. Against the background of the whole story the first stage, that of the itinerant preaching, has a twofold function: the Kingdom of God is proclaimed to the whole of Israel, and in this way the decision is demanded, which will later be made in Jerusalem. Secondly, it is in this period that the 'witnesses' are assembled, who, according to Acts i, 21, must be witnesses of the whole ministry 'from the beginning'. The separate events of this period are depicted with the aid of traditional material. Mark and Q are the main sources, and even the detailed arrangement is not original. It follows Mark, and adds further material. The originality lies rather in the relation of this period as a whole to the two phases which follow. We see in it the outworking of what is in Jesus' mind, as set out in iv, 18 ff. on the basis of Scripture: the good tidings for the poor, deliverance for the captives, sight for the blind, in other words, fulfilment, salvation, 'today'.

of the three phases, but forms a preliminary scene of manifestation for the whole of the Gospel. As we are concerned with the divisions within the ministry of Jesus, we have to start from the sequence of the three scenes of manifestation we have mentioned. The most conspicuous element in Luke's account, that of Jesus' development during the course of his life, depends on this sequence.

Occasionally we find suggestions of further divisions, e.g. iv, 40 f.—cf. vi, 19/ Mark iii, 11. The exorcisms are omitted, and they do not come until later (viii, 26 ff.—in 'foreign' parts). Then follows immediately the conferring of power upon the disciples. Luke xi, 53 contains a new interpolation which emphasizes the note of active hostility. But these are isolated motifs, which are not linked together according to an overall plan.

There is a systematic structure already in Mark, but Luke does not adopt it (on this, cf. ZThK, loc. cit.). What is particularly lacking in Mark is the element of 'development', of a series of psychological stages in Jesus' understanding of himself.

THE CENTRE OF HISTORY

The divisions into which redemptive history falls prove that this 'today' does not extend into the present in which the author lives, but is thought of as a time in the past. What is meant is not an eschatological fulfilment already being realized in the world, however much that may have been the original meaning of the passage, but the manifestation of salvation—real, unrestricted and effective—in a period strictly defined as to its beginning and end, and which now belongs to the past; but through the operation of the Spirit and the record it possesses of the period, the Church still enjoys its blessings. The tone in which Luke speaks of 'today' is anything but that of resignation. It would be a misunderstanding of him and of his eschatology if we were to deduce from his writings a note of resignation resulting from the delay of the Parousia. On the contrary, his whole mind is set on fulfilment, and the outline he gives of the course of events has this very meaning, that one should not surrender that fulfilment of Scripture that has already taken place to eschatological resignation. Luke makes the facts described in iv, 18 ff. independent of the time of the Parousia, by giving them a timeless validity. On the other hand, however, what takes place must be recognized as a unique event in time in order that in the interval one can find consolation in the fact of fulfilment. The present also, standing between the 'today' and the Parousia, is a time of salvation, although in a different sense from the period of Jesus.[1]

---

[1] Vielhauer, *Ev. Th.*, 1950/51, p. 13: 'The early expectation has disappeared, and the delay of the Parousia is no longer a problem.' This is quite correct, but it raises the further question: why is it no longer a problem? 'Luke replaces Paul's apocalyptic eschatology by the pattern of promise and fulfilment which emerges from redemptive history, in which pattern eschatology also has its appropriate place.' We must now consider what is characteristic in the Lucan form of this pattern, and the effect it has on the composition of the biography of Jesus.

If the present is determined by its position between the saving events of past and future, then naturally the pattern of the two advents suggests itself (even though the terminology of it has not yet been developed). Admittedly the Parousia is not yet described by analogy with the first 'appearing' on earth (rather by analogy with the Ascension—Acts i, 11), but the characterization of the present as an in-between time helps to suggest the idea. It should be noted that there is no trace of the typical features of the later Catholic conception, which is characterized in particular by the fact that by virtue of this in-between position man can be held suspended between fear and hope. From the pedagogic point of view this is of the greatest assistance, but there is no evidence of it in Luke. His message is quite definite: the present is a time for hope, not psychological doubt, for it possesses the Spirit. The Catholic system virtually presupposes the absence of the Spirit in the

The complex of events formed by Peter's Confession—the prophecy of the Passion—the Transfiguration marks the next main division. Within this complex there are certain difficulties as regards the order, which are the result of the inadequacy of the available material, and of the fact that Luke has stamped on it his own pattern. The part it plays in the whole story becomes clear if we take the individual incidents as being linked in their meaning.[1] In Luke it is the Transfiguration that forms the climax both as regards the order of events and their inner meaning.[2]

In Mark also the Transfiguration contains the second direct proclamation from Heaven to Jesus. Luke, however, introduces a special motif, in that the scene serves to disclose what is involved in being the Son of God—i.e. it means being destined to suffer.[3] In this sense it is a paradoxical manifestation of glory. Thus the Passion is interpreted in advance, as a gateway to glory, not, as in Paul, as the saving event in a positive sense. The careful assimilation of the Transfiguration and the scene on the Mount of Olives proves that this is an example of conscious composition on Luke's part.[4]

individual Christian, however much it may emphasize the Spirit in theory, in the Church's means of grace.

This present age is for Luke still a secular one, but it is possible to withstand the world. This is good news. It is because the Christian hope is based upon redemptive history that the expectation of the temporal end of the world is not merely a traditional appendage, but an essential part of the hope.

[1] See pp. 55 ff. In spite of all the difficulties, it is plain that the complex formed by Peter's Confession, the prophecy of the Passion and the Transfiguration contains Luke's own conception of the Messiah, in particular the view that suffering is part of the very idea of Messiahship. Again, no distinction is drawn between the titles (Messiah and Son of God). On the vital connection between the journey and the Transfiguration, cf. Ramsey, *The Glory of God*, p. 79: the journey is 'a kind of royal progress'.

[2] Here Luke differs from Mark. Because of his conception of Messiahship, Mark places Peter's Confession in the foreground, Luke, because of his idea of suffering, the Transfiguration. On this subject in general, cf. Riesenfeld and Ramsey, who stresses the connection with the Passion, but does not differentiate sufficiently among the three Synoptics.

[3] This largely accounts for the uncertainty in the composition that we have already mentioned. One cannot of course attempt to discover what was the actual course of events, nor is it satisfactory merely to note the uncertainty, for it is this that shows to what lengths Luke has gone to introduce his motif, and at the same time brings to light the real purpose behind his account.

[4] The construction of a scene in two parts, made up of a communication to Jesus followed by the participation of the disciples, is also part of Luke's composition. Then there is the corresponding parallel formed by the Transfiguration story as a

It is now that the new section, 'the journey', begins. It has as
its goal the Passion, which means that the geographical destination is also fixed. From now on Jesus is 'journeying', but he
does not go by a short route to the city, as the source, Mark,
describes it. He travels according to a plan (Luke xiii, 31 ff.),
and in a definite space of time ('three days').[1]

The fact that the goal is fixed, and that there is no real change
of place for the major part of the period of the journey shows
that the latter is primarily symbolical, and is meant to express
the changed emphasis in Jesus' ministry.[2] In particular it
expresses Jesus' awareness that he must suffer. Once again,
traditional material is employed, and the way in which Jesus acts
is the same as in the preceding period. The new factor is that of
the unfolding of Jesus' nature as his ministry progresses stage
by stage. The original, apologetic demonstration that the
Passion is according to plan is expanded on a grand scale into a
picture of the whole activity of Jesus; thus the explicit confirmation of the 'inevitability' of the Passion emerges directly
from the Gospel account itself.[3]

When we see the real meaning of the journey, it solves the
problem, why Jesus 'journeys' in the same place in which he previously travelled, and why there is no trace of any progress from
place to place, right up to the end of the journey. The journey is
a pattern imposed by the editor, by means of which he expresses
his particular view of the ministry and nature of Jesus.[4]

This second period, like the first, begins with a rejection.
Luke's interpretation again finds expression in the way he emphasizes and alters the misunderstanding which Jesus meets in
his disciples. Again a Marcan motif is employed, but its meaning is altered by the fact that according to Luke it is not

whole and the scene with the people (which Luke makes possible by the omission
of Mark ix, 9 ff.). In the first half of the double scene Jesus speaks of his suffering, and in the second he speaks to the disciples of his nature in general.

[1] For two days he performs miracles, then the third day is the day of fulfilment.
This is in harmony with the fact that in Luke Jesus performs no miracles in the
third period. The saying shows that we must think of the journey as lasting a
considerable time.

[2] pp. 60 ff.

[3] We must not forget that Luke does not adopt the Pauline exegesis, and that
he does not develop a positive doctrine of the redemptive significance of the
Passion and the Cross.

[4] For the relation to the sources, see Part I, ad loc.

Messiahship that is misunderstood, but the suffering attaching to it. Luke ix, 45 and xviii, 34 show the extent to which Mark is altered.[1]

With the approach to Jerusalem, the 'royal' title comes to the foreground. In Luke xix, 38 it is expressed in the form of the acclamation at the Entry, more so than in Mark. Luke mentions the title quite openly. When he repeats it later at the trial before Pilate (xxiii, 3), then it is not a question of the first, paradoxical disclosure—paradoxical, that is, in view of the situation—but of the repetition of what has already been proclaimed before the whole of Jerusalem. Further, Luke has already hinted at the use of the title, for in xix, 11 he raises the problem of Kingship explicitly in connection with the problem of Jerusalem. Its political character is rejected, but the king motif as such is used in a positive sense in the parable which follows. Here again, as in the case of Peter's Confession, a scene of manifestation is interpreted in advance. Its full meaning then appears in v. 37 and its expansion in v. 38b. Verse 37 mentions in summary form 'all the mighty works' and thus marks the close of one epoch and the beginning of another. Verse 38b gives a hint of the transcendent character of Christ's role and of his future exaltation.

The fact that Jesus does not enter the city, but the Temple, is in keeping with the 'royal' manner of the Entry. Even in Luke Jesus' stay in the city is only brief; he does not go into it until the Supper, in other words as a prelude to the Passion. More emphatically than in Mark, Jerusalem is exclusively the scene of this one two-fold event; the Supper and the Passion. It is preceded, however, by the period of teaching in the Temple, a period which, although it is not closely defined, seems longer because of the abandonment of Mark's day by day account. This is the form in which Christ manifests his kingship on earth; but the future glory is proclaimed in the prophetic part of the teaching he gives.

[1] The misunderstanding in Luke is different from that in Mark; its significance is not psychological, but specifically Christological. In Mark the disclosure about the Passion is meant to prepare the disciples. This is the reason for the repetition of the saying. Cf. pp. 64 ff. During the first period in Luke, when according to Mark the Messianic secret is maintained, there is no mention of this secret. The misunderstanding is not seen until the special nature of Messiahship is revealed as that of suffering. The misunderstanding and the journey are based on the same factors, and serve to explain one another.

THE CENTRE OF HISTORY

The counterpart to the teaching by day is Jesus' praying on the Mount of Olives by night (xxi, 37 f., the wording of which suggests a fairly long stay). We can see a two-fold goal, to which Jesus' ministry has been leading: the goal of the journey is Kingship, in other words, the Temple, but the way to glory leads on to the Passion, in other words, into the city of Jerusalem. We shall see later how this connection influences the life of the early Church.

4. THE PASSION

The transition from the activity in the Temple to the Passion is marked, as we have already said, by Jesus' going into the city. The judgement on the city is much more pronounced than in Mark, by means of the sayings which provide the framework for the Passion in Luke (xix, 39 ff. and xxiii, 27 ff.). As early as xiii, 34 it was stated that the prophets die not only in, but through the agency of, Jerusalem. As Luke abandons Mark's day by day arrangement, in xxii, 1 he gives 'at the feast' as the time when the transition takes place.[1] We must bear this in mind when interpreting the account of the Last Supper, which however does not concern us here at least.[2] The symbolism of the anointing at Bethany is missing. Instead, the situation is characterized by the reappearance of Satan (xxii, 3). Thus a new period of 'temptation' begins (xxii, 28, 40, 46), which will continue after Jesus has gone. This fact forms the background of the sayings at the Supper, whatever may be one's view as to their origin and the degree to which they have been adapted by Luke.[3] Chapter xxii vv. 35 ff., mark the break, the transition to a new epoch, in which different conditions prevail than hitherto, for peace under the protection of Jesus is now a thing of the past. The disciples are exposed to temptation, but vv. 31 f. show that they are not deserted.

This idea of one period succeeding the next gives rise to a special feature in Luke's interpretation of the Supper, for he sees

---

[1] *ZThK*, 49, 1952, pp. 28 f.
[2] We assume the longer text to be the original one. Cf. Jeremias, *Abendmahlsworte*, pp. 75 ff.
[3] For a recent examination, cf. K. G. Kuhn, *ZThK*, 49, 1952, pp. 200 ff., and H. Schürmann (see p. 80).

it as something instituted in preparation for the period of conflict which is beginning. It represents the abiding benefits of Jesus' ministry for his disciples when the time comes for him to leave them. Their future temptations will always be surmounted by virtue of the fact that Jesus sits at the right hand of God, by their possession of the Spirit, and by their participation in the Supper. It is instituted in view of the fact that Satan is again present, and thus serves to remind the disciples both of their peril and of their protection, and it also appeals to their perseverance, which in turn is made possible by the sacrament. The immediate practical effect of the sacrament is indirectly expressed by the fact that Luke says nothing of a flight of the disciples; they 'continue' (xxii, 28). Thus the Supper in its Lucan context marks the imminent beginning of the period of the Passion, which is to be distinguished from the period in the Temple. It also symbolizes the abiding benefits of Jesus' ministry. This of course is not meant to imply that Luke interprets the Supper 'symbolically'.[1]

The elements peculiar to Luke's account of the Passion, the apologetic addressed to the Romans and the attitude to the Jews, have already been discussed. Together with the idea of the 'necessity' of the suffering, they represent the modifications which we note in Luke as compared with Mark, and which have given rise to various hypotheses concerning sources. Although the use of new material by Luke cannot be disputed, nevertheless the most important alterations are the result of Luke's editorial work and are the expression of his own views.[2]

---

[1] Luke xxii, 15 expresses Jesus' desire to eat the Passover, but it also suggests the thought that his suffering is voluntary. Is there here a tradition which was originally in opposition to the Gethsemane tradition? It is true that the scene in Gethsemane does not contradict the Church's view of a voluntary suffering (Dibelius, *ZNW*, 1931, pp. 193 ff.), but the emphasis in the two cases seems different. At the same time, vv. 15–18 establish the connection with the coming of the Kingdom. Originally they were an expression of the expectation of an imminent Parousia, but how Luke interpreted them, especially the enigmatic v. 16, is another matter.

[2] Surkau and Dibelius (*Formgeschichte*, pp. 200 ff.) correctly point out the martyr-motif in Luke's account of the Passion. But cf. Bertram, pp. 94 f., for the stylistic difference between the account of the Passion and that of a martyrdom. The main difference is that Jesus' suffering is according to plan. A comparison between Luke's narrative and his dialogue shows that he has not been able to blend all the motifs satisfactorily into a unity.

THE CENTRE OF HISTORY

The most important finding in this connection for our purpose is that there is no trace of any Passion mysticism, nor is any direct soteriological significance drawn from Jesus' suffering or death. There is no suggestion of a connection with the forgiveness of sins.[1]

This is rightly emphasized, e.g., by Dodd, *Apostolic Preaching*, p. 25; Cadbury, *The Making of Luke–Acts*, p. 280, *Beginnings*, 5, p. 366; and also by A. Seeberg, *Der Katechismus der Urchristenheit*, p. 132. For the contrary view, see Lohmeyer, *ThR*, 1937, p. 181. He refers to Acts viii, 32 f., and xx, 28, where he finds the idea of atonement in Luke. The first passage however is irrelevant. Lohmeyer reads the idea into the passage from the source which is quoted. It is in fact significant that even when Luke echoes Isa. liii he is not thinking of atonement and substitution. The second passage probably adopts a turn of phrase current in the Church (perhaps to give a speech a Pauline stamp?—such tendencies are occasionally to be noted in Luke). Neither in the story of the Passion nor in his formulae is there any indication of such ideas—N.B., he omits Mark x, 45. The passage is therefore strange. It should be noted that the idea of the Cross plays no part in the proclamation. Even when Luke uses the word παραδιδόναι there is no trace of the idea of atonement. The technical use of this word seems to be secondary; cf. old phrases which presuppose the simple sense of the word: Mark ix, 31; xiv, 10 f. (and here v. 11 shows how it comes to be used in a technical sense).

Luke's account has in common with all the Gospels the fact that the suffering as such is not contemplated and described. There is in fact a tendency to abbreviate it. Mark already depicts the early arrival of death as a miracle, and Luke only underlines its miraculous nature. The fact that the death itself is not interpreted as a saving event of course determines the account given of it.

1 Cor. xv, 3 ff. shows that the burial soon has its fixed place in the kerygma. But for what purpose is it included? In this particular passage the purpose is to express the reality of the death. Underlying it is the idea of an ascension from the grave.

---

[1] On the terminology of the suffering and dying, cf. Michaelis, *Herkunft und Bedeutung* (see Bibliography), also Jeremias, *ThLZ*, 75, 1950, p. 35.

THE CENTRE OF HISTORY

Luke of course thinks of the event quite differently, but pre-Lucan conceptions are still reflected in his sources, e.g. in the strange statement in Acts xiii, 29. Luke, however, is not aware of the original meaning of this passage. It is true that he alters Mark's account of the burial, but not according to the conception in Acts xiii, 29, and the theological motifs peculiar to Luke do not make their influence felt in this connection. The alteration to Mark is restricted to adapting the account to the part which Pilate plays in the condemnation and execution of Jesus.

5. RESURRECTION AND ASCENSION

In spite of the different wording, there is no fundamental difference between Luke and Mark in their account of the time at which the Resurrection took place.[1] They both allow a definite space of time between the death and the Resurrection, on the basis of ancient tradition. The choice of expressions for stating the time is no doubt influenced by cultic customs. No underlying theme of Luke's can be traced in this passage, but it can be in many other features of his account.

The alteration of Mark xiv, 28 and xvi, 7 in Luke xxiv, 6, and of Mark xvi, 8 in Luke xxiv, 9, shows that Luke is aware that he is not in agreement with Mark. The journey to Galilee is replaced by a prophecy in Galilee about Jerusalem. The witness-motif appears in its 'Galilean' form[2] in xxiii, 49, and is taken up again in the editorial v. 55. The introduction of the Scriptural proof in the characteristic form in Luke xxiv, 25 ff., 44 ff., is typically Lucan.[3] In addition there is the emphasis on the σάρξ, a motif which is another link between the Gospel and

---

[1] On the wording, cf. Mark viii, 31; ix, 31 and x, 34, with Luke ix, 22; xviii, 33; xxiv, 7, 46, and Acts x, 40. The great variation in the written tradition is characteristic. Goguel, *Naissance*, p. 46, correctly points out that in the LXX both forms are used interchangeably: Gen. xlii, 17 f.; Esth. iv, 16; and on the other hand, Hos. vi, 2.

[2] In other words, it refers to the 'Galileans' in Jerusalem; it should be compared with the witness-motif in Acts, in particular with the restriction of the circle to whom the Risen Lord appeared to the 'Galileans' (Acts xiii, 31). There is an unmistakably polemical note here, no doubt reflecting rivalries within the Church.

[3] We have considered this previously. The important thing now is that the meaning of Scripture has been revealed by the Resurrection; as a result, the possibility of knowledge can now be proclaimed as something inescapable.

THE CENTRE OF HISTORY

Acts.[1] At the same time, however, the state of the Risen Lord is described as δόξα.[2]

Against the background of the succeeding phases of redemptive history, the main emphasis is on bringing out the distinctive character and defining the extent of the period of the Resurrection appearances.[3] It becomes a sacred period between the times.[4] This accounts for the difference between these and all later 'appearances'.[5] During the forty days the appearances do not take place from Heaven. Such appearances presuppose the

[1] Luke xxiv, 39 f.; Acts ii, 31. On this point Luke is in agreement on the one hand with John, and on the other with the Apostles' Creed, which is in fact formed almost exclusively from Lucan material. They also have in common the way in which the Resurrection of Jesus and the general resurrection correspond.

[2] Luke xxiv, 26. It is not implied that this glory is still awaited and will not be attained until the Ascension, for it is already present (ἔδει). This is in harmony with the description of the corporeality of the Risen Lord, in Luke xxiv, 36 f., on the one hand, and in vv. 39 f. and Acts x, 41 on the other. Lohmeyer's assertion that only the Exalted, not the Risen Lord, possesses glory (*Markus*, p. 180, n. 1) is certainly not true for Luke. The question arises, of course, whether there might not be traces in this passage of an earlier view, according to which Jesus ascended to Heaven immediately from the grave. In this case it would in fact be an appearance from Heaven. But this is not Luke's view. He sharply divides the appearances on earth of the Risen Lord from his exaltation in Heaven. There is therefore a state in which Jesus is risen and glorified, but not yet exalted.

[3] Luke has taken over the tradition of the empty tomb, which is a specifically Jerusalem tradition, but he scarcely develops it. He is more interested in other aspects.

[4] What is the relation between the forty days and Luke xxiv, 50–3? Is there in either case an interpolation, or did Luke feel there was no discrepancy, and adopt both traditions just as he found them? The textual critical question certainly gives rise to difficulties. If D is almost entirely secondary, then there is at the end of the Gospel a rival account of the Ascension. There are admittedly signs that this has been interpolated. Among them are the non-Lucan setting in Bethany, and the lack of any clear delimitation of the period of the appearances. There are of course indications of this apart from Acts i, e.g. in Acts xiii, 31. The definition of the period in this passage is a traditional expression. Luke is not aware of any difference from the forty days. In any case the statement in this passage fits in as little with Luke xxiv, 50 ff. as the forty days. If we explain the latter as an interpolation, it does not remove the difficulty, but it does if we consider the end of the Gospel to be an interpolation. Ph-H. Menoud holds that there is interpolation in both passages (*Remarques*). Cf. also A. N. Wilder, 'Variant Traditions on the Resurrection in Acts', *J.B.L.*, 62, 1943, p. 311. On the story of the Resurrection: V. Larrañaga, *L'ascension de Notre-Seigneur*, 1938; P. Benoit, 'L'ascension', *RB*, 56, 1949, pp. 161 ff.

[5] It is important to draw a distinction between them. In Luke the Resurrection appearances are more sharply distinguished from activities of the Spirit than elsewhere, because the outpouring of the Spirit is separated even from the Ascension by a further space of time. Luke xxiv, 37 f., is a deliberate apologetic expression of how clearly distinguished the appearances are from any idea of πνεῦμα.

THE CENTRE OF HISTORY

Ascension and are of a different kind, for they establish no relationship with the Lord in the special sense that the Resurrection
appearances do. An example of the 'appearances from Heaven'
is given in the threefold account of the appearance near Damascus.[1]

In making this division into a series of events, each of which
has its own relative meaning and receives its essential character
from its position in the series, Luke has once again used tradition to express his own conception. The Resurrection and the
Ascension follow as stages in Jesus' course, and it is the latter,
not the Resurrection, that marks the limit of his stay on earth,
and the beginning of his heavenly reign. From this moment the
Church needs a substitute for his 'real presence', therefore it
receives the Spirit, and cherishes the hope. The Ascension, by
being linked with the Parousia, is given its place within the
whole course of redemptive history (cf. n. 1 below). Another
division is introduced into the sequence of events by the fact that
there is a further period of time until Pentecost, for the co-
ordination of the Church and the Spirit with the earlier redemptive events of Israel and the period of Jesus, and to make it clear
that the Church is the epoch, the whole character of which is
determined by the conclusion of the Ascension and the arrival of
Pentecost. As a result of this ordering of the events, the Ascension does not form the conclusion of the first, but the beginning
of the second volume of Luke's historical account.

[1] The Ascension has a twofold meaning for Luke: it is the act of exaltation, from
which time Jesus is at the right hand of God, and his appearances now are from
Heaven. The Ascension is also seen as a parallel to the Parousia. Thus it has its
place in the sequence of redemptive history as the penultimate stage in Jesus'
course. The Parousia is still to come. In the meantime the Church lives on earth,
waiting and suffering—but in possession of the Spirit. So we see the relevance of
this story as an introduction to the second book. The event itself is not depicted
in detail. We cannot of course assert that Jesus rose up of his own power (as
Delling does, *TW*, art. ἀναλαμβάνειν). The text is a flat denial of it. It would be
easier to find it in the διέστη at the end of the Gospel.

For the meaning of ὤφθη, cf. Lyder Brun, *ZNW*, 1933, pp. 265 ff. On the idea
of the Parousia on the Mount of Olives, cf. Zech. xiv, 14. In the time of Felix,
the Egyptian leads his people there, Josephus, *Ant.*, XX, 8, 6; *Bell.*, II, 3, 5.

On the significance of the Resurrection from the point of view of redemptive
history, cf. Ramsey, *The Resurrection of Christ*, p. 79; 'For Luke, history and
theology are one; and if he shews us less than does Mark of the Resurrection as a
suprahistorical coming of the Day of the Lord, he draws out instead the important
truth that in the Resurrection one epoch of history, human and divine, reaches its
climax and another epoch has its beginning.'

THE CENTRE OF HISTORY

The question arises, whether the Resurrection has any other direct connection with the existence of the faithful in the present apart from its historical significance, as an event in the sequence of redemptive history. The answer is that it has, and that it is implied in Luke's conception of the Resurrection.

Jesus is called ἀρχηγὸς τῆς ζωῆς (Acts iii, 15; v, 31). The idea is not common, but it is in harmony with Luke's genera. conception. Jesus' Resurrection has significance in the first place for himself, for it is God's vindication of him in view of his murder by the Jews. In addition there is its significance for us: it is the proof of the fact that there is a general resurrection and a judgement. This is the meaning of the ἀρχηγὸς idea. It is the theme of other passages also.[1] Luke starts from the general doctrine of a future resurrection. He is aware that this doctrine already exists in Judaism; it forms part of Scriptural prophecy, and is correctly held by the Pharisees, in contrast to the Sadducees.[2] Luke can adopt a traditional phrase such as that of the 'resurrection of the just' (Luke xiv, 14), but how he understands it is clear from Acts xxiv, 15, where—perhaps for a polemical purpose—he no longer restricts it to the just, but declares that all will rise again. The main motif is that of the universal judgement, of which Luke makes great use in the mission (Acts xvii, 30 ff.). Thus the Christian message can be summed up as the preaching of Jesus and the resurrection; cf. Acts xvii, 18, where the general nature of the doctrine of the resurrection is clear, as it is also in the significant verse Acts iv, 2.[3]

As the general nature of the doctrine of the resurrection is therefore clear, and also its use as a point of contact as an inducement to repentance and as the background to the message of forgiveness, the sayings about the Resurrection of Jesus have to be interpreted along the same lines. What ἀρχηγὸς means in Luke is clear from Acts xxvi, 23, where we read: πρῶτος ἐξ

[1] This is usually interpreted differently, and the word is taken to describe Jesus as the originator (e.g. by Kümmel, *Kirchenbegriff*, p. 47). The alternative cannot be stated in this way. Jesus is the 'first' (Acts xxvi, 23), but he cannot be described strictly speaking as 'originator', as according to Luke he did not 'rise' but was raised by God, and his part in the event was passive.

[2] Luke xx, 27, 33 ff.; cf. Acts xxiii, 8, and the part played by this doctrine in the account of Paul's trial (Acts xxiii, 6; xxiv, 15).

[3] The difficult passage Acts iv, 33 has to be interpreted similarly.

ἀναστάσεως. This is the authentic interpretation of the idea. There is no question of a causal connection.[1] The link between the Resurrection and the individual consists therefore in the fact that it testifies to the truth about his future destiny, that is, to the reality of resurrection, responsibility and judgement. The question then will be, whether he has repented and received forgiveness. The message of the Resurrection, therefore, is not a call to be saved, but is rather of a formal kind. It is now man's concern to draw the consequences, to repent, to be 'converted', baptized, and to live the Christian life. It is obvious that man's response has now gained a significance of its own.

In conclusion, therefore, we may say that the Lord is now in Heaven, whilst on earth there lives the community of the Church equipped with the Spirit, provided with the message which is communicated by the witnesses, and with the abiding blessings of the sacrament. The Church is not 'created' by the Resurrection, for it is created by God, not by a 'saving event' thought of as efficacious in itself—Luke does not yet go so far as this—but the Resurrection does provide the basis for its existence. The next event after the Ascension in the series of mighty acts no longer affects the course of events in Jesus' life, and the Church only secondarily, but it affects the Church directly: the outpouring of the Spirit. We shall now turn to consider the Church and the conveyance of salvation.

[1] As Bultmann correctly states (*N.T.Theol.*, p. 81). We have to beware of importing Pauline ideas.

PART FIVE

Man and Salvation: The Church

I. INTRODUCTION

The bearing of the saving events upon man has to be considered under two aspects: in the first place 'from above', that is, from the doctrinal standpoint, and then 'from below', from the standpoint of 'discipleship'. It is possible to make this distinction only because in Luke the objective salvation that Christ has won and its subjective appropriation no longer form a unity to the same degree as they did before. 'Fides quae' and 'fides qua' are not yet opposed in such a way as to make the question of appropriation a main problem of theology, nevertheless one can trace the more objective emphasis in the description of saving history, and the more subjective emphasis in the account of the Christian way of life. Thus the mediating factor, the Church, gains a greater significance in its own right. As regards the individual, however, there is an increasing tendency to divide the course of conversion into separate events in a definite order. This order is not yet thought of as a fixed principle, and at first it is simply observed as the regular course of development from the moment of hearing the missionary preaching to that of entry into the Church. One can trace, however, new developments which lead in the course of time to the life of the Christian after conversion also being increasingly considered as a separate problem. We shall therefore examine our present topic as follows: the Church as the transmitter of the message, the messengers and their message, their manner of transmission, and finally the recipient of the message and his problems.

207

MAN AND SALVATION: THE CHURCH

Luke does not directly define the position of the individual in the course of redemptive history.[1] Instead his position is defined as a mediated one, for he stands within the Church, and thereby in a definite phase of the story.[2] The Church transmits the message of salvation, in the first place the historical facts to which the eye-witnesses testify, and which are then handed on by the Church after the witnesses have gone. This transmission by the Church makes it possible for the individual's remoteness in time from the saving events of past and future, from the time of Jesus and from the Parousia, to be no hindrance to him. Instead of the nearness of these events there is the Church with its permanent function. In the Church we stand in a mediated relationship to the saving events—mediated by the whole course of redemptive history—and at the same time in an immediate relationship to them, created by the Spirit, in whom we can invoke God and the name of Christ; in other words, the Spirit dwells in the Church, and is imparted through its means of grace and its office-bearers. Prayer, to which Luke attributes a special importance in Jesus' life, represents a timeless form of the relationship. Thus the individual has a link in time through the Church with a definite stage of history, whereby he is granted the assurance of salvation, and he also knows the actual realization of faith in the fellowship, in sacrament and in prayer, which makes him independent of definite periods of time. For Luke the believer must be indissolubly bound to the Church, if he is not to sink either into speculation or into eschatological resignation. Just as Luke's eschatology provided a plan which could stand regardless of time, in his account of the Church we find something similar in regard to the realization of the message in the midst of the continuing world.

The life of the Church in the Spirit, with its fellowship and sacrament, its prayer and endurance in persecution, is illustrated in the description of the primitive community. But here again there is a direct awareness of the historical uniqueness of this

[1] The nature of Luke's whole plan makes it impossible for him to define it in the way in which it is defined in Gnosticism and in apocalyptic.

[2] At first it is the immediate relation of the individual to the saving events that comes to the fore. We can see this in the earliest ideas of faith and of the Spirit, despite the fact that the Spirit unites the individual with a community of those who await the Parousia. Luke emphasizes the other aspect, viz., that the Spirit also has His place allotted within redemptive history.

situation, for this period is the 'arché', when the witnesses are still present. The account does not present a timeless ideal for the Church, for the reproduction or conservation of the conditions prevailing then is obviously not required in the present. There is no trace in Luke of the idea which would form a necessary part of such a programme of reform, i.e. an assertion that the Church has declined from its original high ideal. Further, in his account of Paul's missionary activities he never sets up the primitive community as a model. We can see this in relation to the Law: although the primitive community—including Paul—keeps the Law, Gentile Christians are free from it, and for a reason which is characteristically different from Paul's.

The Church is destined to be the successor to Israel. Beyond that there is no speculation as to her nature. There is no room in Luke's understanding for a doctrine of the pre-existence and transcendence of the Church, and nothing whatever is said about the time after the Parousia. The mediated position, which the individual occupies in regard to the historical events, has its exact counterpart in Luke's idea of the Church, in the fact that God's plan, His act of election, does not concern the individual, but the dispensation of salvation as a whole. On this aspect, see the discussion in Part III.

II. THE CHURCH

1. THE BEGINNINGS

There is an obvious connection between Luke's conception of the Church and the problem of eschatology, i.e. with the situation of the *ecclesia pressa* in the world. Its nature is defined in the light of its historical position: the Church is the third phase, the provision made for the in-between time which is the present, and which makes it possible to endure the time of waiting. Both its task and its equipment spring from this part that it has to play.[1]

At the beginning of Part III we considered the situation of the Church in the world, and saw that it is a situation

---

[1] We need refer here only to the work of v. Baer, who sets out the relation of the Spirit to the Church from the standpoint of redemptive history.

conditioned by persecution. The Church is therefore interpreted as having the task of making endurance possible. The development of an ethic of martyrdom forms an essential element in this conception of the Church.[1]

As the story of the Church continues, the initial period comes to be thought of as a unique kind of period; it belongs, of course, to the epoch of the Church, but it stands apart as the unique period of the witnesses. In the description of it, two motifs are blended, so far as its external fate is concerned: on the one hand it is seen as a period of persecution, and in this respect like the present, with the result that the present can find consolation in this fellowship of suffering and have it before it as an example; on the other hand, however, it is set before us as a time of peace, in which respect it is different from the present, but even this has a consoling effect, as one becomes aware of God's protection, on which the present too can rely.[2]

It should be noted that this contrast of persecution and peace is to be found only in the account of the primitive community. The account of Paul is less stylized and therefore more adapted to the actual circumstances of the author and the purposes he has in mind, but here again we see from time to time the Divine protection. This is to be expected, for such suffering was foretold by the Lord himself, which means that he knows all that

[1] This is less a problem for the individual than for the Church, for persecution and expansion go together. We can see this in the story of Paul's call (Acts ix, 16—following upon v. 15). The prayer in Acts iv, 24 ff. has the same situation in view (v. 29—after the trial of the disciples). It can be seen even more plainly in v, 41, 42. The logia concerning persecution in the Gospel contain the promise of protection. Luke has modified Mark to the extent that it is not the Spirit who speaks, but man—cf. Luke xii, 11 f., and xxi, 14—but it is the Spirit who gives the persuasive power in speaking.

[2] Persecution is mentioned not only in particular instances (e.g. in Acts iv and v, in the story of Stephen and the activities of Saul), but also in summary reports. This gives the motif its fundamental significance. Cf. Acts viii, 1 ff., and xi, 19. Alongside these summaries there are the summary reports of peace (ix, 31; ii, 47). It is impossible, of course, to reconcile the two from the historical point of view. It is a style of description peculiar to redemptive history (cf. viii, 1-3, where Saul appears as the only persecutor in the whole of Jerusalem), which brings out the tension between the persecution the Church experiences and the Divine protection, by setting them both out in the classical form found in the primitive Church. The motif of fear is part of the same style of composition (ii, 43; v, 11, 13—in the case of v, 11, within the Church); here it is shown indirectly how the Church is equipped by God for victory. Chapter iv, vv. 29 ff., shows what form the Divine provision takes in this manner of describing redemptive history.

takes place, and also that the 'necessity' of such suffering can be spoken of (Acts xiv, 22). The difference from the description of the primitive community is that in the latter peace becomes a basic motif, which characterizes the whole period. Later, in the time of Paul, the Divine protection is experienced in particular miraculous interventions (cf. Acts xxvii, 23 f.).

It marks a new stage in historical understanding when one becomes aware of the peculiar character of the period of origin, for only then does the writing of Church history become possible. The separate phenomena can now be grasped as a whole: the change from the Jewish Church to the Gentile Church, the expansion from Israel out into the world, the liberation from the Law. It is now seen that these are by no means accidental events. Of course they had previously been thought of as according to plan, as the outcome of God's will (cf., e.g., Mark xiii, 10), but it is not until now that it can be demonstrated in a continuous account that they are according to plan, or that the place of any single phenomena in the plan can be determined.[1] The task, therefore, is not only to relate the separate events to one another, and to demonstrate the systematic connection between them, but also to bring out the determining factors in each epoch, and show how distinctive they are.

Apart from the way of historical understanding, there are two other possible ways of depicting the original period: by projecting present circumstances into that period or, on the

---

[1] The attitude to the origins is expressed in Luke's use of the idea of the ἀρχή. In Luke i, 2, and also in Acts xi, 15, it is used in the full sense of the beginning of the Church. The 'beginning' in Galilee and the 'beginning' of the Church in Jerusalem are deliberately placed parallel to each other; cf. the formal usage in Luke xxiii, 5 and xxiv, 47, and the way the terminology overlaps into Acts i. The similarity of Luke i, 2 and Acts i, 1 f., is quite intentional.

This pregnant use of ἀρχή for the beginning of the Church, however, is not confined to Luke. The best examples are found in 1 and 2 John, which, compared with the Gospel, show how formal the usage has become in application to the Church (e.g. 1 John ii, 7, 24; iii, 11; 2 John 5). There is no support in the Gospel for such a usage. It is based on the interpretation of the Church as a new creation. (Similar to the use of the related idea ἀπαρχή.) But this element is not brought out in Luke, whereas it is present in the Johannine letters. Luke's account remains firmly within the framework of his general scheme, which, as we have already said, cannot contain any idea of the pre-existence of the Church. This has to be borne in mind, when Luke's conception of the Church is described as 'early Catholic'. Luke differs as regards certain fundamentals not only from Ephesians, but also from tendencies such as we find in Hermas (*Vis.* I, 1, 6; iii, 4) and 2 Clem. (14), which then persist in theology.

contrary, by describing a timeless ideal which is held up to the present as a model for imitation. Luke adopts neither of these courses, for he uses the peace-motif we have mentioned to make the primitive Church stand out as a special period, the distinctive life of which he describes as something unrepeatable, for she has the eye-witnesses in her midst. Although the primitive Church continues to keep the Law and give allegiance to the Temple, Luke does not assume that this must be the attitude of the present. The report of how the Gentile Church is declared free from the Law is one of the highlights of his account. By the quotation of Scriptural proof, Luke shows that this change is part of God's redemptive plan.[1] The same view is expressed in describing as a necessity the turning from the Jews to the Gentiles.[2]

By interpreting this initial period as the historical foundation for the later Church, Luke is able to solve the problems which are raised by his basic scheme: how can the Church abandon the link with Judaism, the Law and the Temple, how can it break away from Jerusalem, its place of origin, and yet remain within the continuity of redemptive history? If Church history is thought of as a development, then the answer is that these factors belong to the initial period, but are not of eternal validity. In fact it is they that embody the principle of continuity, and as the Church develops we see the unity of the present Church with the primitive one, and also the link between the latter and Israel. In this indirect way the Gentile Church of the present is integrated into redemptive history.

[1] The apostolic decree shows the continuity, in that the Law, reduced to an absolute minimum, is applied to the Gentiles. The actual historical meaning of the decree, which is that it made possible table fellowship between Jewish and Gentile Christians, is not stressed by Luke. His conception is fundamentally different from Paul's, in that the Law is described as a burden. There is no trace of the Christological aspect, which plays such an important part in Paul's understanding of the Law, and which underlies the saying about being saved through grace in Acts xv, 11, which has such a Pauline sound. It is clear that by the time of Luke the Law is no longer an acute problem. The whole process of the liberation of the Gentiles is justified by Scripture, particularly by the conception of the 'necessity' of the transition from the Jews to the Gentiles. See next note below.

[2] The idea of 'necessity' can be seen in the significant πρῶτον of Acts iii, 26. It is later set out as a principle in Acts xiii, 46 f. The same motif is used as the conclusion of the whole historical record where the transition is finally justified from Scripture. The idea that this transition is a matter of principle forms a stock pattern in the narrative.

MAN AND SALVATION: THE CHURCH

It is worth noting that although the Church is closely linked with Israel the idea of the 'true' Israel has not yet been developed. One of the most important ways in which this link is shown is the proof that the primitive community is bound to Jerusalem not only as a matter of fact, but also as a matter of necessity (Luke xxiv, 47; Acts i, 4). It is only here that the out-pouring of the Spirit can take place. Pentecost is not only the typological foreshadowing of the mission, but also the historical foundation for it. For this reason the mission spreads out from Jerusalem in concentric circles.

Luke's conception is seen in his language, as well as in his description of the life of the primitive community. This is a matter which we have already discussed (see pp. 162 f.).

2. THE PROGRESS OF THE MISSION

The connection of the Church with the Old Testament prom-ises implies the universal missionary task. This can be seen in the story of Pentecost, which links the Spirit and the mission with prophecy, and also in the conclusion which Paul is com-pelled to draw from the behaviour of the Jews (Acts xiii, 46). If we wish to know how the Church is equipped for the missionary task, then we must of course turn to the Spirit. He gives direct instructions, e.g. in chapter x; viii, 29; xi, 12. The intervention of the Spirit can alternate with that of the angels,[1] although where it is a question of the fundamental principle and not just of interventions in a particular case, then it is always the 'Spirit' that is mentioned.[2] He gives the strength to endure the suffering which begins straight away.[3]

---

[1] Cf. viii, 29 with viii, 26. The juxtaposition leads to reflections such as in xii, 9; xxi, 4 shows that one cannot systematically assess all the expressions (cf. xx, 23).

[2] The linking of the Spirit and public proclamation in the story of Pentecost and in the story of Paul's conversion are part of a basic pattern. Cf. also iv, 31. The external signs, of which accounts are given, also of course belong to this basic pattern; the worse suffering becomes, the more can one find consolation in these. Passages such as viii, 26 and viii, 29 raise the question as to how far Luke's con-ception of the Spirit's activity is still a concrete one.

[3] Suffering is explicitly mentioned in the story of Paul's conversion (Acts ix, 16, 17). The connection between suffering and mission is of course set out in the whole missionary story. Cf. also iv, 31, if we consider together with this vv. 29 and 30, we see how the community was prepared.

MAN AND SALVATION: THE CHURCH

Before the time of Luke the missionary task was thought of as a universal one (cf. Mark xiii, 10[1]), but Luke was the first to build up the picture of a systematic progress of events, the plan of which bears witness to the guidance of God. In the same way the course of Church history from the beginnings until the present is set out as a redemptive process, which God is guiding to His goal.

One can deduce the actual interpretation of the Church from the usage of οἰκοδομεῖν.[2] The typical ecclesiastical application which we find in Acts ix, 31; xx, 32; xv, 16, is of Lucan origin.[3] The fact that God always appears as the subject is the outcome of the view that the missionary expansion is achieved according to God's plan under His direct guidance.[4] We must not forget

---

[1] We can see the shift in eschatology even in Mark. Whereas originally the mission itself was thought of as an eschatological event, Mark already thinks of it as an epoch preceding the Eschaton. Luke, however, severs the connection with the Last Things (he omits Mark's verse). It is a period in its own right, and the Eschaton comes at the close of it, but does not determine its nature.

[2] On this, cf. Vielhauer, *Oikodome*, and Michel's article in *TW*.

[3] Acts xv, 16 presupposes the identity of Israel and the Church—following on the plain statement of v. 14 and in view of the fact that this 'people' is meant to be free from the Law (by the decree of the Holy Spirit and of the assembly of the Church).

The meaning of Acts vii, 49 is connected with the special questions concerning Stephen's speech. Vielhauer, op. cit., p. 113: 'In Acts οἰκοδομεῖν and ἀνοικοδομεῖν are used in their full theological meaning as eschatological and soteriological terms in the Old Testament sense of "God's gracious activity". Even where it is not explicitly stated, the subject is always God, and the object the community, or the community coming into being. The usage is "verbal", that is, it is not determined by the image of a building. The image is not created in Acts, but is assumed, and already has a definite meaning. It is used in fact in the Pauline sense.' This is questionable. However correct it may be to point out the 'verbal' usage and the fact that God is exclusively the subject, one must be cautious in using the term 'eschatological' in connection with Luke; and there is only a formal similarity with Paul's usage. Michel, loc. cit.: 'It is possible to find in Acts an absolute use of οἰκοδομεῖν and ἀνοικοδομεῖν under the influence of the Old Testament. . . . The subject is not the Messiah, but God Himself; the usage in Acts . . . is therefore to be interpreted as a separate new development on an Old Testament basis.'

[4] The technical term δεῖ found in this connection is used among other things for the decision that Paul should go to Rome (xix, 21—cf. the beginning of the verse); in xxiii, 11 the Lord expresses the same idea, and in xxvii, 24 an angel. xxv, 10 is to be interpreted similarly.

It is directly stated in ii, 47, xiv, 27 and xv, 4, 12 that it is God who makes the Church grow (cf. the next note). Alongside these, however, there are sayings about the intervention of Christ, especially in connection with Paul; he appears to him near Damascus, and also in xxiii, 11. In addition there is the intervention of the Spirit, the function of the ὁράματα and the various combinations of these

214

however, that there is a typically Lucan variation of this: in some instances the sayings speak of God acting directly, but at the same time there are reports of what men have done, which is only subsequently referred to God. There is a tendency to make the events as such and man's share in them independent.[1]

III. THE BEARERS OF THE MESSAGE

Both the ideas we meet here and the way in which they are set out bear the stamp of Luke's view of redemptive history. The special nature of the initial period is again made plain. The ministries of the early period are not a model for the later period, for they cannot be repeated. This applies to the position

motifs (ix, 10; xviii, 9; cf. the description of the vision in the story of Cornelius with the statements in x, 20 and xi, 5). From the point of view of the Church the activity of God and of Christ overlap; on this aspect, cf. the section on Christology.

[1] This view can be seen in the usage of προστιθέναι. In ii, 47 the subject is God, but it is used more often in the passive—ii, 41; v, 14; xi, 24. This is a stock turn of phrase which really replaces the simple statement that 'the Church' spread. Sometimes Luke gives a straightforward report, as in iv, 4; xiv, 1; xvii, 12, 34. In vi, 7 we find a combination of the passive turn of phrase and the plain statement of fact; xix, 20 shows the result of a compromise, of which there is another significant example in ix, 31. Whenever such statements are made, it is always God who is thought of as the real agent: it is His 'hand' that is active, but through the name of Christ (iv, 30) or through the hand of those who have received the Spirit (ii, 43; v, 15; xiv, 3; xv, 12). Therefore this gives rise to a tendency to think of their deeds as something independent. The reference to God comes only subsequently, as a result of reflection, and is not always included in the report of what is done by the Spirit-filled man (e.g. vi, 8). Thus we find close together, e.g., xv, 12 and xv, 15, and after xxvi, 29, where the missionary achievement is thought of as something brought about by God, the report of the voyage begins at xxvii, 6, the outstanding example of the thaumaturgic element in Acts, or in fact in the New Testament as a whole.

There are thus two different aspects in the description of God's activity in the history of the Church, and it is the mingling of these two aspects that is characteristic of Luke. We can see it in his reports of miracles. Sometimes it is God who acts directly, sometimes men who act through Him or through the name of Christ. There is here an analogy to Christology, for just as Christ becomes a distinct figure who has to be described as such, so also do the apostles and their deeds, and the Church as a whole.

The development is along the following lines:
(a) iv, 30 (following v. 28): God's hand, and through the name . . .
(b) v, 12 ff., and xix, 11: by the hands of the apostles or of Paul.
(c) The logical outcome is seen in v, 15, xix, 12 and finally in xxviii, 6.

MAN AND SALVATION: THE CHURCH

held by the apostle and the witness.[1] Rather do they form the historical basis for the Church of 'the present'.

Originally the messengers are merely agents, and Luke does not depart from this idea.[2] Their message is not their own, but

---

[1] We are not concerned with the historical circumstances, but with the picture Luke gives. For the historical aspect, reference should be made to the literature on the subject. For a recent contribution, see Goguel, *L'église primitive*, pp. 93 ff. The writer traces the connection between the apostolate and the Spirit—which plays some part in Luke—to Paul, but we must remember that according to Luke the apostolate came into being before the outpouring of the Spirit (Luke vi, 13), therefore we cannot say that the Spirit is constitutive of apostleship. Its range is also different than in Paul, for neither Paul nor James can be apostles (in spite of Acts xiv, 4, 14). On the difficult account of the completion of the circle of the apostles, cf. Ph-H. Menoud, 'Les additions au groupe des douze apôtres d'après le livre des Actes', *RHPhR*, 1957, pp. 71 ff., where the author shows conclusively that here the office of apostle is not thought of as a permanent institution in the Church.

The verb ἀποστέλλω is not quite the same in meaning as the noun. It expresses the act of commission in a broader sense. It is true that the apostles have been commissioned, but not all those who are 'sent' are apostles. Luke vi, 13 is normative for the definition of the noun. For our purpose it is here that we must start, not from the Jewish or Greek origin of the idea. How far this definition agrees with the historical meaning does not affect our enquiry. Against Rengstorf's view (*TW*, I, p. 422) it must be pointed out that it is precisely the restriction of apostleship to the Twelve that is significant for Luke. The two exceptions (Acts xiv, 4, 14) shows the beginnings of a broader usage, and shows that what he describes as Luke's view is an invention of the author. The idea of 'being sent' falls into the background, and the emphasis is on the special position that the apostles occupy. Cf. passages such as Luke xxii, 14 and xxiv, 10. In the story of the mission they do not appear as those who are sent out, but as those who remain. Whenever they engage in missionary work, it has a special significance, as, for example, when they give their sanction to missionary activity as such, by imparting the Spirit in Samaria. Peter anticipates the Gentile mission, but he is not the one who carries it out. What characterizes the apostle is not the missionary commission, but the link with the life of Jesus, that is, with the unique historical facts concerning him. The connection between the idea of apostleship and the motif of the eye-witness proves this. The Twelve are made apostles before they are sent out, and when Jesus sends out 'others' (Luke x, 1), they are not apostles. Rengstorf's assertion (op. cit., p. 434, n. 167) that there are in Acts only miracles of the 'apostles' is in contradiction of the facts.

[2] This can be seen in their call, and is shown by Acts i, 8 and by the story of Pentecost; it is stressed in Acts iii, 12, and maintained throughout the account. The same is true of all the other officials, e.g. the bishops (xx, 28).

They appear as agents in a special sense when they receive a detailed, particular commission. This happens not only repeatedly in the case of Paul, in outstanding passages such as xxi, 10 ff., but also right from the beginning (cf. the instruction to Philip in viii, 26, and the command to Peter in the story of Cornelius).

God and Christ are spoken of interchangeably, and also the Spirit, as those who give the commission. Cf. the juxtaposition of the appearance of the angel (who is always the angel of God) and of being sent by the Spirit (see p. 213). Christ appears particularly in the vision near Damascus. The description of the office as

MAN AND SALVATION: THE CHURCH

God's Word.[1] However, it is part of the process of development that in the course of time the bearers of the message themselves attract greater attention. We must bear in mind that Luke in no way encourages the development of a cult of saints; the very fact that he does not do this, and that he carefully avoids in particular the later stereotype theme of the glorious martyrdom, gives rise to the much-discussed problem of the close of the Acts of the Apostles.[2]

The preface to the Gospel makes it quite clear that the ministry of the initial period is unique. Here we find brought together all the elements in Luke's conception: the connection with the 'arché', and the abiding constitutive function of this uniqueness, in so far as the validity of tradition depends upon it. In this way the constant link of the Church with that ministry—now as far as history is concerned a thing of the past—is expressed. It is by thus defining the connection between present and past that Luke arrives at an understanding of his own position (Luke i, 3, 4).

In view of the uniqueness of the early ministry and the fundamental part it plays, it is surprising that the later idea of the ministries of the Church is so little developed by Luke. Of course he is familiar with the officials in the communities, 'episkopoi' (Acts xx, 28), 'diakonoi' (but this is not a fixed official title) 'presbyteroi' (xi, 30; as a definite appointment, xiv, 23 inter alia), but he is not concerned with precise definitions. These offices are already in existence. Luke's aim, however, is not to describe the constitution of the Church, but to show how the Church as a whole starts from the 'arché' as its

διακονία suggests the idea of commission—Acts i, 17 ff.; xii, 25; xx, 24; xxi, 19 (in the typical form of what God did through the διακονία of Paul); cf. also the significant λαγχάνειν in Acts i, 17. Verse 25 provides further clarification: καὶ ἀποστολῆς.

[1] We shall consider this further when we consider the idea of the message.
[2] This is not to deny that stylistic features connected with the description of martyrdom are present; they can be seen even in the Passion story in the Gospel, as is shown e.g. by Dibelius and Surkau. They are also present of course in Acts, and give a special tone to the description of Paul. But at the same time we must bear in mind that Luke does not develop the fixed terminology of martyrdom (not even in Acts xxii, 20), nor does he build up the stock themes connected with it. Finally, he obviously avoids reporting Paul's death. The often quoted parallelism between the account of the end of Jesus' life and of Paul's consists only in details, and it breaks down at the decisive point. The story of Stephen does not lead us to alter this view.

foundation. Therefore one should not overrate the idea of succession. There is no definite link in the transmission of office. All the emphasis is on the special part played by those who function prominently in the transmission of the Spirit, not of particular offices (viii, 18; note the reservation in v. 20). In this way the connection of the Church of the present with that of the past is guaranteed; and the present office-bearers are authorized by the Spirit, not yet by any particular succession.[1]

In actual fact the unity of the Church of past and present consists in the identity of her message and her sacraments; Baptism confers forgiveness and the Spirit, and the Lord's Supper continually keeps the fellowship in being. The sacraments are the abiding factor which spans the gulf separating the present from the beginnings.

IV. THE MESSAGE

Both the content of the proclamation and also the act of proclaiming are described in stereotype concepts which are current in the Church and therefore do not require any closer definition by the one who employs them. The message takes on a definite shape as the Christological confession and the tradition concerning the ministry of Jesus become established, therefore when any particular detail is mentioned, reference need only be made to what is generally known.

We find one of these typical current phrases in Acts i, 3, where the Risen Lord speaks τὰ περὶ τῆς βασιλείας; xix, 8 contains the same expression as a summary description of the missionary message. It is assumed that the reader knows what the content of this is, or, in practical terms, that he is familiar with the confession of faith and has read Luke's Gospel. When a more detailed definition is given, then it is the Kingdom of God and the name of Jesus Christ that appear as the main elements (viii, 12). There is a further example at the close of the book, in xxviii, 23, and in greater detail in the final verse of the chapter (cf. also xviii, 25 f.).

[1] Unfortunately I could not take advantage of the work of H. Frhr. v. Campenhausen, *Kirchliches Amt und geistliche Vollmacht in den ersten drei Jahrhunderten* (Tübingen, 1953).

MAN AND SALVATION: THE CHURCH

We will now consider some of the most important ideas. The ἀγγέλλειν group of words naturally provides the starting-point.[1] The simple form of the verb is lacking, and similarly the noun ἀγγελία.

ἀναγγέλλειν. In Acts xx, 20 the word is synonymous with διδάσκειν and διαμαρτύρεσθαι. The contents are the συμφέροντα, repentance and faith, the Divine plan. Here we find the strongest analogy with the language of the prophets (Schniewind, *TW*, I, p. 63). Luke draws a distinction here: repentance relates to God, faith to the 'Lord'. Although the terminology of God's βουλή is itself traditional, Luke's special contribution can still be seen. The βουλή idea contains his particular conception, which is linked with tradition, but represents a further development of it. μετάνοια and πίστις represent his interpretation.

The account of confession of sin in Acts xix, 18 is strange. Luke gives an actual description of the process of μετάνοια and conversion. It is to be noted, that faith comes before repentance.

ἀπαγγέλλειν. There is a specifically religious usage as well as an ordinary secular usage. Acts xi, 13; xii, 14; xii, 17; iv, 23 belong to the latter (pace Schniewind). These passages show the same usage as v, 22, 25. On the other hand, the usage in xvii, 30 is specifically religious, although the reading is uncertain. In Acts xxvi, 20 the word is used in the technical sense for preaching. As for the usage in the Gospel, in Luke vii, 22 it is derived from Q (cf. Matt. xi, 4) and has a distinctly solemn sense. In Luke viii, 34, it is derived from Mark, and has a secular meaning. Luke has inserted the word in viii, 36 with a similar meaning; viii, 47 suggests the secular sense, and has a psychological colouring ('she declared')—cf. ἀναγγέλλειν in Acts xix, 18. In Luke ix, 36 it stands in a formal sense for the act of communicating, and can be used for secular or sacred things (cf. Luke xxiv, 9). On the whole this formal usage predominates.

διαγγέλλειν. Schniewind interprets Luke ix, 60 to mean that the eschatological rule of God begins with the word of proclamation, but there is no evidence for this. The meaning is rather that this word makes known future things. Cf. for the

[1] Cf. Schniewind's article in *TW*.

usage and the statement of the object, Luke iv, 43; ix, 2, 11; xvi, 16; xviii, 29; xxi, 31. It must be borne in mind that in part it is a question of editorial adaptation of the sources, that is, of deliberate alteration by Luke. The general nature of the object is typical of Luke, and is to be understood in this passage, in keeping with his other statements. Luke does not suggest an antithesis to the cult of the Emperor in any passage. (Schniewind speaks of 'a parallelism of opposites'.)

καταγγέλλειν. In Acts iii, 18 and vii, 52 we find προκαταγγέλλειν, which is characteristic of Luke's style. In both cases it refers to Christological prophecy, in particular to suffering. Chapter iii, v. 19, brings out the implications, in the familiar terminology of μετανοεῖν and ἐπιστρέφειν, forgiveness appearing as the result of both. In iii, 24 we find a two-fold expression, with λαλεῖν. Once again it is a question of prophecy and fulfilment. In iv, 2 the object is the resurrection, to which Luke no doubt adds that it is a general resurrection, 'in Christ'. Besides this use in connection with redemptive history we find it used also with objects from general ecclesiastical terminology: Acts xiii, 5 and xvii, 13 ('the word of God'); xiii, 38 ('the remission of sins'); xv, 36 and xiii, 5 show how 'God' and 'Lord' are interchangeable. In xvii, 3 the object is simply the relative pronoun, which refers to Christ.[1] In xvii, 18 we find the noun καταγγελεύς, evidently as a general philosophic-religious concept, not specifically Christian. Chapter xvi, v. 21 and xvii, 23 assume the verb also to be in current use outside the Church.

ἐπαγγελία. The word confirms the spread of the general Christian terminology. In Acts xiii, 23 it is used in connection with the promise to Israel, and similarly in vv. 32 f. and in xxvi, 6 (N.B., v. 7). The reference to redemptive history is implied in the word itself, not only when it is defined more precisely, as in Acts vii, 17. Therefore such fuller definition can be omitted. The word is also used for the sending of the Spirit, which is thus thought of as the event of fulfilment in redemptive

---

[1] Cf. the similar use of other verbs, εὐαγγελίζεσθαι (v, 42; viii, 35; xi, 20) and κηρύσσειν (ix, 20; xix, 13, in a formula of exorcism). The comparison shows how impossible it is to draw a sharp distinction between the separate verbs. It is a question of a pious terminology, which has attracted to itself certain favourite phrases. The same is true of Acts xvi, 17.

history. The relation between the two aspects of meaning can
be seen when we compare Acts ii, 33 and ii, 39.

εὐαγγελίζεσθαι and εὐαγγέλιον. The noun does not occur
in Luke's Gospel, which is surprising, as it is present in Mark.
It seems, therefore, that Luke deliberately avoids it.[1] Even in
Acts it is rare, but xv, 7 gives a good example of Luke's usage.
Chapter xx, v. 24 on the other hand is unusual, and has a Pauline
colouring. Is it an intentional adaptation? The verb is relatively
common, but it is missing in the other Synoptics. We meet it as
early as the prologue (Luke i, 19; ii, 10). In Luke iii, 18 it is
used of John, but it is disputed whether it is used here in the
fullest sense, in other words, whether it represents John's
message as a 'Gospel'. This is not so.[2] Luke iv, 18 is one of the
programmatic passages, which describes the ministry of Jesus in
the words of the LXX. Chapter iv, v. 43 and viii, 1 have the
typical object: the Kingdom of God. For the shift of meaning
we may compare the transformation of Mark x, 29 into Luke
xviii, 29. The content of Christian preaching for which it
stands, is set out in Acts viii, 12. We find it used without an
object in Luke ix, 6 and xx, 1, in the latter instance together
with διδάσκειν. The evidence in Acts is the same as in the
Gospel. The word occurs without an object in xiv, 7, that is,
without an actual object (the person addressed being in the
accusative). In viii, 25; viii, 40; xiv, 21, and xiii, 32 it is used
with a double accusative ('τὴν ἐπαγγελίαν'), with an object of
content in v, 42 (cf. viii, 35), xi, 20 (cf. the similar use with
καταγγέλλειν and κηρύσσειν in ix, 20; xix, 13; xvii, 3;
viii, 4); in xv, 35 the object is simply 'the word', to which
there are parallels in the case of the other words just

---

[1] Cf. A. Harnack, *Entstehung und Entwicklung der Kirchenverfassung in den zwei
ersten Jahrhunderten*, 1910, p. 211, n. 1. Mark i, 1 cannot be accepted by Luke
simply because of the different definition of the 'arché'. Does Luke deliberately
avoid the word for the period of Jesus' life? There are other parallels that should
be noted. Mark i, 14 is replaced by the report of the 'call' of Jesus and of his
'teaching'. The word is omitted from Mark viii, 35. Luke's emphasis is on the
person of Jesus. In Mark x, 29 he puts 'the Kingdom of God', which is therefore
his interpretation of Mark's idea. The use of the verb is in keeping with this.
Mark xiii, 10 contradicts Luke's view of the succession of events. Mark xiv, 9
is missing together with the whole scene, which does not fit into the geographical
pattern of the period spent in Jerusalem. As is well known, the word does not
occur in Q.

[2] Bultmann, *N.T.Theol.*, p. 86; cf. above, p. 23, n. 1.

mentioned; x, 36 is a quotation related to Luke iv, 18 ff. The proclamation in xvii, 18—Jesus and the 'anastasis'—is familiar; xiv, 15 gives another definition of the message.

We can trace an increasingly technical usage both in the concept and also in the definition of its content. The other concepts concerning proclamation give the same impression, and the use of two of them together shows that they are losing their distinct meanings.

κηρύσσειν. The noun occurs only in Luke xi, 32, which comes from Q. The verb is found in all the Synoptics.[1] The rhetorical duplications are interesting.[2] In the quotation in Luke iv, 18, the word is parallel to εὐαγγελίζεσθαι; there is no evidence that Luke makes any distinction in meaning. A direct rhetorical duplication by Luke occurs in Luke viii, 1. Such expressions can evidently be combined as one wishes (cf. Acts v, 42). As regards the objects, the evidence is the same as before: cf. Acts viii, 5 (Christ); ix, 20 (a fuller statement, which brings out the meaning of the abbreviated formula); x, 42 is similar; the remaining passages, xix, 13 and xv, 21 add nothing new; xx, 25 should be compared with xxviii, 31.

διδάσκειν. In Luke iv, 32 the noun is derived from Mark i, 22. The parallel verse Mark xi, 18, on the other hand, has been considerably changed in Luke xix, 48. In Luke iv, 36 λόγος occurs, in contrast to Mark i, 27. Here there is an essential difference, for to Luke Jesus' authority does not reside in his teaching, but in his power over the spirits, in his word of command. In Luke viii, 4 also, compared with Mark iv, 2, there seems to be a different view of the 'teaching'; cf. also Mark

---

[1] As far as the relation between Mark and Luke is concerned, Luke sometimes takes over the word, and sometimes replaces it. In Luke iii, 3 (cf. Acts x, 37) the word is retained; Mark i, 38, where κηρύσσειν is used absolutely, is changed into Luke iv, 43. In the next verse, however, Luke leaves the word unchanged. In other words, the two terms are identical in meaning. Luke is not making any special point here. The same is true of Mark vi, 12/Luke ix, 6 (again with an absolute usage). Mark i, 45 is omitted by Luke, who replaces the statement concerning the ministry by one about its effect or the area it covers. Mark v, 20 is taken over (Luke viii, 39). Mark vii, 36 is part of the great omission.

[2] This rhetorical duplication is a common feature, although particularly frequent in Luke in the New Testament. (Cf. the figures given by Morgenthaler.) We must of course distinguish between duplications which are purely rhetorical and those which have real significance. In the group of words we are considering the frequent combination shows how impossible it is to draw any clear distinction. Cf., apart from Luke, Matt. iv, 17; xi, 1; iv, 23; ix, 35.

MAN AND SALVATION: THE CHURCH

xii, 38 and Luke xx, 45. Apart from these instances the noun does not occur in the Gospel. The usage in Acts is in accordance with what we have noted so far. The word occurs in Acts ii, 42 ('the apostles' teaching'), in v, 28; xvii, 19 and in xiii, 12 with an objective genitive—'the teaching of the Lord'. The noun is nowhere used by Jesus himself, as was the case also with the noun 'Gospel'.

The verb is often taken from Mark. Only occasionally does the question arise, as to whether Luke uses it with a different meaning. In Luke iv, 15 he substitutes διδάσκειν for the κηρύσσειν of Mark i, 14 f. Luke iv, 31 derives from Mark i, 21. Mark ii, 13 is altered on account of the setting by the lake, which for Luke precludes the mention of διδάσκειν. The same applies to Mark iv, 1 f. Mark vi, 6 disappears, as Luke replaces this incident with a variant (iv, 16 ff.). Mark vi, 7 does not fit in with Luke's itinerary. Mark vi, 30 refers to what the apostles have done and taught, but Luke mentions only what they have done (ix, 10). In Luke ix, 11 he substitutes for Mark vi, 34 another vague expression, λαλεῖν (cf. Acts xi, 20). Mark vii, 7 is part of the great omission. In the case of Mark viii, 31/Luke ix, 22 the question arises, whether the alteration has any essential significance, in particular whether for Luke 'the prophecy of the Passion is not included in Jesus' public teaching. Mark x, 1 is missing with the whole section. Luke xix, 47 is a stylized form of Mark xi, 17. The origin of the statement is in Mark xiv, 49, but only Luke makes use of it to depict a period of activity of considerable length. Luke xx, 21, compared with Mark xii, 14, shows how the usage has become less distinctive. Mark xii, 35 is missing (Luke xix, 47), but this is not the result of Luke's view of the teaching, for when we compare Luke with Mark we scarcely notice any real difference in interpretation. The remaining passages confirm this view.[1]

[1] The passages are: Luke v, 3, 17 (editorial, but with no special significance); vi, 6 (editorial); xi, 1 (editorial); xii, 12 (the Spirit as teacher, cf. on the other hand Matt. x, 20 and Mark xiii, 11)—cf. Luke xxi, 14 f.; Luke xiii, 10 (editorial); xiii, 26?; xiii, 22 (one of the 'journey references'); xx, 1 (in the Temple, following upon xix, 47); xxi, 37 sums up the two previous passages; xxiii, 5.

ποιεῖν καὶ διδάσκειν is a stock phrase: Acts i, 1 (cf. Matt. v, 19; xxviii, 15).

In Acts, xv, 1 states the content of the teaching, xxi, 21, 28 the connection with the Law. The following are typical statements: xv, 35 and xviii, 11, xviii, 25 (from which it is clear that the genitive in v. 11 is to be understood as an objective genitive) and xxviii, 31. There is a typical duplication in v, 42.

MAN AND SALVATION: THE CHURCH

Luke's description of the time Jesus spent in the Temple provides a detailed, comprehensive account of what Luke understands by the teaching of Jesus. The teaching is public (Luke xiii, 26), and both its themes, the Law and the Last Things, are expounded openly. On this point Luke (xxi, 5 ff.) is in definite opposition to Mark (xiii, 1 ff.). In this period Jesus confines himself to teaching, and no longer performs signs.[1]

λέγειν and διαλέγεσθαι are also used for the process of communication (Acts xvii, 2, 17; xviii, 4, 19; xix, 8 f.; xx, 7, 9; xxiv, 12, 25). There is nothing special to be noted as to their meaning. However, there is still the noun λόγος to consider. Even in Mark we find it used in a technical sense (Mark ii, 2; cf. iv, 33; viii, 32). It seems to be a stock expression of missionary terminology.[2] In the same way passages such as Acts iv, 29, 31; viii, 25; xi, 19; xiii, 46, represent current phraseology.[3]

It is all the more surprising, that in the Gospel (with the exception of Luke i, 2) the absolute use of the word is missing, even where Luke finds it in Mark. The evidence, therefore, is the same as for εὐαγγέλιον and διδαχή: the 'word' is not used by Jesus. The only explanation appears to be that Luke is here deliberately drawing a distinction in order to differentiate the period of Jesus from the period of the Church.[4]

---

[1] Rengstorf's view is that διδάσκειν refers to the teaching of Jesus, not to the proclamation about him. This is not true as far as Luke is concerned (cf. the objects set out above). According to him, in Acts iv, 2, 18; v, 28, 42; xv, 35 διδάσκειν and καταγγέλλειν are not identical. But the way in which such concepts are used in Luke shows that it is a question of a rhetorical form. In iv, 18 διδάσκειν signifies the whole of the proclamation, and in v, 42 and xv, 35 the teaching is identified with the Gospel. In Rengstorf's view, the teaching is the call to repentance, and also the offer of forgiveness (v, 31; xx, 21). There is no support in the text for this restriction of the meaning, and in fact v, 31 suggests just the opposite. Above all it is not possible to find in the 'teaching' the tradition of the sayings, and in the kerygma that of the narrative material. The teaching constantly refers back to Scripture, hence the usage in xviii, 25 and xxviii, 31. The Scriptural proof refers to what has taken place, to the Passion. The evidence of xviii, 11 and xx, 20 does not suggest anything different.

[2] Lohmeyer, *Markus*, p. 50, n. 1.

[3] In addition to the passages mentioned above, cf. also Acts iv, 4; xiv, 25; xvi, 6; vi, 4; viii, 4 and x, 44. The meaning is made plain of course when τοῦ θεοῦ or τοῦ κυρίου, etc., is added.

[4] If on the one hand this 'word' includes the whole account of Jesus, and on the other hand it can be described as the word of the Kingdom, then a definite relation between Christ and the Kingdom is at least implicitly assumed, that relation in fact which we have noted before: in Jesus' ministry the Kingdom is manifest. The report of it gives us a picture of the Kingdom for any period in which the Church exists in the world.

224

MAN AND SALVATION: THE CHURCH

In conclusion, we can confirm that Luke's whole conception of proclamation contains no speculative elements. The media of the message have not yet established themselves as abstract entities with a significance of their own, but the linguistic usage has definitely become more technical. However, it is not yet a matter of vital importance. In fact there is a significant alternation between the absolute use and more detailed definitions. In order to understand them, however, we must take into account the tradition of the Church, the confession of faith, the formulae of which Luke transmits in Acts, and the tradition concerning Jesus, which he sets out fully in his first book.

The Church itself and its history is not yet considered as a factor in salvation in the sense of being an object of faith. It appears as the necessary medium of the message to us, but not as an entity playing a part in its own right in the saving events. The third article is really not yet developed, but the basis for it is created by Luke in so far as he depicts the existence of the Church as history, within the categories of redemptive history.

V. MAN AS THE RECIPIENT OF SALVATION

1. CONVERSION

There is no developed Lucan psychology. The individual is incorporated into the Church, and in this way the acute problems of eschatology and of a continuing life in the world are solved. Luke is therefore not concerned to develop a psychology of the individual's faith. It is true that there is a tendency to draw psychological distinctions, but no complete system is worked out.[1] We shall discover Luke's special emphasis if we consider the encounter of the individual with the message of salvation.

---

[1] Among signs of psychological interest we may mention the following points. Special concepts such as ἐπιθυμία reveal no specific theological significance in Luke, but have their general psychological significance (the noun is found only in Luke xxii, 15, the verb elsewhere). The καρδία appears as a psychological entity in Luke xxi, 34, and Acts xiv, 17; a comparison of Mark iv, 14 f., with Luke viii, 12 ff., brings this out clearly. The ψυχή concept is found more often, but there is no Greek colouring, for it is in harmony with the LXX usage. One should speak with great caution of any Greek, spiritualizing tendency in Luke. On the whole the psychological concepts play no independent part.

MAN AND SALVATION: THE CHURCH

Here again we see Luke's way of making things independent:
the event of conversion becomes an object of greater interest,
and it is therefore more sharply divided into its separate component parts. What we saw earlier about the office-bearers, i.e,
that the 'Spirit-possessed' man becomes an object of special
regard, is of general application, in so far as every Christian has
received the Spirit.[1] Yet we must immediately make this distinction: faith and conversion are thought of as God's work, but
there is no account of Christian possession by the Spirit, for
Luke does not describe the Christian life in pneumatic, but in
ethical categories.[2]

When in this connection man's part is emphasized, in spite of
the reference to God's activity, then we are confronted by a fact
which we have already seen several times to be typical. The
conception of conversion provides evidence of this emphasis. As
God determines the life of the Church, so of course He also
determines the life of the individual. We see this in the fact that
prayer is possible, and it is foreshadowed in the prominence of
the prayer-motif in the life of Jesus. By the time of Luke the
believer hardly expects an angelic revelation—this belongs to
the initial period—but he knows in a general sense how God
acts: through the Spirit, who is imparted in the Church through
the sacrament, in an exceptional way through individual bearers
of the Spirit, and finally by answering prayer.[3]

---

[1] There is a characteristic example of this way of making things independent in
Luke xii, 11 f., and xxi, 14 (by comparison with the source). It is no longer the
Spirit that speaks, but man; the work of the Spirit has been rationalized into
instruction; xxi, 19 shows the ethical tendency which is connected with it.

[2] This is the basis of Acts iii, 16 and xxvi, 29; xvi, 4 states the position from
the psychological angle. On the part played by God or Christ, see the section on
Christology. There are a few definite expressions, e.g. viii, 12, xx, 24, 27;
xviii, 25 f., and there is also the unfolding of mediation by the name. In this way—
according to the theory—it becomes possible to consider man independently.

It is evident that Luke has no personal conception of possession by the Spirit.
We can see this from the way in which he puts together intervention of the Spirit,
of angels and of visions. The process of making independent is seen in the change
from the passive event of being filled by the Spirit to the deliberate selection of
the man who is full of the Spirit, e.g. Acts vi, 3, 5, 8; vii, 55, etc. What Luke
himself has in mind comes out in vi, 5, 8, where he illustrates what he means by
reference to faith and wonders.

[3] The concept of the name plays an important part in this connection. Christians
are those who 'call upon the name' (Acts ii, 21; ix, 14, 21; xxii, 16). This is of
course an old, stock turn of phrase (Rom. x, 13; 1 Cor. i, 2). On the name, its
effect and the significant place it occupies in Luke's thought, cf. above, pp. 177 ff.

MAN AND SALVATION: THE CHURCH

With the decline of the expectation of an imminent Parousia, the theme of the message is no longer the coming of the Kingdom, from which the call to repentance arises of its own accord, but now, in the time of waiting, the important thing is the 'way' of salvation, the 'way' into the Kingdom.[1] The proclamation gives the necessary information about this way. It is then man's responsibility to take this way with God's help. Here Luke gives greater attention to the individual element in the hope, the personal assurance of one's resurrection, than to the cosmological element. The message to man reveals to him his situation, by informing him of the Judgement to come and by revealing the fact that he is a sinner.[2] This can be seen in the fact that the preaching constantly leads into the call to repentance and conversion, motivated by the Judgement.[3]

[1] On Luke's special conception of the 'way', cf. Michaelis, *TW*, art. ὁδός. There are other related images, such as κατανᾶν (see Michel's article in *TW*). The image of the way is of course Jewish, but the particular manner in which it is developed in Acts presents a special problem. In addition to the historical question of the origin of the idea, there is the further question: how does it come about that Christianity is set out as the 'Way'. Quotations such as those in Acts ii, 28 and xiii, 10 give an indication of the origin. Traces of the influence of the LXX can also be seen, the LXX being the strongest influence upon Luke's language. On the details of the concept, cf. Michaelis, loc. cit. We will mention just one particularly clear example, xxiv, 14, where it is used rhetorically. The concept is used in antithesis to αἵρεσις (as Michaelis rightly points out, in contrast to Schlier). This presupposes a usage that is already fixed.

[2] Yet no demonstration of man's sinfulness is attempted in any part of the preaching. In Acts the idea of sin is found only in connection with the declaration of its forgiveness. The idea contains no cosmological or speculative elements whatever. The saying in Acts vii, 60 states the concrete fact of sin. ἁμαρτωλός is not a general declaration about the human situation. There are people who do not need repentance and forgiveness (Luke xv, 3 ff., which is discussed in particular by Schlatter).

Luke xiii, 2, 4; xv, 7, 18; xviii, 3 show the ethical character of sin. Luke v, 30 ff., comes from Mark, but with the significant addition εἰς μετάνοιαν. This reveals the change that has taken place. Mark's paradox has been removed, and repentance has become the condition. Luke v, 8 (S) illustrates what Luke means by the conversion of a sinner. The person is not idealized, but the event becomes the type of the confession which all must make. Luke vii, 34 (S) again makes plain, that sinfulness is not a characteristic of man as such. Luke xiii, 2 (S) is addressed to all, not in the Pauline sense of being inescapable, but on the contrary as an appeal to individual initiative.

[3] In the application of the call to repentance to the Jews we see the continuity with the message of the Old Testament and of John the Baptist. The same facts have to be made plain to the Gentiles, but here a different approach and argument is required. The Areopagus speech provides the pattern. The basis of the appeal is that there is a general resurrection and judgement. It is assumed that this is something we must dread.

227

MAN AND SALVATION: THE CHURCH

The conception of sin, compared with Paul's, has a strong ethical colouring, and the same is true also of deliverance from sin. The idea of 'forgiveness', which recedes right into the background in Paul, is predominant in Luke, but repentance is the condition of forgiveness. Lohmeyer (*Markus*, p. 15) considers μετάνοια and ἄφεσις to be practically synonymous. This is true for Mark, but not for Luke, and the distinction he makes is a characteristic one. Just as redemptive history is unfolded as a process, so also is man's way to deliverance. Forgiveness and repentance are inseparably connected.[1] Whereas in Mark μετάνοια can describe the whole process of conversion, in Luke its meaning is restricted to one definite point. This can be seen in the way in which Luke feels obliged to amplify: Acts v, 31 (καὶ ἄφεσιν); Luke xxiv, 47 (εἰς ἄφεσιν ἁμαρτιῶν); cf. also Luke v, 30, 32. Here again there are duplications, such as we frequently find, but the context points to a special significance in the duplications. We are obviously not to take the two ideas as identical, for μετάνοια alone is not an adequate description of the content of salvation or of the way to salvation.[2] For Luke the content of salvation is ζωή, or σωτηρία,[3] and the basis of it is forgiveness,[4] which in turn is conditional upon repentance (Acts

---

[1] For the alteration from Mark to Luke, cf. the change of tense from Mark ii, 5 to Luke v, 20. Lohmeyer comments that in Mark forgiveness is thought of as something that goes on, and begins at this moment, in Luke as something accomplished in this moment. The latter part of this is true, but the former part is questionable. In both cases forgiveness is not connected with Jesus' death, but with his power. This is not so in Mark x, 45, which is missing in Luke. Acts v, 31 connects forgiveness with Jesus' exaltation. The difference between the two concepts is important for Luke, as it helps him to bring out the contrast between Jesus and John the Baptist. John's preaching and baptism are without the Spirit; the Spirit, Baptism and forgiveness, however, are indissolubly linked.

[2] The old, comprehensive meaning is still seen in expressions which Luke takes from tradition, e.g. Acts v, 31 and xi, 18 (δοῦναι μετάνοιαν). Here repentance is thought of as the gift of salvation. By association with this there are similar expressions in Luke xxiv, 47 and Acts xiii, 38. 2 Tim. ii, 25 and Polyc. Phil. vii, 2 show that in the former instance it is a stock turn of phrase, the meaning of which has been lost. In Acts xiii, 38 there is a popularized form of Pauline terminology. Alongside Acts v, 31 there is v. 32, where obedience is thought of as a condition. How Luke understands the traditional expression can be seen in his interpretation in Acts xvii, 30, according to which the opportunity for repentance is given.

[3] Luke does not develop any special concept of ζωή. In Acts ii, 28, and v, 20 it stands for the message. In xi, 18 the word is connected with repentance. It is clear throughout that there is a parallelism between ζωή and σωτηρία.

[4] In the quotation in Luke iv, 18 this appears itself as the blessing of salvation, but here again we must bear in mind Luke's tendency to draw distinctions.

228

ii, 38; v, 31; viii, 22; Luke xxiv, 47). Acts xix, 18 speaks instead of the confession of sin. This connection and the link between forgiveness and Baptism raises the question whether μετάνοια does not really signify the act of the confession of sin at Baptism; but the fact that the linguistic usage goes beyond this suggests otherwise. The combination which is characteristic of Luke is that of repentance and conversion, which shows that these two go together as the basis for Baptism and forgiveness and indicate the change of attitude and way of life.[1] We can see how the process is split up, and attitude and behaviour are distinguished. Thus the Christian life comes to be thought of alongside correct doctrine as a separate item.

This subdivision is not the outcome of the eschatological call to repentance, but reproduces what actually takes place time after time when men and women come into the Church as a result of the preaching, and shows the conditions fixed by the Church for admission to Baptism. It is in the light of this that the redemptive significance of Baptism is to be understood, and also the continuance in the Christian way of life, which begins with forgiveness and is made possible by the Spirit. There are certain descriptions which give a concrete example of the event of conversion, such as the story of Zacchaeus (Luke xix, 1 ff.); cf. also Acts xix, 18 f., where the factor of confession appears, without being described as μετανοεῖν.

We must make clear the limit of this subdividing and distinguishing of psychological stages: it is not the stages of the psychological development of the Christian that are described, but the stages whereby one becomes a Christian. We must also note that although repentance and conversion are necessary conditions, they are not thought of as an 'achievement'. We can

---

[1] The linking of forgiveness with Baptism makes clear the meaning of ἄφεσις; the word is used, as generally at that time (with a few, but all the more significant, exceptions) for the once-for-all forgiveness of sins at Baptism. This might seem surprising in Luke's case, as he has in mind a long duration for the Christian life, but in fact the problem of a second repentance does not yet exist as far as Luke is concerned. The counterpart to forgiveness is rather the regulation of the Christian life by the Christian ethic.

Acts ii, 38/iii, 19 show the connection of repentance and conversion with forgiveness and Baptism. If 'conversion' is considered as the presupposition for Baptism, then the important thing must be the change in the way of life preceding Baptism. This means that μετάνοια also is an ethical, not a cultic process.

see this in the very passage which most clearly expresses these conditions (Acts xxvi, 18).[1]

The actual significance of the statements concerning the blessings of salvation is connected with the eschatological delay. Just as the Eschaton no longer signifies present, but exclusively future circumstances, so also eternal life is removed into the distance. In the present we do not possess eternal life, but the hope of it, but this hope is not just a formal expectation of future things, but something which has a real bearing upon the present. Its guarantee is the presence of the Spirit, and the indi-'vidual is surrounded by it, by living within the Church. By means of the Spirit and the Church Luke builds a bridge from the present to the future. There is evidence of this in the abbreviated and modified version of Mark x, 29 f. in Luke xviii, 29 f. Therefore it is better to describe the Spirit not as the blessing of salvation, but as the provisional substitute for it. He is the proof of the forgiveness that has been received, by virtue of which one can survive the Judgement to come. The description of Jesus as the ἀρχηγὸς τῆς ζωῆς (Acts iii, 15—cf. v, 31) shows that the 'life' belongs exclusively to the future. In the context of Luke's idea of resurrection, this means that Jesus is the first to be resurrected (Acts xxvi, 23), and as such the guarantor of our own resurrection, which the sinner must dread, whereas the believer has in the Spirit the assurance of forgiveness. Thus the fact of the future life is no longer dependent on the imminence of God's reign, and as a promise it can surmount the passage of time.

[1] No special theory of redemption is evolved. Cf. the use of ἀπολύτρωσις. Luke xxi, 28 speaks of deliverance from the eschatological ordeal. Where the 'blood' is mentioned, as in Acts xx, 28, a traditional phrase is being employed, from which no theological conclusions are drawn. The use of Isaiah liii in Luke is not connected with the idea of substitution and does not prove, but disproves, the presence of any theory of atonement. The decisive thing is that Luke says nothing about the redemptive significance of the Cross, and that he does not link forgiveness with the death of Jesus.

Neither does the isolated passage Acts xiii, 38 f., which shows traces of Pauline terminology, provide evidence of a Lucan doctrine of justification. On this passage, cf. J. H. Roper, *The Synoptic Gospels*, 1934, pp. 77 f., and C. P. M. Jones in *Studies in the Gospels*, 1955, p. 122. Cf. also the use of δικαιοῦν in Luke vii, 29; x, 29; xvi, 15, and xviii, 14. The verb σώζειν is not connected with any doctrine of justification either. Of course there is a connection between faith and salvation, as in Acts xiv, 9, but as a hope of being saved; it is a different matter in Acts xvi, 31 and xv, 11, but it still does not go beyond the general conception of faith and salvation. It is in fact the same conception as in Luke xiii, 23 ff.

MAN AND SALVATION: THE CHURCH

The future life is not depicted in detail, apart from the traditional image of the future feast.[1] The relation of Baptism to the hope is clear from what we have already described, but not that of the Supper.[2] There are still traces of its eschatological character. The 'rejoicing' at the Supper is originally eschatological rapture, but Luke does not develop this. He does not need to make any alterations either. As the manifestation of the Church's fellowship, the Supper itself is transformed as a result of the adaptation of the idea of the Church in view of its continuance. The significance of the Supper for the individual is not explicitly indicated.

2. THE CHRISTIAN LIFE

Because of the extension of the period after conversion, the motifs which are concerned with the ordering of daily life come into prominence. The separation between word and deed, doing and hearing, becomes greater, and the ethical element begins to stand out in its own right.[3] Besides preparing oneself for the future Judgement, one has to deal with the problems of the present (which is characteristically expressed in the idea of ὑπομονή).[4]

[1] The usage of ἐλπίς proves the same. Cf. Acts xxiii, 6; xxvi, 6 f.; xxviii, 20 and, the clearest example, xxiv, 15 (that there shall be a resurrection). Here the point is reached at which the hope of resurrection is completely separated from the early expectation.

[2] Baptism is described primarily of course in terms of its difference from John's baptism, and it is characterized by the Spirit. The motif of the baptism of death (Luke xii, 50) is not developed; there is certainly no connection with Pauline ideas. It is a mistake to overestimate Luke's 'sacramentalism' and the part played in his thought by the cultus.

[3] The following linguistic points should be noted. Luke vi, 47, 49 comes word for word from Q; viii, 15 is derived from Mark, with the significant addition of ὑπομονή. In viii, 21 Luke has τὸν λόγον ἀκούειν καὶ ποιεῖν for Mark's ποιεῖν τὸ θέλημα.
Luke xi, 28: ἀκούειν καὶ φυλάσσειν. On xxi, 33, cf. vv. 34 ff. for what the 'words' are. λόγος — ἔργον: Luke xxiv, 19 (cf. Acts vii, 22).

[4] The influence of Luke's ethical leanings can be seen as early as in the account of John the Baptist, where Luke creates a pattern of ethical exhortation by introducing the account of John's preaching. Already it is taken for granted that the world will continue.
This same ethical tendency can be seen in the usage of single words such as ἀγαθός; in Luke xxiii, 50 and Acts xi, 24 the reference is to Christian virtue. ἅγιος also seems to be given an ethical turn in Acts iii, 14; xvi, 6 and xx, 26 (καθαρός), and ἀδικεῖν is used in the ethical as well as the juridical sense in Luke x, 19 and Acts vii, 24, 26 f. These are of course only isolated examples.

MAN AND SALVATION: THE CHURCH

The shift of emphasis in eschatology brings about of its own accord a change of structure in ethical thinking. Out of the life within the eschatological community with its expectation of an imminent End, there now emerges the 'vita Christiana'. The Judgement still remains a motif, no longer on account of its proximity, but because it is a fact. The real problems which are treated first and foremost are those which arise from the situation of the Church in the continuing life of the world. Besides the regulation of everyday life, the main concern is with the Christian's behaviour in persecution.

The connection between the delay of the Parousia and ethical instruction, which is expressed in the summons to be prepared, can of course be found earlier than Luke, but Luke is the first to consider it closely. We can see the connection, e.g., in Luke xii, 35–8. There is evidence of a deliberate pattern here in the fact that Luke sets out the connection between eschatological instruction and ethical adjustment to a continuance in the world according to a definite scheme. It can be seen in the two apocalypses in Luke xxi and xvii, 20 ff. Eschatology no longer has the immediate effect of a summons, for it has become an idea which now influences ethics indirectly, by means of the idea of judgement. In accordance with this we see how originally eschatological ideas such as ὑπομονή take on an ethical colouring, and others such as θλῖψις a historical colouring.[1]

The statements with an ethical content are naturally made by means of reproducing the sayings of Jesus, which means that there is a considerable agreement with the rest of tradition. But again there are peculiarities. Our aim, however, is not to enumerate the familiar characteristically Lucan motifs such as his attitude to the poor, but to understand the whole structure of his ethical thought.

Luke's ethical teaching is not built up from ideals, but is constructed out of traditional, authoritative material, and the particular emphases which he makes arise from the situation of the time. Luke is aware of the connection between the situation and the demand that is made, which shows his understanding of history; the best example is the connection between the mission charge and Luke xxii, 35 f.: ἀλλὰ νῦν—other rules are in

---

[1] See pp. 98f. above.

232

force. The arming of the disciples follows upon the end of the peace that prevailed during Jesus' ministry. Thus Luke interprets the instructions given in the mission charge not as a timeless ideal of poverty but, in the light of his understanding of history, as a special provision appropriate to the situation of the time. The arming of the disciples symbolizes the Messianic protection; it is neither projected out of the circumstances of the present into the past nor it is held before the present as an ideal.

The 'Ebionism' of Luke vi, 20 comes from the source, and is not developed as a theme by Luke. We cannot speak of an ideal of poverty either in the Gospel or in Acts. The sharing of possessions is not based on such an ideal, but is part of the stylized account of the unity of the Church; it is not an ideal that applies to the present, but belongs to the initial period and is one of its marks. Luke has no intention of demanding that it should be an ideal for his own time.

On account of its historical character, Luke's ethical teaching does not represent an ideal of 'imitatio Christi' either. Jesus does serve as an example, of course (Luke ix, 23 ff.), and there is a parallel between his suffering and that of the disciples in the image of cross-bearing, but the idea of 'imitatio' is immediately blended with other ideas: it is not 'as I do' but 'for my sake'. This emphasis arises from the actual confession made when persecution arises. Luke knows that discipleship today is very different from what it was in the time of Jesus. Then it was literally a question of 'following', as the group of disciples and fellow-pilgrims on the 'journey' shows. One can still be required to leave all (Luke v, 11, 28, similarly xviii, 28 ff.), but this is not made a 'Christian principle'. Luke's ethical thinking is determined not by 'imitatio', but by discipleship, in a form appropriate to the particular time. Therefore there is no ideal of the 'imitatio' of the apostles either.

The confessing of one's faith is no longer thought of as something belonging to the last times, but as an event in the Church's long period of suffering. When the End comes, the suffering will be over (Luke xxi, 28). Thus Luke moves in the direction of an ethic of martyrdom.[1] There is a plain warning of persecution

---

[1] The martyr, however, has not yet been developed into a special figure such as he later becomes, nor has the conception been fully worked out. V. Campenhausen rightly emphasizes this in his account; cf. also Strathmann's article in *TW*. The

at the Last Supper, in the mention of πειρασμός and in the command to the disciples to arm themselves (xxii, 35 ff.). The Christian life is a 'way' and inevitably leads through many tribulations (Acts xiv, 22). The attitude that is required is ὑπομονή (Luke viii, 15), which is what the instructions concerning the future point to. It is the Spirit who makes it possible to endure, and it is the promise of the Spirit that provides the basis for the teaching concerning confessing one's faith.[1]

When we turn to the reward for endurance, it is made quite clear that any claim, any reckoning as to one's desert is excluded (Luke vi, 35; xvii, 10). Alongside these sayings there are others such as Luke xii, 33, and Luke is no more aware of a contradiction than the other Synoptics, for it is part of the expectation that one will be rewarded by the Father; this means, in other words, that the message of salvation speaks on my behalf, and that it is a promise. The Spirit is the guarantee of this salvation, but it is part of one's faith in this very message that one cannot count on a reward.

attitude to be adopted under persecution has to be considered together with the other themes concerning one's attitude to the present world and the immediate situation, in other words, to the Empire.

What the actual situation is can be seen from the logia about persecution. See Riddle, *ZNW*, 1934, pp. 271 ff. On the whole these are fewer in Luke than in Matthew. The allusion in Luke viii, 13 is less vivid than in Matthew, but v. 15 contains 'typical persecution terminology', 'which has no parallel elsewhere' (Riddle, op. cit., p. 274).

[1] There is also of course prayer—cf. Acts iv, 24 ff., and Luke xviii, 1, rather surprisingly following xvii, 20 ff. Just as the Spirit gives the power to withstand, so it is impossible for others to withstand a confession made by this power—cf. Luke xii, 11 with xxi, 15, and also the part played by the Spirit on occasions such as Acts iv, 8 (cf. v. 14, where we see the stereotype nature of the phrase) and Acts vi, 10. Hence the joy, when one is 'counted worthy' of suffering (Acts v, 41; xvi, 25). The 'must' of Acts xiv, 22 is therefore not merely endured, but is accepted with joy.

Bibliography

(Only the more recent literature is referred to in the Bibliography, and only certain of the standard commentaries are listed.)

ALTHAUS, P. *Die Wahrheit des christlichen Osterglaubens*, 1940.

ARMITAGE, A. H. N. *A Portrait of St.·Luke*, 1955.

BACON, B. W. The Chronological Scheme of Acts, *Harvard Theol. Rev.*, 1921, pp. 137 ff.

v. BAER, H. *Der heilige Geist in den Lukasschriften*, 1926.

BARRETT, C. K. *The Holy Spirit and the Gospel Tradition*, 1947.

BAUER, W. Jesus der Galiläer, in *Festgabe für A. Jülicher*, 1927.

BAUERNFEIND, O. *Die Apostelgeschichte (Theol. Handkomm.)*, 1939.

— Die Geschichtsauffassung im Urchristentum, *ZSystTh*, 1938, pp. 347 ff.

— Vom historischen zum lukanischen Paulus, *EvTh*, 13, 1953, pp. 347 ff.

BERTRAM, E. *Die Leidensgeschichte Jesu und der Christuskult*, 1922.

— Die Himmelfahrt Jesu vom Kreuz aus, in *Festgabe für A. Deissmann*, 1927.

·BICKERMANN, E. Das leere Grab. *ZNW*, 1924, pp. 281 ff.

BLINZLER, J. *Die neutestamentlichen Berichte über die Verklärung Jesu*, 1937.

— *Der Prozess Jesu*, 1951.

— Die literarische Eigenart des sogenannten Reiseberichts im Lukasevangelium, in *Synoptische Studien (Festschrift für A. Wikenhauser)*, 1953, pp. 20 ff.

BORNHÄUSER, K. *Studien zum Sondergut des Lukas*, 1934.

BORNKAMM, G. Homologia, *Hermes*, 1936, pp. 377 ff.

— Das Bekenntnis im Hebräerbrief, *ThBl*, 1942, pp. 56 ff.

— Die Verzögerung der Parusie (*Essays in Memory of Lohmeyer*), pp. 116 ff.

— Die Sturmstillung im Matthäus-Evangelium, *Jahrbuch der theol. Schule, Bethel*, 1948, pp. 49 ff.

BOUSSET, W. *Kyrios Christos* (2nd ed.), 1921.

BOUSSET and GRESSMANN. *Die Religion des Judentums* (3rd ed.), 1926.

BRANSCOMB, H. *The Teaching of Jesus*, 1931.

BRUN, L. *Die Auferstehung Christi*, 1925.

BIBLIOGRAPHY

Büchsel, F. *Die Hauptfragen der Synoptikerkritik*, 1939.

Bultmann, R. *Die Geschichte der synoptischen Tradition* (2nd ed.), 1931.

— *Glauben und Verstehen*, 1933.

— Reich Gottes und Menschensohn, *ThR*, 1937, pp. 1 ff.

— *Theologie des Neuen Testaments*, 1948 ff.

— Weissagung und Erfüllung, *ZThK*, 1950, pp. 360 ff.

Buri, F. *Die Bedeutung der neutestamentlichen Eschatologie für die neuere protestantische Theologie*, 1935.

— Das Problem der ausgebliebenen Parusie, *Schweiz. theol. Umschau*, 1946, pp. 97 ff.

Burkitt, F. C. *Christian Beginnings*, 1924.

Burnier, J. Art littéraire, témoignage et histoire chez St. Luc, *Rev. de Théol. et de Phil.*, 38, 1950, pp. 219 ff.

Busch, F. *Zum Verständnis der synoptischen Eschatologie*, 1938.

Bussmann, W. *Synoptische Studien, I–III*, 1925–33.

— Hat es eine schriftliche Logienquelle gegeben? *ZNW*, 1930, pp. 147 ff.

Cadbury, H. J. *The Style and Literary Method of Luke*, 1919–20.

— *The Making of Luke—Acts*, 1927.

— *The Book of Acts in History*, 1955.

v. Campenhausen, H. *Die Idee des Martyriums in der Alten Kirche*, 1936.

— *Der Ablauf der Osterereignisse und das leere Grab*, 1952.

Clark, A. C. *The Acts of the Apostles*, 1933.

Clogg, F. B. *The Christian Character in the Early Church*, 1944.

Conzelmann, H. Zur Lukasanalyse, *ZThK*, 1952, pp. 16 ff.

Creed, J. M. The Conclusion of the Gospel according to St. Mark, *JThS*, 1930.

Cullmann, O. *Die ersten christlichen Glaubensbekenntnisse*, 1943.

— *Königsherrschaft Christi und Kirche im Neuen Testament*, 1941.

— *Urchristentum und Gottesdienst*, 1948.

— *Die Tauflehre des Neuen Testaments*, 1948.

— *Christus und die Zeit*, 1946.

— Das wahre durch die ausgebliebene Parusie gestellte Problem, *ThZ*, 1947, pp. 177 ff.

Dahl, N. A. *Das Volk Gottes*, 1941.

Dalman, G. *Orte und Wege Jesu*, 1924.

Davies, J. G. The Prefigurement of the Ascension in the Third Gospel, *JThS*, N.S., 6, 1955, pp. 229 ff.

Descamps, A. La composition littéraire de Luc 16, 9–13, *Nov. Test.*, 1, 1956, pp. 47 ff.

Dibelius, M. *Aufsätze zur Apostelgeschichte*, 1951.

— *Die Formgeschichte der Evangelien* (2nd ed.), 1933.

236

BIBLIOGRAPHY

— Das historische Problem der Leidensgeschichte, *ZNW*, 1931, pp. 193 ff.

DINKLER, E. Early Christianity, in *The Idea of History in the Ancient Near East*, 1955, pp. 171 ff.

v. DOBSCHÜTZ, E. Kyrios Jesus, *ZNW*, 1931, pp. 97 ff.

— *Das Apostolicum*, 1932.

—Die Berichte über die Bekehrung des Paulus, *ZNW*, 1930, pp. 144 ff.

DODD, C. H. *The Apostolic Preaching*, 1936.

— *History and the Gospel*, 1938.

DOEVE, J. W. L'évangile de Luc, *NedTT*, 9, 1955, pp. 332 ff.

DORNSEIFF, F. Lukas der Schriftsteller, *ZNW*, 1930, pp. 144 ff.

DUPONT, J. *Les problèmes du livre des Actes d'après les travaux récents*, 1950.

— L'utilisation apologétique de l'Ancien Testament dans les discours des Actes, *Eph. Theol. Lov.*, 29, 1953, pp. 280 ff.

— Notes sur les Actes des Apôtres, *RB*, 62, 1955, pp. 45 ff.

EASTON, B. S. *St. Luke*, 1926.

— *Christ in the Gospels*, 1930.

— *The Purpose of the Acts*, 1936.

EBELING, H. J. *Das Messiasgeheimnis*, 1939.

ECK, O. *Urgemeinde und Imperium*, 1940.

ERDMANN, G. *Die Vorgeschichten des Lukas- und Matthäusevangeliums*, 1932.

EVANS, C. F. The Central Section of St. Luke's Gospel, in *Studies in the Gospels* (Essays in memory of R. H. Lightfoot), 1955, pp. 332 ff.

FASCHER, E. *Jesus und der Satan*, 1949.

FINEGAN, J. *Die Überlieferung der Leidens- und Auferstehungsgeschichte Jesu*, 1934.

FLEW, R. N. *Jesus and His Church*, 1938.

FRICK, R. *Geschichte des Reich-Gottes-Gedankens in der Alten Kirche*, 1928.

FUCHS, E. Christus das Ende der Geschichte, *EvTh*, 1949, pp. 447 ff.

— Jesus Christus in Person, in *Festschift für R. Bultmann*, 1949, pp. 48 ff.

— Review of Kümmel's *Verheissung und Erfüllung*, in *Verkündigung und Forschung*, 1949, pp. 75 ff.

GASSE, W. Zum Reisebericht des Lukas, *ZNW*, 1935, pp. 293 ff.

GEWEISS, J. *Die Urapostolische Heilsverkündigung nach der Apostelgeschichte*, 1939.

GIRARD, L. *L'évangile des voyages de Jésus*, 1951.

GOGUEL, M. *Introduction au Nouveau Testament, III*, 1922.

— *La foi à la résurrection*, 1939.

BIBLIOGRAPHY

GOGUEL, M. *La vie de Jésus*, 1932.
— *La naissance du christianisme*, 1946.
— *L'église primitive*, 1947.
— Luke and Mark, *Harvard Theol. Rev.*, 1933, pp. 1 ff.
— Le charactère de la foi à la résurrection, *RHPhR*, 1931, pp. 329 ff.
— Eschatologie et apocalyptique, *Rev. de l'hist. des rel.*, 1932, pp. 381 ff., 490 ff.
— Quelques observations sur l'œuvre de Luc, *RHPhR*, 33, 1953, pp. 37 ff.

GOPPELT, L. *Typos*, 1939.

GRANT, F. C. *The Growth of the Gospels*, 1933.
— *The Earliest Gospel*, 1943.

GROBEL, K. *Formgeschichte und synoptische Quellenanalyse*, 1937.

GRUNDMANN, W. Das Problem des hellenistischen Christentums, *ZNW*, 1939, pp. 45 ff.
— Die Apostel zwischen Jerusalem und Antiochen, *ZNW*, 1940, pp. 110 ff.

HAENCHEN, E. Tradition und Komposition in der Apostelgeschichte, *ZThK*, 52, 1955, pp. 205 ff.
— *Die Apostelgeschichte* (*Kritisch-exegetischer Kommentar über das Neue Testament*, Section 3, 10th ed.), 1956.

HARNACK, A. *Die Apostelgeschichte* (*Beiträge zur Einleitung in das Neue Testament*, III), 1908.
— *Neue Untersuchungen zur Apostelgeschichte* (*Beiträge*, IV), 1911.
— *Sprüche und Reden Jesu* (*Beiträge*, II), 1907.

HARTMANN, G. *Der Aufbau des Markusevangeliums*, 1936.

HAUCK, F. *Das Lukas-Evangelium* (*Theol. Handkomm.*), 1934.

HERING, J. *Le royaume de Dieu et sa venue*, 1937.

HIRSCH, E. *Frühgeschichte des Evangeliums*, 2 vols., 1941. (See also *ZNW*, 1942, pp. 106 ff.)

HILLMANN, W. *Aufbau und Deutung der synoptischen Leidensberichte*, 1941.

HÖLLER, J. *Die Verklärung Jesu*, 1937.

HOOKER, C. J. *The Work of the Holy Spirit in the Acts of the Apostles* (Princeton Dissertation), 1952.

JACKSON and LAKE. *The Beginnings of Christianity*, Part I, vols. 1–5, 1920–33.

JACQUIER, E. *Les Actes des Apôtres*, 1926.

JEREMIAS, J. *Jesus als Weltvollender*, 1930.
— *Die Abendmahlsworte Jesu* (2nd ed.), 1949.
— *Golgotha*, 1926.
— Eine neue Schau der Zukunftsaussagen Jesu, *ThBl*, 1941, pp. 216 ff.

BIBLIOGRAPHY

— Zur Hypothese einer schriftlichen Logienquelle, *ZNW*, 1930, pp. 147 ff.

— Untersuchungen zum Quellenproblem der Apostelgeschichte, *ZNW*, 1937, pp. 205 ff.

— *Die Gleichnisse Jesu* (2nd ed.), 1952.

JONAS, H. *Gnosis und spätantiker Geist*, 1934.

JÜLICHER, A. *Einleitung in das Neue Testament* (7th ed.), 1931.

KITTEL, G. *Die Probleme des palästinischen Spätjudentums*, 1926.

— (ed.). *Theologisches Wörterbuch zum Neuen Testament*, 1933 ff.

— Die Auferstehung Jesu, *DTh*, 1937, pp. 133 ff.

KLOSTERMANN, E. *Das Lukasevangelium* (*Handbuch zum Neuen Testament*), 1929.

KNOX, J. *The Man Christ Jesus*, 1942.

KOH, R. *The Writings of St. Luke*, 1953.

KRAGERUND, A. Itirariet in Apostelens gjärninger, *NorskTT*, 56, 1955, pp. 249 ff.

KÜMMEL, W. G. Jesus und der jüdische Traditionsgedanke, *ZNW*, 1931, pp. 105 ff.

— Die Eschatologie der Evangelien, *ThBl*, 1936, pp. 225 ff.

— *Verheissung und Erfüllung* (2nd ed.), 1953.

— Kirchenbegriff und Geschichtsbewusstsein in der Urgemeinde, *Symb. Bibl. Upps.*, I, 1943.

— Das Urchristentum, *ThR*, NF, 22, 1954, pp. 138 ff., 191 ff.

KUNDSINN, K. *Topologische Überlieferungsstoffe im Johannesevangelium*, 1925.

LAMPE, G. W. H. The Holy Spirit in the Writings of St. Luke, in *Studies in the Gospels* (Essays in memory of R. H. Lightfoot), 1955, pp. 159 ff.

LEAL, J. El plan literario del III Evangelio y la geographía, *Estudios Ecclesiasticos*, 29, 1955, pp. 197 ff.

LEIVESTAD, R. Der Pietist unter den Evangelisten, *NorskTT*, 55, 1954, pp. 185 ff.

LIETZMANN, H. *Messe und Herrenmahl*, 1926.

— Der Prozess Jesu, *SBA*, 1931, pp. 313 ff.

— Bemerkungen zum Prozess Jesu, *ZNW*, 1931, pp. 211 ff.

— Symbolstudien, *ZNW*, 1922, pp. 1 ff., 1923, pp. 208 ff.

LIGHTFOOT, R. H. *History and Interpretation in the Gospels*, 1935.

— *Locality and Doctrine in the Gospels*, 1938.

LOHMEYER, E. *Galiläa und Jerusalem*, 1936.

— *Markus* (Meyerscher Komm.), 1937.

— *Kultus und Evangelium*, 1942.

— Vom urchristlichen Abendmahl, *ThR*, 1937, pp. 168 ff., 1938, pp. 81 ff.

BIBLIOGRAPHY

LOHMEYER, E. Die Reingung des Tempels, *ThBl*, 1941, pp. 257 ff.
— Die Idee des Martyriums im Judentum und Urchristentum, *ZSystTh*, 1927–8, pp. 232 ff.
— *Gottesknecht und Davidssohn*, 1945.
LOHSE, E. Lukas als Theologe der Heilsgeschichte, *EvTh*, 14, 1954, pp. 185 ff.
— Missionarisches Handeln Jesu nach dem Evangelium des Lukas, *ThZ*, 10, 1954, pp. 1 ff.
LOISY, A. *L'évangile selon Luc*, 1924.
— *Les Actes des Apôtres*, 1920.
— *La naissance du christianisme*, 1933.
MANSON, T. W. *The Sayings of Jesus*, 1949.
MANSON, W. *The Gospel of Luke*, 1930.
MARSH, J. *The Fullness of Time*, 1952.
MARXSEN, W. *Der Evangelist Markus*, 1956.
McCOWN, C. C. Studies of Palestinian Geography in the Gospels, *JBL*, 50, pp. 107 ff., 57, pp. 51 ff., 59, pp. 113 ff., 60, pp. 1 ff.
MENOUD, PH.-H. Le plan des Actes des Apôtres, *NTStud.*, 1, 1954, pp. 44 ff.
— Remarques sur les textes de l'ascension dans Luc—Actes, in *Neutestamentliche Studien für Bultmann*, 1954, pp. 148 ff.
MEYER, R. *Der Prophet aus Galiläa*, 1940.
MICHAELIS, W. *Täufer, Jesus, Urgemeinde*, 1928.
— *Reich Gottes und Geist Gottes im Neuen Testament*, 1931.
— *Zur Engelchristologie im Urchristentum*, 1942.
— *Der Herr verzieht nicht die Verheissung*, 1942.
— *Herkunft und Bedeutung des Ausdrucks ,,Leiden und Sterben Christi''* 1945.
— Kennen die Synoptiker eine Verzögerung der Parusie? in *Synoptische Studien (Festschrift für A. Wikenhauser)*, 1953, pp. 107 ff.
MONTEFIORE, C. G. *The Synoptic Gospels* (2nd ed.), 1927.
MORGENTHALER, R. *Die lukanische Geschichtschreibung als Zeugnis*, Parts 1 and 2, 1949.
MUNCK, J. *Paulus und die Heilsgeschichte*, 1954
MUSSNER, F. Das ,,Gleichnis'' vom gestrengen Mahlherrn (Luke xiii, 22–30), *TrThZ*, 68, 1956, pp. 129 ff.
NOACK, B. *Satanas und Soteria*, 1948.
— Das Gottesreich bei Lukas, *Symb. Bibl. Upps.*, 10, 1948.
O'NEILL, J. C. The Use of Kyrios in the Book of Acts, *Scottish J. Th.*, 8, 1955, pp. 155 ff.
OTTO, R. *Reich Gottes und Menschensohn*, 1934.
POHLENZ, M. Paulus und die Stoa, *ZNW*, 1949, pp. 69 ff.

BIBLIOGRAPHY

PRICE, J. L. Studia Biblica XXII. The Gospel according to Luke, *Interpretation*, 7, 1953, pp. 195 ff.

RAMSEY, A. M. *The Resurrection of Christ*, 1945.

— *The Glory of God and the Transfiguration of Christ*, 1949.

RÉTIF, A. Témoignage et prédication missionaire dans les Actes des Apôtres, *NRTh*, 1951, pp. 152 ff.

RIDDLE, D. W. Die Verfolgungslogien, *ZNW*, 1931, pp. 271 ff.

RIESENFELD, H. *Jesus transfiguré*, 1947.

SAHLIN, H. *Der Messias und das Gottesvolk*, 1945.

— Studien zum dritten Kapitel des Lukasevangeliums, *Uppsala universitets Arsskrift*, 1942.

— Zwei Lukasstellen, Lk. 6, 43–5; 18, 7. *Symb. Bibl. Upps.*, 4, 1945.

SCHELKLE, K. H. *Die Passion Jesu*, 1949.

SCHICK, E. *Formgeschichte und Synoptikerexegese*, 1940.

SCHLATTER, A. *Das Evangelium des Lukas*, 1931.

SCHMID, J. *Matthäus und Lukas*, 1930.

SCHMIDT, K. L. *Der Rahmen der Geschichte Jesu*, 1919.

SCHNEIDER, J. Zur Analyse des lukanischen Reiseberichtes, in *Synoptische Studien (Festschrift für A. Wikenhauser)*, 1953, pp. 207 ff.

SCHUBERT, P. The Structure and Significance of Luke 24, in *Neutestamentliche Studien für Bultmann*, 1954, pp. 165 ff.

SCHÜRMANN, H. Die Dublettenvermeidung im Lukasevangelium, *ZThK*, 76, 1954, pp. 83 ff.

SCHWEITZER, A. *Geschichte der Leben-Jesu-Forschung* (5th ed.), 1933.

SCHWEIZER, E. Zur Frage der Lukas-Quellen, *ThZ*, 1948, pp. 469 ff.

— Eine hebraisierende Sonderquelle des Lukas? *ThZ*, 1951, pp. 161 ff.

— Art. πνεῦμα (NT) in *TW*, VI, pp. 394 ff.

SCOTT, E. F. *The Varieties of New Testament Religion*, 1946.

SEEBERG, A. *Der Katechismus der Urchristenheit*, 1903.

STARKY, J. Obfirmavit faciem suam, *RScRel*, 39, 1951, pp. 197 ff.

STONEHOUSE, N. B. *The Witness of Luke to Christ*, 1951.

STREETER, B. H. *The Four Gospels*, 1924.

SUNDKLER, B. Jésus et les païens, *Arb. und Mitt. des ntl. Sem. Upps.*, VI, 1947.

SURKAU, H. W. *Martyrien in jüdischer und frühchristlicher Zeit*, 1938.

TAYLOR, V. *Behind the Third Gospel*, 1926.

— *The First Draft of St. Luke's Gospel*, 1927.

— *The Formation of the Gospel Tradition*, 1933.

— *The Atonement in New Testament Teaching*, 1940.

— *Jesus and His Sacrifice*, 1921.

THEISSING, J. *Die Lehre Jesus von der ewigen Seligkeit*, Breslau Dissertation, 1940.

TORREY, C. C. *The Composition and Date of Acts*, 1916.

BIBLIOGRAPHY

van Unnik, W. C. Opmerkingen over het doel van Lukas' geschied-werk (Lk. 1, 4), *NedTT*, 9, 1955, pp. 223 ff.

Veit, M. *Die Auffassung von der Person Christi im Urchristentum*, Marburg Dissertation, 1946.

Vielhauer, P. Zum „Paulinismus" der Apostelgeschichte, *EvTh*, 1950, pp. 1 ff.

Violet, B. Zum rechten Verständnis der Nazarethperikope. Lk. 4, 16–30, *ZNW*, 1938.

Vögeli, A. Lukas und Euripides, *ThZ*, 9, 1953, pp. 415 ff.

Wellhagen, J. *Anden och riket*, 1941.

Wellhausen, J. *Das Evangelium Lucae*, 1904.

— *Kritische Analyse der Apostelgeschichte*, 1914.

Wendland, H. D. *Die Eschatologie des Reiches Gottes*, 1931.

— *Geschichtsanschauung und Geschichtsbewusstsein im Neuen Testament*, 1938.

Werner, M. *Die Entstehung des christlichen Dogmas*, 1941.

Wifstrand, A. Lukas och den grekiska klassicismen, *SvEvÅrsb*, 5, 1940, pp. 139 ff.

Wilder, A. N. Variant Traditions of the Resurrection in Acts, *JBL*, 1943, pp. 307 ff.

Williams, C. S. C. The Date of Luke—Acts, *Exp. Times*, 64, 1953, pp. 283 f.

Winter, P. The Treatment of his Sources by the Third Evangelist in Luke 21-24, *Studia Theologica* 8, 1954, pp. 138 ff.

— On Luke and Lucan Sources, *ZNW*, 47, 1956, pp. 217 ff.

List of Abbreviations

EvTh   *Evangelische Theologie*
DTh   *Deutsche Theologie*
JBL   *Journal of Biblical Literature*
JThS   *Journal of Theological Studies*
RB   *Revue Biblique*
RHPhR   *Revue d'Histoire et de Philosophie Religieuses*
RScR   *Recherches de Science Religieuse*
TW   *Theologisches Wörterbuch zum Neuen Testament*
ThBl   *Theologische Blätter*
ThLZ   *Theologische Literaturzeitung*
ThR   *Theologische Rundschau*
ThZ   *Theologische Zeitschrift*
ZNW   *Zeitschrift für neutestamentliche Wissenschaft*
ZSystTh   *Zeitschrift für systematische Theologie*
ZThK   *Zeitschrift für Theologie und Kirche*

Index of Authors

244

INDEX OF AUTHORS

Index of Scripture Passages

INDEX OF SCRIPTURE PASSAGES

INDEX OF SCRIPTURE PASSAGES

INDEX OF SCRIPTURE PASSAGES

251

INDEX OF SCRIPTURE PASSAGES

INDEX OF SCRIPTURE PASSAGES

INDEX OF SCRIPTURE PASSAGES

INDEX OF SCRIPTURE PASSAGES

71 72 73 74 75 10 9